PRAISE FOR *THE SEARCH FOR MEANING AT WORK*

"An excellent field guide for becoming a better leader by creating a path to purpose and meaning to engage employees at every level."

—**Henry DeVries**, Forbes.com columnist and author of the bestselling book *How to Close a Deal Like Warren Buffett*

"Ideas are the currency of your future. Steve VanValin helps you see ideas that others don't see and turns those ideas into your reality."

—**Chic Thompson**, Batten Fellow of Entrepreneurship, University of Virginia Darden Business School Founder

"A must read for anyone who is looking for clarity of purpose and meaning at work. With VanValin's storytelling, the book is impossible to put down, and the plethora of examples and visuals bring meaning into focus. For the first time, instead of thinking about meaning at work, I felt meaning and its impact on the working world. You will too."

—**Jess Podgajny**, co-founder and CEO, LLUNA

"Steve VanValin's new book, *The Search for Meaning at Work*, is a powerful and timely book for both individuals and leaders—one that provides a practical road map to capture long-term meaning and engagement in the workplace. VanValin makes a compelling case that purpose, empathy, and one's supervisor are essential components of a meaningful career. Weaving effective and easy-to-understand visuals, prompt questions, case studies, and best practices, *The Search for Meaning at Work* is a must-read for anyone looking to use purpose and personal engagement as foundational pillars for a successful career and life."

—**Bob Kelleher**, President, The Employee Engagement Group and author of *Employee Engagement for Dummies*

"Experiencing meaningful work is a fundamental human desire and leaders play a crucial role in facilitating it. In *The Search for Meaning at Work*, Steve VanValin gives leaders an immediately actionable playbook for how to amplify meaning from any position—which I believe is *the* most important skill of any modern leader."

—**Zach Mercurio,** PhD, author of
The Invisible Leader, meaningful work researcher

"Steve VanValin does a masterful job in connecting the dots of meaningful purpose in a practical way. If you are a leader looking to squeeze as much out of life and leadership, this book is a must-read!"

—**Robb Holman**, Global Leadership Speaker and
author of *Lead the Way*, *All In*, and *Move the Needle*

"*The Search for Meaning at Work* is a master class on how to create deep meaning and purpose in the workplace, which ultimately leads to higher performance."

—**Steve Blue**, CEO of Miller Ingenuity and best-selling author

THE SEARCH FOR
MEANING
AT WORK

THE SEARCH FOR
MEANING
AT WORK

*Unleashing the Hidden Power of Purpose
to Engage and Fulfill Your Workforce*

STEPHEN VAN VALIN

ROWMAN & LITTLEFIELD
Lanham • Boulder • New York • London

Published by Rowman & Littlefield
An imprint of The Rowman & Littlefield Publishing Group, Inc.
4501 Forbes Boulevard, Suite 200, Lanham, Maryland 20706
www.rowman.com

86-90 Paul Street, London EC2A 4NE

British Library Cataloguing in Publication Information Available

Library of Congress Cataloging-in-Publication Data

Names: VanValin, Steve, 1961– author.
Title: The search for meaning at work : the definitive guide to amplify purpose, inspire performance, and engage your workforce / Steve VanValin.
Description: Lanham, Maryland : Rowman & Littlefield Publishing Group, [2022] | Includes bibliographical references and index. | Summary: "Retaining top talent and encouraging engagement and motivation at work is always difficult but even more so at a time of remote or hybrid work, mass resignations, and the uncertainties of the future of work. Here, Steve VanValin offers a playbook for managers and leaders for cultivating meaning and engagement at work for the success of everyone"—Provided by publisher.
Identifiers: LCCN 2022013175 (print) | LCCN 2022013176 (ebook) | ISBN 9781538152119 (cloth) | ISBN 9781538152126 (epub)
Subjects: LCSH: Employee motivation. | Job satisfaction. | Quality of work life.
Classification: LCC HF5549.5.M63 V33 2022 (print) | LCC HF5549.5.M63. (ebook) | DDC 658.3/14—dc23/eng/20220706
LC record available at https://lccn.loc.gov/2022013175
LC ebook record available at https://lccn.loc.gov/2022013176

Contents

Acknowledgments

This book is only possible because of the amazing people who have amplified purpose in my life. I'm so grateful to be surrounded by talented, loving people who have supported me in my journey. Thank you to my wife Kara, son Ryan, and daughter Julianna for contributing their immense talents and for helping me when I needed it most. Thank you to Chris Murray, the world's best editor and coach, who combines wisdom and kindness in his craft. You gave me meaning throughout this venture and cared for this subject as your own. To Connie Rose, my graphic artist, thank you for your patience with my tedious perfectionism. To Christine Alexy, thank you for the deep-dive research and the writing skill that brought the stories to the surface. To my agent, Leticia Gomez, and Suzanne Staszak-Silva with the team at Rowman & Littlefield, thank you for believing in me and this subject.

I extend a special thank you to the coauthors of *The Progress Principle*, Teresa Amabile and Steven Kramer, for your kindness in sharing your incredible insights with me that inspired this book.

The mentors, clients, and friends who have graced my life and given me inspiration are almost too many to list, but I admit it was fun just to think of each one of them and the special meaning they have gifted to me. They include Dr. Mike Brenner, Chic Thompson, Jennifer Ayres and all my incredible partners at Concinnity, Jessica Podgajny of Lluna, Dan Calista of Vynamic, Meredith Toole of Talent Point, Jim Lucas and my Vistage team members, Hendrick-Jan Franke, Gerry Lantz, my colleagues at QVC, Eleanor Gathany, Dan Kerkel, Ronnie DeMarco, Bob Schulman, Terry Harmon, Beth Rubino, Nan Russell, Jeff Charney, Doug Thompson, John Thalheimer, Wade Walton, Matty Dalrymple, Michelle Alexander, Kurt Kampf of Senn-Delaney, Dan Kerr and Matt Rafferty of Burns Mechanical, Robb Holman, Charlie Poznek, David Newman, Henry DeVries, Robb Holman, Melanie Boor, Dr. Ayyappan Rajasekaran, Tom Gill, Zach Zones, Donna Teitelman, Robb Holman, and Lauren Williams.

To the thought leaders who paved the way on the subject of purpose, culture, and leadership, thank you for your inspiration and commitment to change the world of work: Dan Pink, Simon Sinek, Aaron Hurst of Imperative, Adam Grant of Wharton, Davin Salvagno of Purpose Point, David Friedman of High Performance Culture, Dr. Zach Mercurio, Bob Kelleher of Employee Engagement Group, Dr. Amy Wrzesniewski, Hubert Jolly, Patrick Lencioni, Ryan Estes, John Izzo, Marshal Goldsmith, Jim Collins, Ken Blanchard, Brené Brown, Seth Godin, Pastor Chris Swansen, Larry Hawkins II of Hawkins Consulting, Kelly Stewart of the *Doing (Good) Business* podcast, and Kathleen Brady. All of us are forever grateful for Viktor Frankl who opened our eyes to the impact of meaning on our humanity.

And thank you to the thousands of people who have openly shared their thoughts, concerns, passions, and hopes with me in the hundreds of workshops I've led. I hope that I have advocated for you through this book and that your voice has been heard.

Introduction

My purpose is to be a positive force that forever changes the experience of work. Everything I do is anchored on creating cultures rich in meaningful relationships that are positive, creative, energizing, and deeply fulfilling. Through this book, I am the voice for people at every level who are searching for meaning at work.

For more than 25 years, I've had the unique opportunity to hear and absorb thousands upon thousands of expressions from people on the subject of purpose and meaning at work. I experienced the corporate world from the inside with QVC, the multimedia shopping network. My prime vantage point as the lead facilitator of the QVC Difference—QVC's marquee leadership program to shape a high-performance, values-centered culture—showed me something remarkable: the inner workings of the human spirit at work.

Leading the culture at QVC, I collaborated with and learned the perspectives of employees at all levels, and from all regions in the United States and around the globe. Together we explored a full repertoire of deeply personal leadership and cultural subjects that invited introspection of the human spirit. People responded in ways that spanned a vast spectrum of emotions—from self-revelation to gratitude. The opportunity to learn from people going through their own discovery has been an incredible blessing. It was almost impossible to walk away from one of those experiences without feeling moved to reflect on my own state of purpose and meaning. It was a deep immersion into my own state of emotional intelligence, as well as a continuous stretch of my comfort zone as a leader.

I've conducted firsthand intake through hundreds of workshops at QVC and through the many others I've created and led with my current consulting firm Culturology. I estimate that I've led experiences with approximately

25,000 participants throughout a 20-year time frame. Each workshop has been like a Petri dish experiment on what drives people to do the things they do. It has been an amazing journey to witness these things from the proverbial front row.

At unforgettable moments in the workshops, I heard the unvarnished truth on the core beliefs people have that drive behavior—based on their own stories and experiences. This is where the rubber meets the road on motivation, and for me, it's not just theory in a vacuum. These workshop experiences have been a two-way street that invited people to share their thoughts, feelings, and insights. I'm now their voice through this book.

I've also had the opportunity to read thousands of open-ended comments about the work experience from engagement survey data. The comments ran the gamut from heartfelt appreciation about their work experience to cries for help in desperate emotional conundrums involving injustice with a boss or coworker. These mostly no-holds-barred reflections and cathartic outpourings of opinions have shaped my thinking on this subject. I only hope I can do right by them by helping to influence a better future for the work experience. Learning people's deep desire for something meaningful at work has shaped my own personal purpose.

Through my consulting role with Culturology, I've explored the deepest challenges with leaders at all levels through coaching and intake. They've shared their frustrations about the drama of their culture and the people who report to them, as well as the leaders above them who seem oblivious to their emotional needs. I've also heard great uplifting examples from HR leaders and CEOs about incredible people who influenced them in a positive and meaningful way. Many of them give credit to a specific person who forever changed their approach through powerful coaching or by setting an incredible example. I'll share some of these cases throughout the book as an inspiration for the high bar of what's possible and as a warning for what not to do.

IT'S PERSONAL

My commitment to helping you bring meaning and purpose into your workplace is not just professional. It's personal.

I believe I may be uniquely qualified to write on the subject of meaning. Purpose and meaning have always had a strong gravitational pull in my life.

I'm only half joking by confessing to you that I've been having a mid-life crisis since I was six years old. I've searched for the reckoning in just about everything I do. I bombarded and exasperated my parents and grandparents with the *why, why, why* question to everything. I had the nerve to question my seventh-grade algebra teacher as to *why* learning about equations would make a difference in my life. He was not amused.

Looking back on my life and career, I can say with confidence that if I was stoked, jazzed, excited, or deeply engaged with anything I've done, it was a result of feeling that my work mattered, and that I mattered. It's that basic. Those positive experiences had a purpose, and that purpose gave me the meaning I required to be at the top of my game.

I found I could endure almost anything if I was with a cool team or a boss I respected. Whether the job task itself was actually exciting seemed to matter less to me than the element of fun from relationships and the people surrounding me. One of my most positively memorable experiences was packing boxes in a hot warehouse at QVC with my fellow sales team members in an "all-hands-on-deck" effort. Being "in it together" wins the day even on jobs that appeared to be menial and physically brutal from an outsider's perspective. Since I enjoyed the camaraderie of the people "suffering" through it with me, the actual task didn't seem to matter. The conditions for meaning were still present.

On the dark side of the equation, sometimes my idealism has made me deeply frustrated to the point of being on the edge of depression. I've had times where I felt like an invisible cog in a big Orwellian wheel of futility. Somewhere along your journey, have you felt this way, too? If I didn't have a work partner or team to commiserate with, then the mundane, uncreative nature of the work would dominate my thinking and add to my feeling of meaninglessness. Or, in my worst scenario ever, I felt I was actually playing a role in degrading society by proliferating vulgar and profanity-laced gangster rap videos to urban markets in my position as director of affiliate sales for an interactive music video service. I literally felt sick at times coming and going to that meaningless job and what it represented. If it weren't for one trusted friendship there, I don't think I could have survived long enough to escape to another company.

I had another barf-bag-worthy job a couple years later. The company and my role looked like a dream job on paper; however, my toxic boss and the culture of backstabbing she proliferated took me completely by surprise and destroyed my self-confidence. I had my mojo completely sucked out of me. The only purpose that remained for me was to get out of there as soon as feasible.

So I've experienced the good, bad, and ugly up close and personal in the trenches. And I've seen the effect it has had on the people directly in my circle, and the thousands of others who have openly shared their opinions to me in workshops and anonymously through surveys. Purpose and meaning will always have a profound impact on my success for better and worse. It wouldn't be a stretch to say I'm certain it has been that way for you, too. Let's start applying our lessons in life on this subject to the way we lead people. Why would they be any different in the things that motivate them?

We're learning more and more every year about the impact of purpose and meaning on the psyche of workers at every level. We are in the midst of a movement that is being driven by a greater awareness and compunction to have purpose-driven lives. At the same time, millennials and Generation Z are creating demand for purpose and meaning-rich cultures acting upon utopian-level idealism. Purpose has become their core rallying point, which fuels the employee experience and their brand promise. I love it! Millennials and Gen Zers are savvy to the power of purpose earlier in their careers than we have ever seen. Baby boomers and Generation Xers are there too (finally), completing the perfect storm tsunami of the purpose movement.

A SENSE OF URGENCY

I assume that I'm not alone in experiencing the dynamic tug-of-war for purpose and meaning in life. That's probably why you picked up this book in the first place. If you believe, like I do, that life is too short to waste a single moment, then we owe it to ourselves to act *now* upon our purpose, so that rich meaning and satisfaction are amplified through our life. That prize is available to all of us, yet it's the rare few who reflect with enough desire and humility to fully realize it. I believe our purpose for being here on this planet can be elevated to a new level of consciousness. Here's the best part: since we can do that for ourselves, it means we can do it for others, too. That could possibly be the greatest gift I could personally bestow upon you and the world—helping people fulfill their ultimate purpose.

I've intended from the very start to be flat-out candid with you in this book and not pull any punches. You may disagree with my thoughts and opinions, and that's great! If it moves you to think it through for yourself and to form your own quantifiable opinion, then mission accomplished. In the end, it's all about gaining a greater level of emotional intelligence. If you know yourself, then you can do a better job of the choices to manage yourself. If you can empathize more with others, then you can do a better job on the choices to positively influence them. It's that simple, and that's the purpose of this book. Let's not waste another second. Let's get into it.

1

Meaning at Work

The Holy Grail of Engagement

Challenging the meaning of life is the truest expression of the state of being human.

—Viktor Frankl (Holocaust survivor), *Man's Search for Meaning*

Employee engagement will forever be a hot topic in the world of business and with good reason: the mountain of evidence proving your company's performance is going to suffer if your employees' disengagement continues to grow. Different academic studies have shown that companies with high levels of engagement have 40 percent less turnover, half the absenteeism rate, and double the net profit compared to companies with low engagement.[1] One Gallup study of 23,000 business units showed an 18 percent higher productivity output in companies with higher engagement.[2] In another Gallup poll, 59 percent of the more engaged employees said that work brings out their most creative ideas—only 3 percent of the less engaged said the same.[3] And according to PricewaterhouseCoopers, 70 percent of engaged employees will have a good understanding of their customer needs, compared to just 17 percent of disengaged employees.[4]

It's no wonder leaders are intent on increasing employee engagement. But the fact is that, in the United States and throughout the world, companies are failing badly. According to Gallup's latest State of the US Workplace report, employee engagement dropped in 2021 for the first time since 2009.[5]

We are losing the battle despite the near obsession that employers have in increasing engagement. So what's going on? It's obvious that most companies know what they want, but they don't know how to get there. No matter how many initiatives they launch, no matter how many motivational and pro-ductivity consultants they might bring in, these companies seem unable to engage their employees. The reason is that they are failing to get to the heart of engagement; there's a missing sense of *meaning* and *purpose*. If meaning and purpose are missing in the workplace, no consultant or program is going to effectively change how employees feel about their work.

What's most important to American employees in today's post-pandemic workplace? According to a 2022 survey, "purpose" is at the top of the list, topped only by "benefits" and "flexible hours."[6] This underscores the recent shift in employees' personal and professional priorities, reinforcing the need for employers to look beyond the symbols of perks and benefits, placing equal importance on the substance of purpose and its impact on engagement.

ENGAGEMENT: A CHOICE THAT MATTERS

It's important to get calibrated on the definition of the term *engagement*. I see it as a choice. It's a conscious and subconscious choice to apply our energy, talent, and care to any effort, large or small. I estimate we make hundreds of these choices throughout a given day—whether to speak up in a meeting, check your e-mail a third time for grammar and tone before pressing "send," or serve a customer in a way that will delight them. These are choices that matter. When you add up these positive choices across the total organization, you create and scale a high-performance culture with an entirely new set of accountable expectations.

Although there are many other engagement definitions out there by cred-ible sources, most of them seem to miss the mark on engagement by not seeing it as a living, organic, and active element in the psyche of employees. Engagement is highly variable. The truth is I might be totally fired up and engaged at 8 a.m. to start my day, but after a discouraging conference call, I'm completely checked out and watching the clock to escape for lunch by 11 a.m. Then, after a great exchange with my boss at 3 p.m., I'm recharged to take on a tough challenge to finish the day with a victory.

How do you possibly measure something as variable as engagement by doing a once-a-year survey? I always tell my clients that a yearly engagement survey is just a small snapshot in time to give you a feel for how things are

ENGAGEMENT: The extent to which a person chooses to apply their energy, talent, and care.

Energy

The vibrant acts of diligence and enthusiasm. The mojo that get things done and makes working with them an uplifting experience. The grit and determination to work through challenges and make progress. Having a sense of urgency and willingness to act NOW.

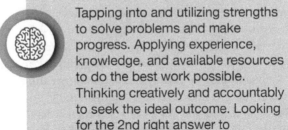

Talent

Tapping into and utilizing strengths to solve problems and make progress. Applying experience, knowledge, and available resources to do the best work possible. Thinking creatively and accountably to seek the ideal outcome. Looking for the 2nd right answer to achieve excellence.

Care

Applying deeply held values through empathy and pride to go the extra mile. Thinking and acting on behalf of others. The distinctly human emotional connection only they can deliver through their unique personality. Being authentic and transparent in ways that earn trust.

Figure 1.1 Engagement definition.

trending. A more relevant measure of engagement is to review the outcome of the individual choices people make every day. Are people making progress, getting things done, exceeding goals with their energy, talent, and care? That's the irrefutable evidence of engagement.

Here's the big payoff and the reason the definition matters. If you view engagement as a choice, then it opens up our potential to influence the choice. We have the power to apply our own choices and, as managers, the accountability to influence better choices in others. If we view engagement as something that is done *to* us or someone else's job (in HR), then we have completely missed the point.

In this book, I will show you how to amplify meaning and purpose for your team of employees in ways that bring creativity, engagement, and fulfillment to the work you're doing together. This is a book of ideas—ideas that you can act upon immediately. Some ideas will be brand new to you, and others will confirm and refresh principles you know to be true but seemed challenging to apply consistently.

Get ready to go deep to explore the dynamics of beliefs and behavior at work, and how you can positively influence people by making the work experience rich and meaning filled. This book will challenge you to think differently about your role as a leader and escape the swirling vortex of busyness to become highly effective in ways that are deeply gratifying. Imagine the satisfaction of creating meaningful experiences that influence the choice people make to apply their energy, talent, and care (see figure 1.1).

The Search for Meaning at Work will activate a new level of emotional intelligence in you—an attribute that inspirational leaders possess and express with grace and ease to amplify meaning. The everyday, practical action steps and relevant ideas will energize you to be a difference maker for the people you lead. And, best of all, it will elevate your own level of engagement and meaning while leading with newfound energy, confidence, and satisfaction.

THE PROGRESS PRINCIPLE: THE ULTIMATE CONTEXT FOR MEANING

The meaning of things lies not in the things themselves but in our attitudes towards them.

—Antoine de Saint-Exupéry (French pioneer aviator, journalist, and author), *The Wisdom of the Sands*

In their landmark book, *The Progress Principle*, Harvard Business School professor Teresa Amabile and psychologist Steven Kramer share a vivid discovery that should impact every manager's approach to engagement.[7] Their research is considered the most in-depth study ever conducted on the actual events that take place in a person's work life that engage or disengage them from performing at a high level. They discovered that *making progress in meaningful work* was the number one driver of the positive *perceptions, emotions,* and *motivation* at work. *The Progress Principle* identifies these three factors as a person's "Inner Work Life" (see figure 1.2). Their research clearly demonstrates that inner work life had a profound and vivid impact on engagement leading to performance. When these aspects were elevated by events at work, a person's performance had higher output in *creativity, productivity, commitment,* and *collegiality.* All four of these highly coveted performance dimensions serve as a strategic competitive advantage—especially when you scale them across an entire organization.

 The Progress Principle research also points out that the manager has the greatest control over events that facilitate or undermine progress. Engagement is won or lost based on the relationship between managers and their direct

Figure 1.2 Inner Work Life.

reports. For most managers and organizations, this is both good and challenging news. The good news is that engagement practices can indeed be influenced directly to provide a high return on investment. The challenging news is
that advancing engagement takes more than a masterstroke from upper-level
leadership. It requires leaders at all levels to participate in a concerted effort to
drive progress on meaningful work.

So, inevitably, it comes down to the one-on-one, everyday events that shape
culture and individual engagement. The battle for engagement is won or lost
in the trenches, by the granular and seemingly innocuous exchanges and
choices that take place in the course of working through the day. Who is the
primary shaper of these exchanges? It's the manager. Managers play the crucial
role in determining whether the events positively or negatively impact people's
ability to make progress in meaningful work.

So what's a manager to do? The idea of making progress probably feels
very tangible to you. But what about meaningful work? How do you inspire meaning to your team members without sounding disingenuous or a
Pollyannaish rah-rah cheerleader of the company? The ole' "Let's win one
for the Gipper!" speeches and short-term incentives to gain commitment are
risks that potentially have the opposite effect in our current environment that
lacks psychological safety. People on the team sniff these out immediately as
being phony ploys. Many managers feel this risk, sense their own inadequacy
to make a sincere connection, and therefore hopelessly surrender to the fate
of cynicism.

To avoid this fate, you as a manager and leader must understand how to
make work meaningful. In many ways, *The Search for Meaning at Work* answers the *how* question raised by the insights of *The Progress Principle*. Amabile
and Kramer reveal that *meaningful work* is the linchpin of engagement, and
that "small wins"—again, the granular and seemingly innocuous exchanges
that take place in the course of working through the day—is the process
through which meaningful work is created.

But the questions remain: *How do you make those granular, innocuous
exchanges meaningful? What makes some work tasks, conversations, and events
meaningful, and others not meaningful?*

The short and powerful answer is *purpose*. Where there is a purpose, there
is an opportunity to amplify meaning. And where there is meaning, there is
engagement. Understanding the dynamic relationship between purpose and
meaning and how to use purpose in the workplace as the source of meaningful
work and employee engagement is what this book is about.

WHAT IS "PURPOSE"?

The minute we wake up, we move forward with a sense of purpose. There is a reason for our actions. Why do we take a shower and get dressed in appropriate clothes for our work every workday morning? We do it to be presentable at work. Why do we drive down a crowded highway every morning? We do it to get to our workplace.

Because it gives the reason for an action or an event, a purpose answers a *why* question. In other words, a purpose is the *what* that answers the *why* question, with the *what* answer usually beginning with the word *to*: "*Why* do you set your alarm every morning?" The purpose is, "*To* arrive at work on time."

The examples I've used so far are simple and mundane and really obvious, but purpose, of course, can be on a much higher plane. Instead of asking, for example, "Why do I drive to work?" what if you asked, "Why do I work?" The *what* answer is no longer so obvious, is it?

And if we go to an even higher plane and ask the question "Why am I on this planet?" the answer is even less obvious. In fact, many people don't take the time to think such a question through; they don't take the time to reflect, consider, and have insights on the purpose of their existence. They chalk it up to fate, or something so mystical that they can't get their arms around it. Their *why* question sadly becomes, "Why bother?"

But let's say your answer to the question "Why are you on the planet?" is simply, "to be kind to people." That's great! One would assume that as life presents itself, that you would take the opportunity to be purposefully kind to people along the way. But what do you do when life gets so complicated, busy, and distracting that your purpose gets applied only in convenient and serendipitous ways? It may feel like the opportunity to live out your purpose of being kind to people is somewhat out of your control. Your great intent can become diluted over time and simply evolve into a general life philosophy, and not a focused purpose. *Ugh*. We can't let that happen.

Here's how to bring your purpose back into clarity and relevance with a sharpened focus. Take your purpose of being kind to people and get specific on the *action steps* that you can do to make it happen, which could include the following choices:

- becoming a door greeter at your church
- volunteering for Meals on Wheels or another helpful volunteer service
- creating a blog dedicated to encouraging people

- setting a goal of making eye contact with all strangers on the street and saying, "hi"
- starting a pay-it-forward initiative
- participating in a five-kilometer run for charity
- committing to always be the person who smiles and then waves in the other car in the merge lane
- scheduling time to have coffee every week with someone at work to just talk about life issues
- sponsoring a disadvantaged exchange student
- as a surprise and delight for your partner, doing a chore he or she normally takes on

The list is endless, but hopefully you get the idea. It can consist of actions large or small, but getting clear on how you can deliver the *what* of your purpose (in this case, to be kind to people) has a big payoff.

To sum up, purpose is driven by an intentional outcome, a desire to achieve or contribute something. This could apply to the simplest of desires or goals (such as making a special birthday cake this afternoon), or to the loftiest of aspirations (such as giving back to others in a way that creates a lasting legacy for your family name).

Aaron Hurst, the founder of Imperative and author of *The Purpose Economy*, constantly reminds people that purpose doesn't have to be a "cause."[8] In other words, it's not just a single, grandiose purpose that is in play for people. Purpose takes many forms and is valued differently from person to person in the way it provides fulfillment.

DO I HAVE TO CHOOSE BETWEEN PASSION AND PURPOSE?

I've seen too many people (myself included) put too much credence on doing work that we're "passionate" about. There's nothing wrong with that except that it sets us up for a big potential disappointment.

Passion is not always sustainable. Soon the weeds and hairballs of the work itself that are required to be successful look nothing like the "passion" aspects we were idealistically seeking.

Purpose, on the other hand, weathers the storm of the hard work and obstacles, and serves as a springboard to help us overcome and persevere. Ironically, it's the pursuit of purpose that we can become passionate for, and not the other way around. I wonder if Thomas Jefferson considered "pursuit of purpose" versus "pursuit of happiness" in his word choices. Now we know for certain that the "pursuit of purpose" is one of the few things that gives us the capacity to be happy.

If we reframe our passion to be about our pursuit of purpose, then all the wonderful meaning-filled experiences that come from our journey add up to a passion for life, and not a fleeting aspect of work that is often out of our control.

THE THREE HIERARCHIES OF PURPOSE

I've identified three hierarchical types of purpose to demonstrate how the role of purpose is varied in its impact on our lives. Purpose can be both deep and wide, yet it can also be highly focused and driven by the dimension of time. The following are examples in action.

1. The *transcendent* type of purpose, which is a purpose for life and for your being. Examples of transcendent purpose:
   a. To leave the world a better place
   b. To give back to others
   c. To glorify God

2. The *transformative* purpose, which is a purpose that leads to significant change. Examples of transformative purpose:
   a. To take care of your body through healthy living and exercise
   b. To build a family vacation home
   c. To launch a charitable trust

3. The *transactional* purpose, which is the type of purpose related to accomplishing specific goals and objectives.
   Examples of transactional purpose:
   a. To hit a sales goal for the month
   b. To declutter the house over the weekend
   c. To complete a nagging project assignment by Friday

Although they might be widely different (compare "to glorify God" with "to declutter your house over the weekend"), the three types of purpose follow the same rules: They answer a *why* question, and you'll need action steps to achieve them.

I see distinct characteristics in people who are most successful in life. They are confident, fulfilled, and driven. They have a clear personal vision for purpose emanating from all three purpose types. In a sense, it seems they have a full repertoire of unified and interconnected conditions for their success. They live their life in constant movement forward toward fulfillment of these purposes. The way their multiple purposes harmonize together creates their unique character and unique personality.

Other Examples of the Three Types of Purpose

Transcendent Purpose Examples

- To leave a positive legacy for your family
- To bring hope to those who are hopeless
- To be an influential leader others are willing to follow
- To inspire others to achieve the unimaginable
- To change the world
- To serve and defend your country
- To be a generous, giving person

Transformative Purpose Examples

- To have a high impact in your role at work
- To reduce your carbon footprint
- To earn an advanced degree
- To write a book
- To simplify your life by downsizing
- To volunteer at church or school
- To save money for your child's education
- To achieve work-life balance
- To become an entrepreneur
- To create a scholarship fund
- To be the best parent possible

Transactional Purpose Examples

- To complete a work project
- To lose 10 pounds
- To take a cooking class
- To hit a sales goal

- To get promoted
- To teach English as a second language
- To coach youth soccer
- To plant an organic vegetable garden
- To redecorate your family room
- To spend more time with your kids this week

HOW PURPOSE CREATES MEANING

For work to have meaning, it must have a special significance to the worker. How does a worker know that something has special significance? The answer reveals the fundamental difference between meaning and purpose: the worker knows that something has special significance because he or she *feels* it. Meaning, unlike purpose, is an emotional response, not a rational, intentional target.

When someone says, "I have a strong *sense of purpose* doing this work," what they are probably describing is *meaning*. "This work is meaningful" is the feeling and emotion we seek to influence so that people are engaged and fulfilled to do incredible work.

Too many managers and leaders think they have no control over meaning in their workplaces. "What am I supposed to do?" they ask. "Tell my people what to feel?"

The answer, of course, is "no." You can't tell people what to feel. But you can create the conditions that lead to a certain feeling. That applies to all feelings and emotions. For example, you're not going to walk into someone's office and say, "Be angry." You, as a leader, however, can create the conditions for anger—for example, by being a complete jerk.

In much the same way, you can create the conditions for meaning. The question is *how* do you create the conditions? You might know how to avoid making an employee angry, but do you know how to fill an employee with a sense of meaning?

Here, Amabile and Kramer offer an answer when they describe "meaningful work" as work that "contributes value to something or someone important to the worker."[9] In other words, if through their work workers are contributing value to *something* or *someone* important to them, they will emotionally respond to that activity with a sense of meaning.

For example, let's say someone works for the transcendent purpose of providing her children with a standard of living that she never had as a child. It doesn't matter what that person does at work. Her purpose of providing her children with a higher standard of living gives whatever she does meaning. She is creating a legacy through her work. Without a doubt, that is the motivational and sustainable force in her life and work.

As I pondered Amabile and Kramer's definition of meaningful work, I realized the role that *purpose* plays in the creation of meaning. The reason the worker I just described finds *meaning* in her work is because she has a *purpose*: to give her children a higher standard of living.

THE PRINTER'S SHOP

A watershed moment in my thinking about meaning and purpose came a number of years ago in one of my Progress Principle workshops. We were discussing how to make work more meaningful when the CEO of a printing company asked a very important question. She asked, "Most of my people work all day on collating machines making advertising supplements for the newspaper. How is it possible to give that type of work meaning?" I quickly asked the group what they thought (to admittedly give myself time to think of a clever answer). One person suggested explaining to workers that the supplements helped newspaper readers save money. Someone else recommended telling the workers how much revenue the supplements generated for the printing firm.

All good suggestions, but I knew that they weren't good enough based on the unsatisfied look on her face. I asked, "How long have they worked there?" She said, "All of them have been with us for over 20 years." I probed some more for the reason they would be so loyal doing such a menial job. I saw her face light up when she made the connection. They were working almost in a self-sacrificial way for their families. That was the purpose that gave them meaning: to give their families a better life. She immediately seemed relieved seeing her opportunity to amplify the family connection for these hard-working, loyal workers. Her game plan was to talk to them more about their kids and the things they were proud to describe about their family. To fully understand what their paycheck truly meant to them was a game changer for her. It gave her an entirely new, empathetic approach for amplifying meaning. Now, she would communicate everything through the positive filter of their family perspective first. What a powerful connection.

She was feeling what Amabile and Kramer delineated. Meaningful work depended on contributing value to someone important—and that someone important wasn't necessarily just the *company* nor the *customer*. It was *family*.

This event caused me to think more broadly about the sources of purpose and meaning, and to begin analyzing new, creative possibilities that were playing out in people's lives at work. People have the instinct and ability to multitask when it comes to purpose in their lives.

MEANING AND THE IMPORTANT SOMEONES

Through an innovative study, Professor Adam Grant demonstrated the motivational power of understanding how you're adding value to people's lives.[10] The study involved a group of students raising money from alumni. He took one group of these students to the end-users of the money—the scholarship recipients and other people who were benefiting from the money raised. When these students returned to their work of doing outbound calls, they were eight times more successful than the students who had not visited end-users.

At QVC, I did a similar exercise by inviting employees to meet with our red-carpet customers (our best customers who were ferociously loyal to QVC). This face-to-face meeting had a significant impact on how those employees felt about customers and their role at QVC. Customers went from being statistics to real-life personalities. The customers were such fun to be around, and the meeting gave our employees a chance to see QVC through their eyes. It amplified meaning because employees made the connection to how their work at QVC created an experience for customers that they truly loved.

DISCOVERING PURPOSE BY ACCIDENT

Sometimes, we have serendipitous events in our lives that provide purpose and meaning. One morning, Anne Mahlum, who worked for a political watchdog group in Philadelphia, was on her usual run through the streets of Philadelphia.[11] As always, her route took her past a men's homeless shelter. That morning, she had the idea that perhaps running could help the men in the shelter. "Everything about it made sense to me," she later told the *Washington Post*. "Running is so powerful. It was absolute therapy for me when my parents went through a divorce."

She enlisted the help of the shelter director, found nine men who were interested in running, and got a local shoe retailer to donate running shoes for the men. Mahlum had found her purpose. She decided to create a nonprofit group called Back on My Feet, creating programs for the homeless that start with running and include job placement and other initiatives to, in the words of the *Washington Post*, "bring order and purpose" to their lives.

Within six years, Back on My Feet had chapters in 12 cities and a budget of $6 million, funded through private donations. Always physically active, Mahlum found meaning through her purpose: to help others by getting them involved in physical activities. Eventually Mahlum would be inspired by that same purpose and the meaning it gave her to launch a successful chain of fitness centers.

Understanding that *purpose drives meaning* is essential for leaders seeking to inspire their workers to be more engaged. If, in our role as leaders, we articulate purpose in smart ways to make it more conscious for other people—by defining purpose in terms of making a contribution of value to someone or something that is important to them—then it will increase the chances of them gaining an emotional return through meaning.

I call this process of articulating the inspiring purpose that helps workers gain meaning from their work *amplifying meaning*.

MULTIPLYING THE IMPACT
OF PURPOSE AND MEANING

In some ways, leaders of the past instinctively, if not consciously, understood the link among purpose, meaning, and engagement; however, they looked at the source of meaning at work only from one dimension. They focused on identifying the extent to which a person sees their work as having an impact on the success of the *company*. Indeed, the success of the company can be a powerful purpose for working.

Well-intended managers, however, have been confounded to make a relevant meaning connection if it's not clearly evident in the nature of the work itself. For example, what if your people do routine work like take calls in a call center, run a piece of machinery, pack trucks with boxes, or something else that is granular work behind the scenes? Meaning as a motivating factor is just as important to the people in these roles. It's a mistake to underestimate that fact. We certainly want them to be engaged to perform. Do we have other options to consider, beyond helping the company to succeed, that would give them the sense of meaning they deserve? The answer is yes.

I am happy to report that managers don't have to limit their efforts to amplify meaning to the single dimension of the *company*. Hopefully, that might provide some relief for you if you've struggled to do so. Instead of assuming that meaning is too far-fetched and ignoring it, you can set yourself apart as a leader by identifying and tapping into factors that matter greatly to people.

Think about the workers at the printing company. Were they driven by an overriding desire for the company to succeed? Not so much. It was the purpose of doing right by their families that gave their work meaning. *Family* is one of the *amplifiers of meaning*. Are there more? You bet.

Distilling my experiences and knowledge by asking *who* or *what* could be the important someone or something that workers are contributing value to, I identified 11 amplifiers of meaning:

1. **Self-satisfaction:** Making progress toward feeling positively challenged and respected in the daily grind of the work.
2. **Family:** Making progress toward benefiting your family as a result of the work.
3. **Work partner:** Making progress in strengthening the closest working relationship(s) at work by being supportive and investing in each other's success.
4. **Team:** Making progress toward a sense of belonging as an integral team contributor and valued member.
5. **Manager:** Making progress by satisfying the boss in ways that earn back respect and advocacy.
6. **Department:** Making progress by being unified in achieving the departmental objectives that support the goals and strategies of the organization.
7. **Company:** Making progress by aligning your role and work priorities to impact the overall success of the organization.
8. **Customer:** Making progress by being a difference maker in the customer experience.
9. **Community:** Making progress toward growing the health and strength of the local community.
10. **World society:** Making progress toward benefitting others by improving the condition of humanity and the world.
11. **Spirituality:** Making progress toward living out the highest-level ideals and beliefs that govern your life.

If their work enables a person to contribute value to *themselves*, their *families*, their *work partners*, their *teams*, or their *managers* or *departments*, for example, that work will be meaningful.

The "Purpose Amplifies Meaning" model, which I will explain in detail in the next chapter, provides new facets to consider and unlocks your creativity as a manager. For example, instead of attempting to generate meaning solely on the purview of "the Company," there are a host of other possibilities at play that may have a greater impact. I believe the amplifiers represent a full repertoire of factors that play out in people's psychological perspective of the workplace. The amplifiers define the key emotional touchpoints in the work experience. They deliver a wider opportunity of choices to amplify meaning. This is especially important because the meaning of work is deeply personal and unique to every individual.

As a manager who really wants to move the needle on meaning, don't limit yourself to one facet. This model evokes a creative exercise in thinking more broadly about the possibilities. The most savvy, creative leaders seek the second right answer and beyond.

So if you identify some low-hanging fruit that you can act on right away and get results—great! I would also challenge you to think through some new perspectives that inevitably could spark a complete transformation of the way your team members respond to you and the work they are doing. It's a matter of blending the curiosity to *learn* with the discipline to *act*. The exploration itself should be deeply satisfying to you as a leader. At the very least, you'll learn things about them and yourself that would otherwise have remained hidden.

Is Meaning Lost for Some People?

When it comes to finding meaning these days, some people seem to have given up looking. The work experience in too many cases has become a bitter pill of exchanging time for income. The year 2008, when the bottom fell out of the economy and businesses executed wholesale layoffs and budget cuts, was a tipping point for meaning at work for many people. The impact is still felt today and has been amplified by the pandemic. People began to lose their naiveté about their company's loyalty to them as employees. The idealism of employees and culture coming first gave way to survival of the fiscally fittest. It's been a huge blow to our psyche that has changed our hierarchy of needs at work.

The scar tissue of this change will likely last a very long time for the generation that experienced the betrayal. Leaders of organizations have been duped just as the people at the "doer level." Many leaders believed the organization would be loyal to their employees no matter what, but the harsh economic reality betrayed the huge investment they made into shaping their culture around employee-centric values. Those values typically hang on the wall in a mocking irony to what people experience as the "true" values of the organization. People saw nothing but dollar signs mocking them as they walked out the door.

When the COVID-19 pandemic hit in earnest in 2020, workers again stopped to consider whether their work had a purpose that gave them the meaning they desired. All of a sudden, working at home in a virtual world changed the equation and turbo-charged what was most important in their lives. Some rediscovered their families, and a sense of autonomous freedom that was a deal breaker to the previously assumed "9 to 5 and beyond" lifestyle in the office. The "Great Resignation" of job shifting resulted in hybridized work schedules to accommodate workers who were not willing to give up the newly amplified meaning they experienced, even through the worst of times.

But without meaning there is no engagement. In many cases at the ground level, people's confidence and optimism for finding meaning at work has lost out to a sense of self-preservation that now seeks personal safety and security first. This belief translates into the behavior of not making waves, not standing out for any particular reason, and certainly not taking any risks in that type of environment. People describe their situation using the warfare reference of being in the trenches, keeping their heads down, and making the doughnuts. We repeatedly see a high percentage of these disengaged people every year in the survey data if they feel stuck and without freedom.

Ironically, at a time when companies need innovation the most as a competitive advantage, their fearful cultures have all but pulled the plug on the motivation to try something new. In reality, it's not a bad short-term strategy for some companies that have no other options; however, this book is for leaders and people looking for a long-term answer.

For the "have-not" cultures still out there in corporate America, a loud wake-up call is needed. The COVID-19 pandemic proved that the role of purpose and meaning has *not* lost its potency as a motivating factor; it has simply lost the badly needed attention that keeps it healthy and alive. If it feels far-fetched as a leader to amplify meaning, then you are inadvertently leaving a key driver of your business unattended and undernourished. If meaning is in the rear-view mirror, people will lose the impetus to do something great for themselves and their organizations. Engagement will take a beating, and performance will pay the price. We have an opportunity to amplify meaning and keep it front and center.

2

The Amplifiers of Meaning

As planes start to make their approach to an airport runway, a transmitter along the designated runway sends out a radio signal that generates a "beam" on the pilots' instrument panel. This beam creates a "glide path" to the runway: in aviation terms, the glide path is the steady, downward-sloping final path to a destination. By staying within the glide path, the pilots steadily proceed to the touch-down zone where they can safely land.

The glide path constantly tells pilots where they are in relationship to having a safe and successful landing. It provides confidence they are "on course." Their ultimate purpose is to land the plane and passengers safely, *period*.

I see our personal *purpose* as providing the same function as the glide path instrument at airports. Our source of purpose transmits a signal that creates a glide path that guides us to our destination. In other words, each of the 11 amplifiers of meaning is a transmitter that creates its own distinct glide path of purpose.

How do you know if you are staying within your path of purpose, that you have not strayed off your glide path? This is where *meaning* comes in. If what you are doing—your job, your task, your activity, whatever it may be—gives you a sense of meaning, then you are on course and making progress toward your purpose. If you can feel it, then you can be assured that you are still on your glide path.

Glide Path to Purpose

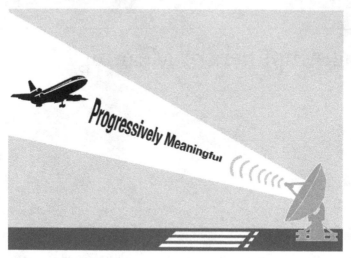

Figure 2.1 Glide Path to Purpose.

While the workers in the printing shop may never have visualized the glide path of purpose as shown in figure 2.1, no doubt that they felt their work had meaning, and their sense of purpose toward the goal of benefiting their family is what kept them motivated to come to work for decades. They stayed on course to fulfill their purpose.

THE JOURNEY IS THE DESTINATION

You know for certain you're within the beam or the path to purpose when you feel an event is meaningful. That is the emotional signal you receive as you make progress toward your destination. What is your destination? It is the purpose you've identified that is uniquely yours.

Let's apply what we categorized earlier regarding *transcendent*, *transformative*, and *transactional* purpose types. All transactional purposes and most transformative purposes have a finite destination or end date as the goal. You'll clearly know when you've arrived. But a transcendent purpose consists of a continuous effort throughout a lifetime. The fruits of your labor often live beyond your mortal being. So, even though you never technically arrive at a transcendent purpose destination, it's the progress toward the purpose that matters. It can be said that the journey itself is the destination.

GETTING LOST

Not everything we do keeps us in the glide path. Life is not so generous. Instead, our daily lives, including our lives at work, are filled with commitments, tasks, responsibilities, setbacks, and unforeseen events from which we draw no meaning, because these life events are not helping us progress toward our purpose.

If we are not on a glide path to purpose, then we are technically lost. In life, we may flounder or grope to regain our direction. We are lost in the clouds or find ourselves in a holding pattern. I think of these life events as "passively meaningless." An example from the workplace would be continuously doing work that has no challenge to it, or that doesn't require you to use any creativity or discretionary effort to complete.

There are also "painfully meaningless" experiences in life that cause us to feel like we've crashed and burned (see figure 2.2). These can come from a

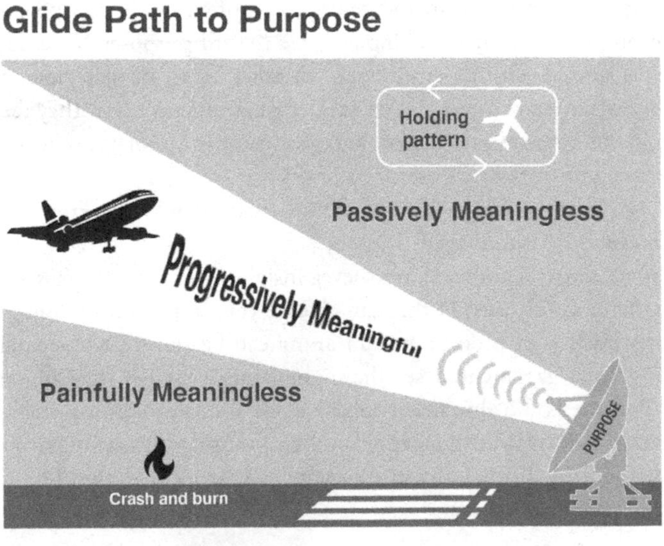

Glide Path to Purpose

Figure 2.2 Glide Path to Purpose.

toxic relationship with a boss or coworker. It can also come from doing work that is completely out of alignment with your personal value system.

Early in my career, I was way off course and felt I was headed for a crash landing. One of my purposes in work (and one I probably share with most of you) is to be a *positive* force for change in the world. It doesn't have to be a contribution of Nobel Prize–winning caliber—I will never cure cancer, for example—but it does have to be positive. That's not negotiable for me. In other words, I want my work to keep me within the glide path to "world society." When I worked at the interactive video music service, I knew that I was way outside of my glide path, because the work had no meaning for me. I felt the void, and it was alarming. That lack of meaning was as clear as a blinking red light on my instrument panel, telling me that I needed a serious course correction. That's exactly what I did.

THE EMOTIONAL IMPACT
OF PURPOSE AND PROGRESS

I believe it's possible to recognize whether people are on track toward their purpose at work. If you observe the emotions they display, those emotions may reveal their glide path location, plus predict behavior and performance.

What do you observe from the descriptors in figure 2.3? Do people have clarity of purpose? Are they making progress toward purpose? Note that each quadrant is labeled with an emotion, a "persona," a set of behaviors, and an outcome. Awareness will give you choices. If you're not sure how they feel, why not ask? It will demonstrate respect and give you the opportunity to work on what's missing from their experience at work.

I am convinced of the validity of the following statement: *Progress toward purpose makes work meaningful.*

This is my most significant next-level insight from *The Progress Principle* research (noted in chapter 1) that can change your approach to engagement. Here's why. Although progress and meaning can be scrutinized separately as conditions for engagement, I see the highest impact when they function in synergy. Purpose is the glue that holds progress and meaning together. Here's the important takeaway, and great news. We *can* absolutely clarify purpose. It's within our control. I believe as an engagement strategy, it should become our number one focus as leaders.

Emotional Impact
of Purpose and Progress

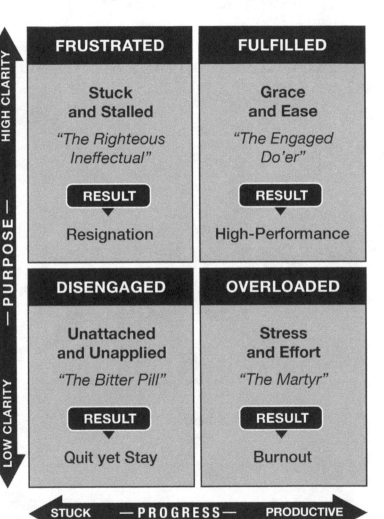

Figure 2.3 Emotional Impact of Purpose and Progress.

THE PURPOSE AMPLIFIES MEANING MODEL

The Purpose Amplifies Meaning model (see figure 2.4) shows all 11 amplifiers of meaning. Each amplifier represents a distinct glide path of purpose that creates the conditions for work to be meaningful.

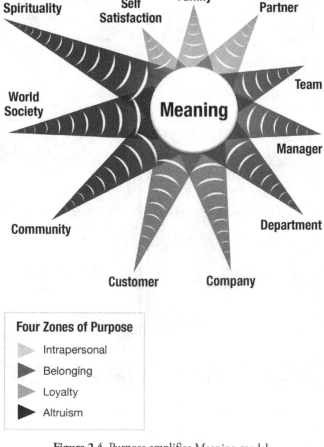

Figure 2.4 Purpose amplifies Meaning model.

You'll notice that some of the paths of purpose are shorter, and some are longer. Metaphorically, the length of the beam or glide path is relevant to the nature of the amplifier and the time it takes to act upon its signal. *Self-satisfaction* casts a very short yet broad beam that is felt and received immediately and frequently (multiple times a day). I believe we take hundreds of flights in a given day that fall within the shorter amplifier beams. They happen constantly as events occur throughout the day. As you move further out in the nautilus of the model, the less flights you take because these typically are made up of transcendent purposes. Most of the flights are long-term transcendent ventures that have many stopovers in the journey. For example, the purpose of *spirituality* emits a long beam that is more symbolic of an entire life's work.

In aviation, the airport must make sure that the ground instruments are functioning properly so that pilots can receive the signal and have a glide path to follow. In the workplace, you as a manager have direct control on whether the purpose "transmitters" are turned on and amplified to create the glide path or paths of purpose for your employees. In other words, you must communicate the purpose connection for people so they can see it for themselves. Learning how to turn on all the transmitters in the model is what you'll discover in this book.

Simply turning on the glide path of purpose doesn't guarantee people will use it. In the end, people on the receiving end must be accountable for switching on their receiver in a way that allows meaning to be heard (i.e., felt). In many workplaces, the problem is not workers who don't care about finding meaning in their work; the problem is companies and organizations where the purpose that could give the work meaning is a weak signal or is turned off altogether by poor leadership. That's why the model is called *Purpose Amplifies Meaning* because it's your job to *amplify*—to make loud and clear—the purposes that guide and fulfill individuals and your entire organization with deeply satisfying meaning.

THE FOUR ZONES OF PURPOSE

The 11 amplifiers I identified earlier fall within four overlapping "zones of purpose." As shown in figure 2.5, the zones of purpose identify the sense of relevance the amplifiers have upon a person's perspective of the work and their environment. The first zone of purpose, the intrapersonal zone, is typified by frequent everyday events that are embedded in the work experience. Many of those events provide meaning through emotional intimacy. As you move further from the everyday, the zones of purpose become broader in scope and, in a sense, larger than oneself and the granular elements of work.

The Four Zones of Purpose

Zones of Purpose Amplifiers	Driven by:	Inspires:	Meaning expressed:
INTRAPERSONAL Self Satisfaction Family Work Partner	Emotional intimacy	Self-respect, pride, accountability, and personal relationships.	"It's fulfilling."
BELONGING Team Manager Department	Membership	Collegiality, collaboration and teamwork.	"We're in this together."
LOYALTY Company Customer	Patriotism	Commitment to excellence and creativity.	"It's my duty."
ALTRUISM Community World Society Spirituality	Love	Fulfilling one's calling. Giving back to benefit others. Selfless acts of kindness.	"It's doing the right thing."

Figure 2.5 The Four Zones of Purpose.

Intrapersonal Zone

The quality of our relationships is what determines the quality of our lives.

—Esther Perel, Belgian psychotherapist and author[1]

The *self-satisfaction*, *family*, and *work partner* amplifiers are anchored in the intrapersonal zone because they represent an everyday component of the work. They could also be described as highly intimate because they influence us at an emotional level due to the dynamics of the close-knit relationships involved. If work were a football game, then the amplifiers in this sphere represent the play-by-play you'd hear from an announcer. These amplifiers are powered by the intimate and familiar daily routine of the job itself, plus our common personal encounters that happen at work and home. If a person's work is not providing at least a rudimentary level of fulfillment, self-respect, or pride through these amplifiers, then achieving a positive sense of meaning would be a steep, uphill climb for them. They'd have to have some of the other remaining amplifiers turned up to full power to overcome a deficiency in the intrapersonal amplifiers.

Belonging Zone

> The most basic human desire is to feel like you belong. Fitting in is important.
>
> —Simon Sinek, author of *Start with Why*

Team, *manager*, and *department* are amplifiers that lie within the belonging zone. These amplifiers are entities that we connect with, feel a part of, and participate in. They become our identity within our companies. Even the *manager* amplifier qualifies for this zone of purpose because, within a company, it's often the first filter we use to describe our role or position. If a coworker asked what we do, we would probably say something like, "I work for Jane Jones in IT." We are members of what celebrated social scientist and author Seth Godin calls "tribes."[2] Membership and participation in a tribe gives us a real sense of belonging. As a result, we form a common bond for what we are working on together. We recognize that our personal performance has a great impact on our manager, team, and department, and we are motivated to succeed for them, because we are a part of them. The sense of belonging and collegiality of membership in the tribe is a strong and motivating influence on the meaning we derive from work.

Loyalty Zone

> If we communicate the vision behind our ideas, the purpose guiding our products, people will flock to us.
>
> —Adam Grant, *Originals: How Non-conformists Change the World*

The *company* and *customer* are amplifiers that fall within the loyalty zone. In many ways, we may see our work as a duty to perform in the service of these two important entities. Much of the culture work training that has been done in business over the past several decades has been centered upon building loyalty and commitment to the company and customer. This has been propelled ever since the books *Built to Last* and *Good to Great* became corporate Bibles confirming the high impact of creating a customer-centric culture. Once this valuable connection is established for employees, they are predisposed to make decisions that are in the best interest of the company and the customer. People who do this exceedingly well are said to "wear the company hat" and are trustworthy advocates for the customer. The majority of organizations have established a customer focus–themed value for that purpose because it has such a robust ROI (return on investment). It's almost a sure bet that your company has a value, or even two values, that puts a stake in the ground to declare the importance of customer focus. Companies love to trumpet their patriotism to both employees and the outside audience about their unwavering duty to serve the customer.

Altruism Zone

> I think people get satisfaction from living for a cause that's greater than themselves. They want to leave an imprint.
>
> —Dan Pink

The amplifiers of *community*, *world society*, and *spirituality* are influenced by altruism. We connect and value these amplifiers out of a sense of love for others and a desire to give back. Altruism feels good to us in a very deep way that is rooted in the emotion of satisfaction. It's often hard for people to describe why they do such amazing things within this sphere. Altruism seems to be motivated by an internal value and attitude that is a type of higher calling in its selflessness. People who experience the joy that comes from these amplifiers are often driven to focus their entire life's work around them. In some cases, it gives them such a profound new sense of perspective that everything else seems far less important. The power of transcendent purpose is clearly evident through the amplifiers in the altruism zone.

I should note here that whole new generations of employees (millennials and Generation Z) are asking deeper questions (even in interviews) about the altruism amplifiers. They want to find a match for themselves. It's not just about nailing a job, making money, and raising 2.5 kids in a suburban cul-de-sac anymore. Millennials are seeking meaning from the get-go as a qualifying factor for their loyalty. The savvy organizations that "get it" (and probably created their business from the start for this same reason) are separating themselves from the herd. They are able to attract incredible talent and are shaping cultures that almost sound like fairy-tale fiction in their level of commitment to idealism.

WHEN PURPOSE BECOMES SUSTAINABLE

As a diagnosis tool, it would be fair to surmise that the further out individuals go from the center of the model, in terms of making the connection to their work, the more profoundly engaged they would be through the meaning of their work. In other words, the work itself provides such a positively steadfast sense of meaning that people can withstand temporary setbacks, hardships, a jerk boss, and other disappointments more readily. They stay in the game and remain engaged due to the sustainable nature of meaning found through the work. It's less likely they will be out shopping their resume every time a negative event happens at work.

Think of what a missionary typically goes through in terms of sacrifice and potential physical harm. Missionaries and people volunteering for Peace Corps projects describe being fully engaged in ways that allow them to persevere. They carry out their transcendent purpose and mission even in the face of tremendous hardships and would do it all over again if given the chance. Many even risk their lives because their beliefs about the nature of their work are indivisibly strong.

If you create a culture that is rich in meaning within the outermost zone of altruism, then you'll create "sticking power" for your very best talent. That's a priceless investment in performance security.

If none of this seems possible, and the outlying zones of purpose don't seem to be a viable factor for your organization, all is not lost. Purpose does not have to be connected to a cause. Individuals can indeed still be fully engaged through the meaning of their work if the other amplifiers are activated and accentuated.

UNIQUE DIFFERENCES IN AMPLIFIER POWER

Every person is unique in terms of which amplifiers are most valuable or powerful to him or her. Each of us has our own set of values that we continuously attempt to fulfill. This quest inevitably governs our lives and is our anchor point to meaning.

Others may see the value of the amplifiers quite differently than you. What's most important is our ability to learn this about each other with a great sense of empathy. We can then make better choices on how to influence the amplifiers that are vital to each of us. Are you willing to see the work and the world through their eyes?

THERE'S NO EXCUSE FOR INACTION

You may be saying to yourself, "Our organization doesn't make cancer drugs, heart valves, or impact world hunger; how can I realistically leverage meaning for my team?" Let's face it, most of us are not in the business of fighting cancer or reducing world hunger. Yet many leaders and managers use this reason to opt out of efforts to instill meaning and purpose in their companies. If the nature of your work does not have an obvious built-in meaning factor, then you will need to create connections by considering new possibilities. This was the motivating factor for identifying the Purpose Amplifies Meaning model in the first place. I recognized that people were really struggling with the topic of meaning. The amplifiers provide managers with a whole new consideration set from which to generate meaning for teammates. You don't have to be in the business of philanthropy or solving world problems to amplify meaning. There are so many other more relevant possibilities.

In the early 1980s, there was an amazingly campy and satirical movie called *This Is Spinal Tap* (1984). The movie documented the outrageous exploits of a fictitious British heavy metal band. In one of the most memorable scenes, lead guitarist Nigel Tufnel proudly shows an interviewer that his amplifiers had volume knobs that went up to 11. All other amps only go to 10, but he had the ability to push his audience over the sonic cliff by going to 11. The interviewer asks with stone logic, "Why don't you just make 10 louder, and make 10 be the top number, and make that a little louder?" Nigel pauses to think about it and says with startling credulity, "These go to 11."

With this simple phrase—"These go to 11"—Nigel was not just cranking up the music, he was cranking up two of the amplifiers in our model. First, he had his own vital sense of self-pride, one of the core facets of the *self-satisfaction* amplifier. He had something special at work to help him overachieve (an amplifier that goes to 11). Who else has an amplifier like that? People love having a unique expression of themselves.

Second, he recognized that pushing his volume to a new level would make a difference in the experience for his audience. He was, in other words, amplifying his own *customer* amplifier.

You could make the assumption that Nigel found a high level of self-satisfying meaning in his own work and created a unique way to share it with others to help *them* amplify their meaning—literally. We should be so lucky. Isn't that what we're all seeking? Everyone has a sense of pride and the desire to reach mastery of their art form. We can all be rock stars of meaning if we really want to and are willing to work at it. What does "11" look like for you in the work you do?

If you're a manager looking to engage your employees with a higher level of meaning at work, there is good news. In a stroke of serendipitous irony, I have identified 11 amplifiers that can be activated to bring meaning into symphonic harmony. Nigel Tufnel would be proud!

The model I've constructed shows the distinction and context of the amplifiers and serves as the foundation for this book. My discovery is intended to give you new ideas and options on how to find meaning at work. We'll explore each amplifier one at a time by looking at its psychological ramifications but, most important, what *you* can do about it. Whether you crank the amplifiers up to 11 is totally up to you. I want to show you how it is possible. Let's take meaning to 11!

3

The Self-Satisfaction Amplifier

We were more concerned with diversity, self-satisfaction, creativity. We were trying to entertain ourselves first and foremost.

—Robert Plant, Led Zeppelin

In *The Progress Principle*, as noted in chapter 1, Teresa Amabile and Steven Kramer unveiled a key touchstone through their breakthrough research. In order for work to be meaningful, the person must perceive it as contributing value to something or someone who matters. That "something or someone" could be your family, your boss, your company, or even your community or society in general. But the first "someone" to whom your work should contribute value and, therefore, be meaningful is *you*. Thus, the first amplifier that gives meaning to work is *self-satisfaction*.

That is, the actual work itself, in the trenches, must provide an aspect of self-satisfaction or its meaning is lost. This is a key factor of consideration for elevating engagement in ways that motivate performance.

Wouldn't you automatically be self-satisfied if you "had it all" in life? Maybe not. It's mind blowing that rock 'n' roll icon Mick Jagger recently said, "Teaching may have been more gratifying than being in the music business." Are you kidding me? This is coming from a multibillionaire who is the very embodiment of what it means to be a rock star. If Mick could step back after all these years and reflect on what is so fundamentally important to him, then we all have a shot. In a twist of ironic prophecy, Mick and the Stones' most recognizable song has the hook line, "I can't get no satisfaction." Yes, it's true that no matter what we do or achieve, we all seek a sense of satisfaction at the very core of our being. Apparently, material possessions, worldwide fame, and even living a life in the center of the limelight don't necessarily guarantee self-satisfaction.

Do you know what people are looking for from their experience at work to be satisfied? How might you gain awareness of the elements in your corporate culture or business goals that amplify self-satisfaction? This chapter will open up some creative options. The goal is to elevate your emotional intelligence (EQ), which will reveal new opportunities to strengthen and grow the self-satisfaction of your employees and how they feel about their work.

To frame our exploration, let's first identify the *key self-satisfaction questions* your people ask themselves about their work and their experience through work:

- Do I feel respected here?
- Does the work stir my interest and challenge me in a positive way?
- Can I capitalize on my true talent and use my strengths doing this work?
- Am I proud of the way my work reflects on me as an individual?
- Does the work provide an intrinsic value that goes beyond the exchange of my time for extrinsic compensation?
- Do I have the ability to influence and change the way the work is done?

These questions are all about discovering self-satisfaction, and you should seek to learn the answer to these questions from your team members' perspective. Empathy is key. Self-satisfaction is perhaps the most imperative of all the amplifiers. It is the closest to a team member's core in terms of direct impact on work being meaningful. At the end of this chapter is a playbook to guide you on one specific action you can take to impact their mind-set—and allow them to answer "yes" to the questions posed earlier.

Everyone requires a degree of self-satisfaction at work to be fully engaged. This amplifier is wired into the granular nature of the work itself. Dynamics that amplify (or stifle) self-satisfaction in the workplace happen multiple times every day. If your team members are lacking in self-satisfaction, then you must start addressing these questions to bring out the best in them and their performance.

The self-satisfaction amplifier falls within the intrapersonal zone of our model. It might also be the most nuanced, fragile, and emotionally driven amplifier as well. Self-satisfaction has a subtle and ephemeral quality to it that has the potential to change rapidly with the slightest nudge. Managers can impact self-satisfaction with as little as a smile, an acknowledgment, or virtual pat on the back. Or, alternatively, they can crush it with the opposite—a frown, a tactless outburst of criticism, or ignoring a person's humanity. So where do we start?

SELF-SATISFACTION BEGINS WITH RESPECT

Self-satisfaction is anchored on a foundation of respect. When we perceive that our teammates, boss, or even our customers respect us, then we feel our presence and contribution are valued. Respect gives us dignity. Respect tells us that we matter as human beings and colleagues. What could be more basic as a confirmation of our purpose for being?

It would be easy to assume everyone knows that respect is essential as a motivating force and therefore given in great abundance. The proof says otherwise. Sadly, I've seen so many people simply seeking dignity at work yet leave feeling used or treated like a small replacement part in a big machine. I've also seen people willing to run through a wall for a manager because they craved the respect they received when challenged to think and do something meaningful.

It is sobering to see the shockingly low scores coming from engagement surveys on the question of being respected at work. I've never seen more than 50 percent of employees indicate they are respected on a regular basis by their leaders. You'd think respect would be the most valued of all values. We should be putting the full energy of our effort into making it the norm within our cultures by doing deep-level training on the psychology of respect and the behaviors that cause people to feel respected.

Respect, however, is a very personal thing and can't be fully "instituted" with masterstrokes of policy or programs from the C-suite (e.g., CEOs). Those certainly help set the right expectation, but respect is established from everyday conversations and encounters—one at a time. That's good news if you desire to have people feel more respected because those conversations and encounters are mostly within your direct control. Respect is your most important consideration if you want to turn on the self-satisfaction amplifier.

The Little Radio Station That Could

I feel extremely fortunate. The first real job I had right out of college amplified meaning for me in the self-satisfaction realm. I landed a DJ position doing the overnights at radio station WSQV-FM in the media metropolis of Jersey Shore, a time-forgotten town deep in the heart of Pennsylvania.

Most of the things that went on at the radio station were better than fiction. WSQV had the weakest signal in the entire market and was originally dead last in any Arbitron ratings. The only thing going for it was that it was located on the second floor of an old house, and the first floor was a bar. The young owners of the radio station, who were all in their 20s, bought the station on the cheap. Through brilliant branding, marketing, promotions, and a new rock format, they turned the station into number one in the market in less than six months. All of us on the staff became friends inside and outside of work, which created a highly energized team.

The culture that the leadership team created was truly remarkable. Every Wednesday afternoon, the entire radio station staff was invited to an all-hands on-deck brainstorming session to generate ideas to pitch to new and existing clients. We'd pack the little two-desk sales office with people sitting on any available object, windowsill, or crammed spot on the floor. It was the first time I ever heard the "rules" of brainstorming—and they were enforced! If anyone was negative or judged an idea, they were instantly pelted with wadded-up notebook paper balls. We got the message.

The team generated tons of ideas that literally increased the fortunes of our clients. For me, it was a total joy to take part and have an impact as a 22-year-old business rookie. During my time at WSQV, I learned I was talented when it came to the generation of ideas. My teammates responded so positively that I began to take more chances. My creative muscles were being flexed. And it was all because I felt respected, simply by being given the opportunity to contribute.

That first job at WSQV changed my life because it changed the way I thought about myself. I discovered that I was highly creative and loved engaging in the electrifying exchange of thoughts and ideas. In every place I've worked since then, I've sought that same sense of purpose. It's an unshakable passion. The experience of self-satisfaction can do that for each of us.

Looking back, this positive experience probably spoiled me by setting a super-high bar for the type of open, collaborative, and creative culture that I needed to thrive. Here's a truth that likely applies to you, too: Once you know what is deeply satisfying for you within a culture, it's almost impossible to be content without that element being present in the everyday nature of the work environment.

Why Respect Matters

Don't just tell people what to do. Just giving orders does not show respect. For that reason, be relentless in communicating the *why*. Explain to them why their tasks are important, how their tasks contribute to the success of the organization or the business unit, and why it's personally important to you.

This habit or practice applies to each of the 11 amplifiers of meaning but is especially core to the self-satisfaction amplifier. Here's why. (Pun intended.)

- Taking the time to communicate the bigger picture of the *why* is a sure sign to others that they matter. You're investing time and effort in them.
- The *why* helps people feel they have a stake in the game and are included.
- The *why* galvanizes resolve—a feeling of being in it together as a larger unit.
- Communicating the *why* demonstrates that you have respectful empathy for others (and that respect will be reciprocal). If you are viewed as a manager who "cares," you will set yourself apart.
- The *why* is the most emotionally centered aspect of work and, therefore, has the greatest impact on intrinsic motivation.
- The quest to satisfy the *why* opens the runway to new thinking, approaches, ideas, and innovations. Revealing the clear purpose of the work activates a type of organic creativity in people seeking to make progress.

Making the *why* an absolute must-have within your communication repertoire is the key to unlocking respect. For everything you communicate, in all mediums, consider the best way to articulate the *why*. If you need to put a sign on your wall or desk as a reminder, it will be worth it. This is an opportunity to brand yourself as a purpose-driven leader and communicator. Soon, others will be speaking the same language as well as letting you know that you've changed your culture from the inside out with your influence.

Respect Unlocks Authenticity

Respect helps us feel confident we are working within the glide path of our purpose at work. As a result, that greater sense of meaning and inclusion adds to the vital psychological safety that is necessary to act as our *authentic self*—and this relieves our stress. It might seem obvious, but it's hard work to constantly try to be something that you're not.

Being our authentic self is the only sustainable path to long-term effectiveness. Respect gives us permission to let our hair down and buys us a sense of priceless security. Respect is a form of relationship equity.

If, as leaders, we want others to be highly effective, less stressed, and more fulfilled, then being a champion of respect is essential within our leadership repertoire. We must let others know that they are free to be themselves, without judgment or repercussions.

INCLUSION IS CORE TO FEELING RESPECTED

The lowest-hanging fruit to impact respect in ways that turn on the self-satisfaction amplifier stems from an empathetic orientation. Do you realize most people are dying to share their opinions and to feel important enough that you care? They want to matter by feeling included.

The key challenge is being emotionally intelligent enough to be aware. Awareness unlocks choices on how to adjust and manage to be more socially savvy. It's a matter of putting yourself "in their shoes." How do you do that if it doesn't come naturally to you? I recommend getting disciplined at asking "includer questions"—questions that help others feel included, involved, respected, and that they *belong*.

Asking includer questions is a discipline you can practice so that it becomes a common behavior in the way you lead. I can almost guarantee the positive reaction you'll receive will reinforce the practice and encourage you to make includer questions an everyday element of your communication style.

Here are examples of includer questions:

1. What is your opinion on . . .?
2. What is one thing that could make your job easier?
3. What ideas have you been thinking about?
4. What are the barriers or pinch points in the way we work that add stress to your job?
5. How might I be more effective for you as your supervisor?
6. How do you think we could improve things around here?
7. What would you like to learn that would help you grow?
8. What would you like to know more about that I could communicate to you?
9. If you were your own boss, how might you change things?
10. What are some of your strengths and passions that you'd like to tap into more often?
11. What gets you jazzed about your role here?
12. What do you see happening here from your unique vantage point that I should know?
13. What else could I do differently to be a more effective leader for our team?

All of these questions come from a place of empathy blended with open curiosity. Just taking the time to ask them, and then listening with patience and interest, is a huge demonstration of respect in and of itself. The positive expression on people's faces will confirm it for you.

Inclusion in a Tough Neighborhood

I experienced a game-changing event in my life where I witnessed the power of giving dignity and respect where it was least expected. At the time, I was leading the culture for Vynamic, a rapid-growth health care consultancy. Our team at Vynamic sponsored a technology room for the RW Brown Community Center in North Philadelphia as one of our give-back initiatives. We supplied desperately needed laptops and internet for the middle school kids who came to the center every day after school. This was a tough neighborhood where many kids grew up too fast. Access to a safe environment and learning computer skills were potential game changers for them.

We came up with a plan to include the kids in a brainstorming session to completely redesign the technology room and to turn it into a place they could call their own—with ideas and a design they could be proud of because it was uniquely theirs.

I led the session with roughly 15 of the kids and began by introducing them to the rules of brainstorming. Keep in mind that I had done this procedure hundreds of times with adults, but never with kids—especially kids having a vastly diverse experience from my own growing up in suburbia. I was nervous, and the brainstorm was off to a shaky start. The kids weren't responding to my questions or even making eye contact with me. It was then I realized with some sadness they rarely had been asked to share their opinion or participate in a creative free-for-all before. Plus, they didn't fully trust me, the enthusiastic stranger they just met.

I wasn't going to give up, so I kept smiling and asked them to share their names. It took a very anxious 20 minutes on my part, but things started to open up. Someone had a funny idea, and everyone laughed. I laughed, too, and shared how fun and humor were the key to creativity and good ideas. It gave me a chance to change the brainstorm question about the design of the room to "What might we do to make the room fun?" The kids completely rocked the rest of the brainstorm and came up with amazing ideas and seemed to enjoy the entire experience.

What does this experience teach us? These kids didn't trust me at first and were thrust into a peculiar challenge. Does that sound familiar when you think about the people you work with? But they ended up performing. Here's what I learned:

- The simple practice of asking questions and opinions makes others feel like they matter. We included the kids in the process every step of the way—and they owned the outcome.
- Never underestimate the power of mattering. My Vynamic team members and I treated the kids like creative rock stars in training. It took patience, but it got through to the kids and they rose to the occasion.
- Don't give up on winning people over. Inclusion is the key. Trust your instinct that people will respond positively if given respect.

When our team came back to the community center a couple weeks later to paint the walls and move furniture, some of the kids greeted me with a high five and big smiles. I was deeply moved. They made me feel I was included.

Inclusion Retains Your Best Talent

All of us are probably familiar with the concept of doing "exit interviews" when people resign. Exit interviews are a good practice to surface potential retention issues. But why wait until it's too late to learn these things? It seems silly, doesn't it?

All of the includer questions I mentioned can serve double duty as "stay interview" questions because they reveal self-satisfaction factors that would cause a person to want to stay with the organization. It's so much better to be proactive—especially with the people whose resignation would break your heart. Don't wait.

Virtually Excluded?

The COVID-19 pandemic surfaced the essential need to remove the isolated feeling of working from home. All of a sudden Zoom meetings became the daily norm, and the organic conversations about work, personal life, shared frustrations, shared laughs, and relationship building vaporized. The pandemic required leaders to be purposeful in pulling people together to build relationships instead of drifting away into the digital abyss of endless virtual meetings.

If you have a virtual team, it's especially important to help them feel included. What's the opposite of that? It's feeling isolated, out of the loop, and unimportant. All these emotions are a potential default mode for people working outside of their core team in the new work-from-home megatrend.

Pull remote team members into the scene by seeking their opinions. Also, some of the most progressive organizations are scheduling time for calls to simply connect with each other on a personal level—talking about family, career history, things they like to do, and so on. Doing so is a very proactive and purposeful way to help them feel included and respected even if it's from afar. In the "Team Amplifier" chapter (chapter 6), I share a specific playbook of actions you can take to build valuable rapport by facilitating relationship-building conversations.

Sometimes we make things so complicated. Respecting people by including them is truly basic, 101-level leadership, yet it is too often neglected or underestimated. Begin asking the includer questions to activate respect. The self-satisfaction amplifier will be jump-started in the process.

Managing Up with Inclusion

Nearly everyone has their doubts about being accepted as part of the group, no matter what their level of authority. You'd assume position-power gets you an automatic "buy-in" of acceptance. Surprisingly, I've heard expressions of frustration many times from high-level leaders—a concern of feeling isolated or separated, of not being on the proverbial inside with their team members. When they spontaneously join an organic conversation, they notice the dynamics change. Suddenly, people clam up, take the edge off their comments, or lose the candor in favor of norming to the type of organizational political correctness that seems appropriate to team members given the new high-level participant in the crowd—you! In other words, people get a little more uptight. Most leaders can't stand this dynamic because it causes them to feel separated. They want others simply to be themselves in their presence.

Being effective at managing "up" starts with your recognition of this dynamic. Your opportunity is to find creative ways to include leaders into the tribe. It might come from asking questions to pull them into the candid dialogue of the group. (Most of the includer questions I've mentioned apply to them, too.)

The most effective technique I've seen that should come naturally, however, is simply to demonstrate that you are happy to be around them. How do you do that? Offer a warm smile, a gracious welcome, or even a comment that entails lighthearted ribbing. Nothing helps a person gain a foothold faster on being included in the group than the opportunity to express self-deprecation. It helps them be authentic. It's the high EQ members of the group who have the tact to set up the right conditions of safety for that to happen for someone else—including the boss. They will love you for it and reciprocate with a higher level of authentic rapport.

SELF-SATISFACTION THROUGH AUTONOMY

Workers need both headroom and elbowroom to be productive.
—Peter Drucker, founder of Modern Management

Have you ever experienced feeling a sense of freedom at work? Brendon Burchard, performance coach and *New York Times* bestselling author, said, "Humans have a natural instinct for freedom and independence."[1]

The screenwriters of the movie *Jerry Maguire* (1996) hit the nail on the head. Jerry's character is the poster child for this amplifier. The white paper he wrote on his vision for how work should be conducted at his sports agency got him fired. But for the remainder of the movie, he never gave up on his deep passion and commitment, and that dynamic struggle among Jerry, the agency, and his client Rod Tidwell (Cuba Gooding Jr.) made the movie compelling. His drive to attain that self-defined level of satisfaction took him to rock bottom. Of course, it's Hollywood, so ultimately he prevailed, winning back his career and the girl of his dreams. The one and only client who stuck with Jerry, Rod Tidwell, in contrast had the family amplifier playing at full blast.

The fictional Jerry attests to our inherent drive for self-satisfaction through autonomy. In fact, Jerry was willing to sacrifice everything to get it. He sought—to his detriment—the freedom to make his own decisions and function at peak performance.

Research shows that most people have an inherent drive for autonomy. Autonomy, as described by researchers James Adie, Joan Duda, and Nikos Ntoumanis, is "fulfilled when people perceive that they are the origin of their choices and decisions, and that they are acting in accord with their integrated sense of self."[2] In other words, when we are free or given latitude to make decisions, we get both the satisfaction of making those decisions and the satisfaction of being left to our own devices.

Dan Pink's research, described in his groundbreaking book *Drive*, also identifies autonomy as a key component of motivation. People need to feel they have control and some authority to make decisions and influence the way work is performed. There is great satisfaction in feeling our creativity and discretionary effort truly make a difference. I have found that managers are mostly tone deaf to this amplifier factor.

Unwittingly, managers often create the opposite conditions in the name of compliance and consistency. They've removed the impetus to innovate and instead have implemented rigid controls and procedures that treat people like automatons that simply crank out the work. Being placed in the proverbial box and treated like a commodity is a sure-fire way to destroy self-satisfaction and meaning.

Autonomy is why Jerry Maguire prevailed in the end. Hollywood got it right.

Job Crafting

> The key to creativity is giving people autonomy concerning the means— that is, concerning the *process*—but not necessarily the ends.
>
> —Teresa Amabile (Harvard Business School), "How to Kill Creativity"

Job crafting is something you can start doing immediately by simply giving employees more flexibility, a higher degree of freedom, and greater decision-making authority. Job crafting allows employees to modify how they perform their tasks. Each member of your team not only will feel empowered with the vested autonomy that comes from job crafting but also will have the opportunity to discover meaning in their work.

I'm not talking about being a laissez-faire leader; I'm talking about purposeful leadership. You still need to set team expectations, goals, individual key performance indicators (KPIs), and deadlines, but give employees leeway on the process and let them determine the best route to the outcome. If you have a project, hold back your own ideas, ask for theirs, and watch how engaged, motivated, and satisfied people will become. Teresa Amabile states the following:

> People will be more creative if you give them freedom to decide how to climb a particular mountain. You needn't let them choose *which* mountain to climb. In fact, clearly specified strategic goals often enhance people's creativity.[3]

The power of crafting your job is vividly demonstrated by Yale professor Amy Wrzesniewski, a pioneer researcher in job crafting. Wrzesniewski describes the stark differences between the cleaning staff at a hospital.[4] One group of cleaners described their work as highly skilled. The other group described their work as low-skilled work that just about anybody could do. The group who felt their jobs required a high skill level followed the job description to a T, paying close attention to their responsibilities but also to the limits of their responsibilities. For example, cleaners were not supposed to interact with the patients and their families. Thus, the cleaners who considered their jobs to be highly skilled came into work, did the required cleaning, and left.

But one group of cleaners, who believed that their jobs were low-skilled jobs, approached their jobs differently. This group interacted freely with the patients and their families. One cleaner even rearranged the pictures hanging in the room of a patient in a coma, believing that perhaps that pictures might in some way help the patient recover. By developing relationships with the patients and their families, these cleaners were extending the job description of cleaner from cleaning staff to *caregiver* or *healer*. As cleaners, they were contributing to the care of the patient. This perspective of cleaner as part of the caregiving staff in the hospital gave their job much more meaning.

Wrzesniewski says those cleaners were job crafting—that is, crafting the boundaries of their jobs in ways that made work more meaningful to them. What an amazing difference that is. Imagine the quality of patient care you'd get with people who describe their role as "healers"! I know if I were a patient, I would want to be around healers versus a staff following a tactical job description.

The point is that the cleaners who considered their jobs high skilled drew some sense of meaning from the accomplishment of doing a high-skilled job. But those who considered their jobs low skilled needed another source of meaning; they found it by "changing" the job description ("recrafting the job" in Wrzesniewski's terminology): they were "healers" not "cleaners." As Steve Jobs once said, "Design is not just what it looks like or feels like. Design is how it works."

Lisa Bodell, the CEO of Future Think and author of *Kill the Company*, uses one very clever question to rally an entire team to recraft their jobs. She famously employs the "What's a stupid rule?"[5] question to unearth the assumptions of work rules and bureaucracy that frustrate people. Try using it at your next staff meeting to invite participation. Be willing to act upon the "stupid rules" people call out.

Autonomy and Trust

Trust, but verify.—Ronald Reagan

I've always found that when employees of any generation have a trusting relationship with their manager, they also have a high level of respect for the manager that compels them to perform beyond expectations.

In short, we must extend trust because it will usually be returned. If we walk around suspicious that our teams and employees are abusing the internet or social media, we end up with a self-fulfilling prophecy. The best solution is to address work from home, flex time, and smartphone usage abuse on an individual basis.

Stephen M. R. Covey talks about using smart trust. In his book *The Speed of Trust*, he writes that, on the one hand, we can't be gullible; but he says that, on the other hand, if we "treat people . . . as if they can't be trusted," we will incur a 'low-trust tax'—including bureaucracy, politics, disengagement, and turnover—and lose high-trust dividends such as innovation, collaboration, partnering, and loyalty."[6]

Distrust of your employees (suspicion and monitoring) doesn't add up to self-satisfaction. Manager suspicion, Covey writes, "sometimes even helps produce the very behaviors they fear, which further validates their suspicion."[7] In the end, it's not worth going against the grain.

The Pull of Entrepreneurism

Millennials in greater numbers than any previous generation have felt the gravitational attraction of entrepreneurism for self-satisfaction—an attraction more easily fulfilled thanks to easy access to the marketplace via social media.

Based on a survey by Bentley University, 67 percent of millennials aspire to start their own business. In fact, according to the Bentley researchers, "Millennials are eager to make their own pathways because they suspect the traditional ones may lead nowhere. Millennials see chaos, distrust of management, breaking of contracts and bad news associated with business. They've watched their relatives get fired and their peers sit in cubicles and they think, 'There has to be a better way.'"[8]

This high risk–high return syndrome is not entirely isolated to millennials and Generation Z. I've embraced it, along with so many of my peers who started their own companies in search of fulfillment. I have started five corporations and hold a patent certificate for a garden tool invention. That's a lot of embracing! The entrepreneurism allure has only mushroomed since the early 2000s, particularly in light of easier access through the online gig economy.

The new gig economy mind-set is that nothing stands in a person's way of making it happen. Ask any person under 35 and they can give you countless stories of people they know who hit it big early in life. All their business heroes are the hipsters who disrupted the social media sphere or used breakthrough technology to create entirely new vertical business segments. My son had a middle-school friend who made enough money doing YouTube hacking tips for the video game *Call of Duty* that he was able to buy a Mercedes when he turned 16. Your most-talented employees likely feel they can do it too and are constantly on search mode for these self-satisfying opportunities.

This may be the greatest threat to your ability to retain millennials and Generation Z. You must provide them ways to be "entrepreneurs" inside of your organization or they will quickly be going outside.

WHEN WORK IS A CALLING

Pleasure in the job puts perfection in the work.

—Aristotle

Yale professor Amy Wrzesniewski argues that people who see their work as a *calling* are significantly more satisfied with their jobs and with their lives. They're more engaged in what they're doing and tend to be better performers—regardless of what the work is. Not everyone sees their work as a calling, but we can help people get satisfaction.

Wrzesniewski pointed to the stark contrast between a corporate securities lawyer and a small-town taxidermist. On the one hand, the lawyer described his job as "dealing with the devil." He said the only reason he stayed was because of the proximity and benefits to his family. On the other hand, the taxidermist felt his job was a little slice of heaven: "I did a duck for a guy the other day, and when he came and picked it up, he almost started crying because it looked so nice. He was just happy, and that made me feel good that he thought I'd done a good job."[9]

Not too many deals with the devil make anyone feel good.

Are you surprised that the taxidermist felt self-satisfaction with his job—one that might seem barbaric to most of us? It's these seemingly minute details like the impact the taxidermist made on his client that bring people meaning and satisfaction. At first glance, one would think the corporate attorney would have had the more satisfying job compared to the taxidermist. It's law! It's prestige! It's affluence! But to the attorney, it's dreadful.

Wrzesniewski suggests the telltale signs of recognizing job satisfaction are in the way team members think about their work, and how they describe the tasks of their job. The lawyer and taxidermist had polar opposite descriptions of their work.

Pride: Welcome to Apple

Apple is the most respected brand in the universe. It's probably not a huge surprise that an organization like Apple plugs into the power of their purpose to amplify meaning. They have been among the business cultural elite for decades and have legendary results to show for it. Their innovations have indeed changed our world and how we communicate.

Have you ever wondered what happens within the Apple culture that allows and encourages them to famously *think different* in ways that drive innovation? What I find fascinating is that they not only have purpose radiating from their company, customer, and even world society amplifiers but also leverage the self-satisfaction amplifier. Apple clearly understands the underlying psychology that sets their workforce apart and articulates the connection. They call out the everyday challenge that comes from the very nature of the work as the factor that leads to greatness. For example, here is a note that new employees used to receive as a part of their onboarding:

> There's work and there's your life's work.
>
> The kind of work that has your fingerprints all over it. The kind of work that you'd never compromise on. That you'd sacrifice a weekend for. You can do that kind of work at Apple. People don't come here to play it safe. They come here to swim in the deep end.
>
> They want their work to add up to something.
>
> Something big. Something that couldn't happen anywhere else.
>
> Welcome to Apple.[10]

What's the message you can send to new employees to get them amped to work for you? How might you clarify your expectations for the unique attitude that leads to success? Just simply having the cultural EQ to know that about your organization is valuable. But, taking it to the next level of acting upon it is key. The best of the best organizations and leaders amplify meaning by communicating in overt ways. They clarify purpose at every opportunity, and the possibilities are endless. The great news is that people will rise to the challenge if given the vision and autonomy to do something they can ultimately be proud of.

You can write a welcome message at any level. Whether it's just for the individual working with you one on one, a small team, your department, or the entire organization, what's the message that clarifies your purpose-driven expectations?

Write your "welcome message" here:

_____

_____

_____

_____

_____

_____

THE HIGHEST PROOF OF SELF-SATISFACTION: WORKING FOR FREE

People yearn for satisfaction to such a degree they will go to extremes to get it, even going so far as to work without pay.

Now that sounds like far-fetched hyperbole, but consider for a moment the digital phenomenon of crowdsourcing. How else can you explain why thousands of gainfully employed IT programmers dedicate personal, uncompensated time and effort solving code issues via crowdsourcing sites like crowdspring.com?[11] Without compensation, it seems to come down to these developers exercising their creative muscles to gain a formidable sense of pride and achievement.

Aaron Hurst, the founder and CEO of Imperative (an organization focused on helping individuals and organizations identify and act upon their purpose), launched a deep exploration into the psychology of purpose as a result of repeatedly hearing reactions from high-level leaders doing pro bono work through his Taproot Foundation. The evidence Hurst quantified and described in his book *The Purpose Economy* was extraordinary in terms of the level of fulfillment these leaders were expressing.[12] They had transforming experiences by literally giving away their time and expertise, expecting nothing in return. What they received was priceless: fulfillment and satisfaction.

So what kind of work will you do for free? What kind of work do you think your team members would do for free? If you know that answer, then you can amplify your own satisfaction and meaning by doggedly pursuing that type of work. And, if you know the answer to the second question, (and, as manager, you should) you can design or craft your team's duties so that they too derive self-satisfaction and meaning.

What I do for free:

_____

_____

What do I "get back" for doing it?

_____

_____

_____

_____

What aspect of work do my team members love doing so much, they would nearly do it for free?

_____

_____

_____

_____

What makes the work so satisfying for my team members?

_____

_____

_____

_____

How might I increase the percentage of work for my team members that is self-satisfying for them?

_____

_____

_____

_____

SELF-SATISFACTION PLAYBOOK

I can live two months on a good compliment.

—Mark Twain

My "Self-Satisfaction Playbook" will give you one powerful tactical amplifier to get immediate results. Essentially, the playbook reveals the single best actionable idea you can apply to amplify self-satisfaction. Every amplifier chapter in the book will end with a similar playbook.

A Game-Changing Attitude and Skill

We can directly influence self-satisfaction as a leader or coworker with recognition and appreciation. It's the most potent game changer we possess. Becoming skilled at this tactic will transform you into an inspirational meaning maker.

Self-satisfaction is amplified by reflecting on how our work matters and feeling proud of it. Did you ever produce or accomplish something and step back and say to yourself, "Dang, that's really good stuff"? I hope so, because when we reflect and appreciate our work, the self-satisfaction amplifier gets turned on. The problem is, we typically don't do it enough, or we blow it off by taking it for granted.

Sadly, a lot of people lose sight of their own good work, or the pride of doing it melts away over time as it becomes part of their routine. We have an opportunity to step up and amplify self-satisfaction as their advocate.

Step 1: Developing the Winning Attitude of "Catching People Doing Things Right"

Call out the winning behavior and attitude of others. Focusing your employees' attention on what they are doing right helps them more clearly see what they are doing that is important and meaningful. More important, the fact that you explicitly acknowledged and appreciated their work increases their sense that the work is meaningful.

Recognition and appreciation—the act of catching people doing things right—is a mind-set we can develop by training ourselves to recognize superior employee performance and articulating our appreciation with purposeful intent. It's about looking for the positive in people, the exceptional choices they make, and the discretionary effort they exhibit.

When our filter for the way we view people is focused on catching them doing things right, we will begin to see it happen everywhere we go. The encounters of everyday life provide countless examples worthy of recognition and appreciation. Here are some examples:

- The grocery store checker who carefully bags your groceries with the delicate items on top
- The security guard with the warm, friendly attitude who makes you feel welcome with a greeting
- The neighbor who called to see if you needed anything when they were out running errands before a storm
- The child who takes the family dog for a walk without being asked
- The waitress who gives amazing service even when the restaurant is packed
- The contractor who did the extra little things to get the project done perfectly even though no one else would have noticed

These people made choices that brought us joy and fulfillment. Our accountability is to simply let them know that it mattered.

Step 2: Tell the Story That Makes It Meaningful

I've noticed that many people seem to avoid giving appreciation because it's uncomfortable for them. They either don't have the words, or they fear expressing sentiment to others. As a default, they use the safest expression possible and only say, "Great job." We hear that all the time and often say it as an autopilot reaction like "Have a nice day." Saying "great job" is certainly better than saying nothing at all, but it lacks the positive stickiness of connecting emotionally. To make that connection, we need the specifics of a great job story.

Here's how we can get comfortable in telling a great job story and build muscle memory to become masterful at doing it well every single time. Express appreciation by following a proven pattern to unfold a meaningful story, which I call the "Meaning Maker" narrative. The pattern is a guide to express the story with specific, detailed recognition elements, plus the appreciation component that amplifies meaning.

1. Start by recognizing the *what*. What did the person do right? What was the action they took to make a difference?

2. Recognize the nuanced details with the *how*. How did they make it happen? How was their winning behavior carried out?
3. Finish with appreciation by making the meaningful connection with the *why*. Why does it matter? Why did their action have a positive impact on people or the situation?

The Meaning Maker narrative model shown in figure 3.1 gives brief examples of what the elements of a story might sound like in each column. Use the model to prime your thinking on how you can express appreciation by telling the complete and meaningful story.

The *Meaning Maker* narrative
"Catch people doing things right" with recognition and appreciation

THE *WHAT* What did the person do right?	THE *HOW* How did they make it happen?	THE *WHY* Why does it matter?
Met or exceeded a goal	Positive attitude	Made me and others feel valued
Delivered on-time or under budget	Highly accountable ownership	Took the burden off the team
Sparked a new idea	Respectful to others	Reduced stress for everyone
Led an initiative	Collaborative approach	Established a new expectation
Chaired a successful meeting	Professionalism	Created a better relationship
Conducted research or analysis	Calm in the storm	Demonstrated growth as a leader
Took on a new challenge	Proactive leadership	Built trust, respect, and inclusion
Communicated with clarity	Probed with effective questions	Made me proud/grateful to work with you
Resolved a difficult problem	Asked for help	Elevated everyone's creativity
Addressed a customer issue	Assumed innocence	Created an example of excellence
Identified lessons learned	Willingness to learn and grow	Provided valuable feedback for me
Helped a team member	Thinking creatively	Positively challenged the status quo
Initiated a proposal	Highly energized and engaged	Elevated the image of the company
Received a go-ahead approval	Set an example of teamwork	Got results when we needed them most
Made a tough yet smart decision	Demonstrated being self-empowered	Stretched your zone of comfort

Figure 3.1 The Meaning Maker narrative.

Who have you caught doing things right that deserves appreciation? Put the Meaning Maker narrative into practice right away by identifying a person and the story elements you will share with them.

Who will you recognize and appreciate?

_____

_____

_____

What did the person do right?

_____

_____

_____

How did they make it happen?

_____

_____

_____

Why does it matter?

_____

_____

_____

When will I communicate with them? (Be specific.)

_____

_____

_____

Shaping Culture One Conversation at a Time

> Talk about changing people. If you and I will inspire the people with whom we come in contact with a realization of the hidden treasures they possess, we can do far more than change people. We can literally transform them.
>
> —Dale Carnegie, *How to Win Friends and Influence People*

I firmly believe that culture change happens one conversation at a time and is most powerful when it comes from the inside out. Appreciation is a catalyst for identifying and making clear what is valued within your relationships, your team, and organization. If you want others to have clarity on the winning behaviors that make a difference, then the mind-set and skill of catching people doing things right and presenting your recognition and appreciation through a story will be a game changer for you.

4

The Family Amplifier

The achievement-focused relationship of Tiger Woods and his father Earl Woods is one of the most documented family affairs in the history of sports. The video images of Tiger hitting golf balls on *The Merv Griffin Show* as a two-year-old are jaw-dropping. Even then, you can see the sparkle in the little boy's eyes as his proud "Pop" introduced the world to a future phenom. Tiger and Earl Woods formed an inseparable father-son bond—and a transcendent purpose for Tiger to become the greatest golfer the world had ever known.

There are three vivid and confirming moments in Tiger's illustrious career that show the power of the *family* amplifier driving him to a stunning achievement. First, Tiger competes at the 1997 Masters at age 21 and comes away with a record-breaking victory. The voice of the Masters, iconic commentator Jim Nance, described Tiger's victory as "one for the ages" as Tiger walked off the 18th green with his first major title and into the arms of his father with a long, tearful embrace. It was clear that winning the Masters represented a victory for both of them, and a major milestone to honor their family journey.

The second moment occurred when Tiger somehow summoned all his talent and moxie to win the British Open at St. Andrews, just weeks after his father Earl had passed away. Tiger clung onto his caddie after the final putt, weeping inconsolably from the void. He dedicated the victory to his Pop and let us know his father was on his mind the entire time.

And third, as life comes full circle, Tiger did what no one thought possible in winning the 2019 Masters after recovering from back fusion surgery. Most thought he'd never play golf again, let alone win a major title at age 43. When Tiger walked off the 18th green, this time he melted into the arms of his daughter Sam and son Charlie. When they asked Tiger what it meant to win the Masters, he said he did it for his kids. His motivation came from realizing his kids had never actually seen him win a major. At that point in his life, he was just a "storybook legend" dad to them. Tiger desperately wanted to relive the glory in front of them to make it real. The family amplifier went into sonic boom in the most inspiring way that beautiful April day in Georgia.

So what could the power of this amplifier do for you and your people at work as a motivating force? Have you considered family as a factor to help people discover meaning? It might even surprise you that family is one of the amplifiers of meaning at work because it might seem outside of our control to influence. Our family is front and center in our psyche, even if they aren't physically present with us. If you ask people why they work so hard and want to succeed, many will tell you they are doing it for their family. This amplifier turns the false assumption that people are primarily motivated by extrinsic rewards upside down when we consider where their money goes, and who it is spent upon.

Here are some search-for-meaning questions people ask themselves:

- Is my family proud of me because of the work I do and who I work for?
- Does my job live up to the standard of respect that reflects my family values?
- Does my work allow me to pursue and fulfill my family priorities?
- Do I feel I'm a good provider for my family?
- Does my family think favorably about the people and organization where I work?
- Does my family believe I am treated fairly and with respect at work?

FLIPPING THE SCRIPT ON MOTIVATION

Some managers are never able to shake their old paradigm that people are motivated by money first and foremost. For them, everything else is a waste of time or too fluffy. It is wise to not hit this dead end with your thinking.

I believe that the extrinsic motivation of money doesn't truly exist in its purest form. Why? Because it is possible to probe deeply with anyone, on any extrinsic award they receive, and discover it always connects directly to an intrinsic desire that is a family-focused purpose. I've experienced this phenomenon many times as a coach when probing for the *why* behind a person's true motivation; in other words, the motivation that has sticking power.

Here's a quick example. Picture a new manager who seems to be extrinsically motivated by a cash bonus for hitting a goal. She works incredibly hard and with great discipline to get there. On the surface, you'd assume it has to be the bonus money. But after probing the real reason (behind the curtain), you discover it's her intrinsic desire that causes her to work hard for the bonus. She's highly motivated to move her kids to a great school district. She needs the ability to cover the costs of the move. That's the outcome of the bonus money. We'd typically never know that unless we cared enough to ask.

How can this insight be leveraged? If you knew this about her, then the conversation about the bonus completely changes to being about her family goal. That's deeply meaningful and motivating. Now, your actions as her manager are inclusive and create a sense of belonging. This knowledge sets up the conditions for you to be her advocate on something intrinsic and meaningful for her at an emotional level.

CONVERTING COMPENSATION INTO INTRINSIC MOTIVATION

What are people doing with their money? What purpose does money help them achieve? Even if people say, "I'm just here for the paycheck," there is far more to it. I'm suggesting that most of it connects back to family as the driver. The paycheck is intended to make progress on a family goal or purpose. The paycheck moves them forward in their purpose path. As a manager, do you have a sense for what their paycheck helps them accomplish? It's not about being nosey and prying into their lives. It's about expressing a sense of care (your EQ, or emotional intelligence) and showing that you understand why they are in this job from a practical standpoint. Once you know that, then you have the power to amplify meaning when it counts. In times of crisis when work is extremely tough, or you're asking people to go above and beyond, or you're requiring people to go through extreme change, remind them of the *why*. Here is what you might say: "We'll get through this. I understand the situation sucks, but our temporary sacrifice will be worth it in the end because it is about securing the output for the sake of our families." Keep in mind how it will make a difference for them. Play this trump card with great care and reserve. It's not a subject to use as "shotgun" coaching or a phony rah-rah speech. This must be communicated one on one in most cases.

WHATEVER IT TAKES

There are countless heroic stories of people who have worked sacrificial schedules or juggled several different jobs just so they could make ends meet or put one of their kids through college. For example, founder of Forever 21 Don Won Chang worked three separate jobs every day to feed his family. Prior to becoming successful, he worked as a custodian, a gas station attendant, and a barista, some of the most disrespected, underpaid, underappreciated jobs on the planet. In my own experience, living the glamorous life of an entrepreneur required that I worked several part-time jobs just to cover the never-ending expenses of starting Culturology and of my family. I've been a bartender, a professional gardener, and a salesperson in the seasonal department at the local Lowe's. Whatever it takes to keep our family going is what any of us are highly motivated to do regardless of the sacrifice.

FAMILY HAPPINESS AT WORK

Family is a loud and powerful amplifier for many people, yet in the corporate world, it is often overlooked. Julian Barling, a professor of organizational behavior and psychology at Queen's University in Kingston, Ontario, suggests that the prevailing school of thought in the 1950s was that work and family were independent. Recent studies, however, provide empirical evidence that work and home life are inextricably linked and, as a result, influence each other. Blessing White, an international consulting firm, "dedicated to creating sustainable high-performance organizations" through positive culture initiatives such as leadership development and employee engagement, revealed the vital importance of family through survey results collected from more than 15,000 people between 2004 and 2013. The survey asked participants to rank 15 attributes on a scale from 1 to 100 and found that people throughout the nation ranked the importance of "family happiness" at a whopping 60 percent. Throughout a nine-year span, the statistics show that family happiness consistently outranked all other qualities. Maybe more surprising, it outranked economic security by 25 percent. The gap between the prominent desire to realize both family happiness and achievement (60 and 45 percent, respectively) compared to the low importance placed on personal development (approximately 22 percent) is in part what this book aims to close.

FAMILY AND YOUR CULTURE

How does family tie into work culture and vice versa? According to Paul Muchinsky, a PhD graduate of Purdue University with a degree in industrial/organizational psychology, "culture is the language, values, attitudes, beliefs, and customs of an organization." Each attribute can and often does influence the other, which tends to have a spillover effect. Muchinsky suggests that, while a person's work culture and experiences influence their home environment, the inverse also holds true; the home environment influences their work environment.[1] Likewise, it is reasonable to believe that while research (e.g., Pfeffer 1983; Weick, Sutcliffe, and Obstfeld 2005) reveals that "employee perceptions, attitudes, and behaviors are influenced by informational cues present in their immediate work environments," informational cues are equally present in their immediate home environments.[2]

The point is that our families play a very important role in how we feel about our job, our managers, and ourselves. The feeling of meaning we get, or don't get, influences our performance. We typically look at our role through the filter of the family and the informational cues that they communicate. After all, what is typically the first thing our significant others ask when we come home from work, even if you've been texting with each other all day? Perhaps it's something like this, "How was your day, honey?" This loaded question triggers a verbal download of our authentic thoughts and reflections of work each and every day. If the engagement survey gurus such as Gallup, Energage, TalentKeepers, McKinsey, and countless others could simply monitor the answers to this question across the corporate world, they would possess the ultimate treasure trove of truth about employee engagement and harness the solutions that improve employee attitudes and social norms, which manifest within the workplace culture. Is there an app for that? Wow, what an opportunity.[3]

Their reaction has an impact on how we in turn see ourselves, the work we do, and the meaning we associate to our role. Research performed by William B. Swann Jr. (professor of social and personality psychology at the University of Texas), Chris De La Ronde (professor of psychology at the University of Texas at Austin), and John G. Hixon (lecturer of social psychology at the University of Texas) established that there is a high probability that the views and feelings that your employees carry home are supported and perpetuated by their significant others. Since spouses and family are the most important people in our lives, their feedback can have either a positive or a negative effect on our self-view and psychological well-being, which consequently reinforces certain work attitudes, motivations, and behaviors.[4]

FLEXING THE FAMILY MUSCLE

Flexibility to work one's life is now the most universal "want" from workers at all levels. It comes down to a loud call for freedom to reprioritize family as the unconditional preference when managing time choices. The COVID-19 pandemic turbocharged this mega-movement into an enormous dilemma for all employers. But most organizations weren't ready and didn't know how to deliver on flexibility as an employee value proposition. This sets up a prime opportunity to turn up the family amplifier by addressing this factor head-on in ways that are deeply meaningful.

Imagine if there was a platform that could make flexibility scalable in a way that personalizes work experiences and benefits that mattered most to people. This blink of an idea was the brainchild of consulting executive Jess Podgajny. And it was born, with perfect timing, right in the middle of the pandemic. She and cofounder Aaron Kamholtz created Lluna, a technology platform that enables managers or their companies to offer employees flexibility and choice to meet them where they are now and in the future. You can easily tell from their tagline—"Work designed for life"—that they are all about delivering flexibility.

I asked Jess how the search for meaning at work was influenced by the family amplifier. She had some key insights that should influence how we view the work experience through the filter of family and flexibility. Jess told me, "We all needed to determine how to come back together after the pandemic. People reevaluated and began listening to their priorities tied to family goals. It created a demand for flexibility and choice" (personal communication with the author, February 2, 2022). She highlighted two inclusive choices people wanted for themselves: first, accelerating their career and leaning in more to provide for their family and, second, controlling how they spend their time. According to Jess, people want permission for a type of "fluidity" that creates the space to attend key events involving the family and, notably, feeling supported in those moments. The Lluna platform they created gives employers control over the choices offered across 10 dimensions that shape the employer/ employee relationship—it's a way to structure flexibility. The technology is supported by a repeating process, where employees refresh their choices periodically to match work/life priorities. Data derived from the platform gives employers—and, notably, managers—real-time insights to enhance their leadership and, by extension, their team's engagement and performance.

Flexibility has an impact on performance. Jess shared, "Especially for parents, the pandemic elevated the challenge of juggling schedules and added super stress to work and home. A work schedule that has customized predictability is a deal maker for people. We're seeing workers with more engagement, confidence, and a focus to perform when their work schedule is predictable and fits their unique needs." Flexibility opens up the opportunity for people to pursue purpose. Survey data show that 86 percent of people say they'd be less stressed with more flexibility at work, and more than 78 percent feel they would be healthier.[5]

I asked Jess how the emphasis on equity applies when people are given extremely different schedules and work arrangements. She said, "When it comes to equity, flexible choices need to be offered to all, but individual choices will vary. It's not about having the same virtual arrangement or schedule. Individuals determine what they are comfortable with, and establish their own boundaries. People still need to collaborate and communicate to stay aligned. Different job types will have different job-flexible options, and at times employers will need to get creative."

So how can a manager amplify meaning with these factors in play? Jess gave direct and actionable advice, saying, "People need permission. Managers can be proactive and address it openly with their team members, saying, 'Just talk to me—we can make it work.'" Doing so eliminates their trepidation of looking uncommitted or entitled. A manager who has this empathetic conversation sets themselves apart and gains loyalty."

Here is another significant reason why the future for Lluna is trending so positively. Nearly 90 percent of knowledge workers say that, when they search for a new position, they will look for one that offers complete flexibility in their hours and geographic location, according to Citrix Research. In addition, 76 percent of the workers polled believe that employees will be more likely to prioritize family and personal interests over proximity to work. According to Citrix, it's expected that workers will pursue jobs in locations where they can focus on lifestyle factors (family, friends, personal interests) even if it means taking a pay cut.[6]

"BRING YOUR DAUGHTER TO WORK!"

Erica, a front desk agent at a Springhill Marriott, is also a single mom. She's working as many hours as she can to cover living costs, plus the extra expense to send her four-year-old daughter to a terrific preschool. She wants the absolute best for her. What mother wouldn't?

One day when the preschool was closed for a holiday, and her mother wasn't able to watch her daughter, Erica was faced with a tough choice. Would she need to take an unexpected day off, or scramble to find someone to watch her daughter at the last minute? A "someone" that she didn't know?

Erica calls her manager to give her a heads-up about the dilemma. Erica's manager knows Erica well enough and is aware of her family situation, and instead of saying, "Too bad for you, you've got to come in no matter what!" she finds a creative solution. She asks Erica if she'd like to bring in her daughter for the shift this one time.

Although Erica likes most of the team at the Marriott, and the banter with the hotel guests, her family amplifier creates the glide path for everything she does. Her manager's awareness revealed a brilliant choice that amplified meaning for Erica. The result of Erica's daughter coming to work conveyed a feeling of respect and dignity. It also sparked another important payoff. All her coworkers were enchanted by her adorable daughter, bringing their knowledge of Erica and her family life to the next level. Some of the guests checking in or out also had fun conversations with her daughter and seemed delighted. Erica was a front-row witness to all of it.

How do you think she feels about her role at the Springhill Marriott now? Is she more fulfilled and likely to go the extra mile? Is Erica more or less likely to jump to another job for an extra $1 per hour bump? Will Erica refer her best friend to apply for a job there? One empathetic decision by the manager changed everything.

TAPPING INTO FAMILY PRIDE

Gratitude unlocks the fullness of life. It turns what we have into enough, and more. It turns denial into acceptance, chaos to order, confusion to clarity. It can turn a meal into a feast, a house into a home, a stranger into a friend. It turns problems into gifts, failures into successes, the unexpected into perfect timing, and mistakes into important events. It can turn an existence into a real life, and disconnected situations into important and beneficial lessons. Gratitude makes sense of our past, brings peace for today, and creates a vision for tomorrow.

—Melody Beattie[7]

It can be incredibly gratifying for people to share a proud moment with their family. As a manager, expand your thinking on recognition and appreciation events to include the family. They usually can't stop talking about it long after the fact, and they continue to amplify meaning even further on their own and within their communities. The pictures of their smiling faces will end up on Facebook or Instagram where a hundred others will congratulate them, adding to their sense of pride. Some managers have been known to send a kind note home to an employee's significant other to laud their employee's performance. These easy-to-do acts are thoughtful gestures that personify value and instill meaning for both the employee and his or her family. The note resonates even louder when it includes two movie tickets or a certificate to their favorite restaurant. Let them share in the glory together, as it simultaneously increases organizational engagement, loyalty, and motivation.

Get creative with the type of recognition or rewards you provide at your organization. If you're investing budget money on incentives, then consider compensation that your employee would share directly with their spouse or kids. Receiving restaurant certificates, movie tickets, and passes to a big sporting event or a theme park are likely to be even more exciting for the family member than it is for your employee because of the surprise factor. When you make an employee a hero or heroine with their family, then you activate a meaning-rich amplifier as an employer who creates lasting memories and experiences they are highly unlikely to get anywhere else.

Here's one of the most creative examples I've ever experienced: The doorbell rings, and it's a flower delivery person with a beautiful bouquet of flowers two days before Mother's Day. Here's what the note tucked within the arrangement said: "Thank you for raising an awesome member of our Seer team! Sincerely, the Seer Management Team." After being blown away with their generosity, I *was amazed* that anyone could be so savvy and smart to know who the major influencer was in our 21-year-old son's life at that point. Yes, Mom (and Dad). Seer is an interactive agency specializing in SEO (search engine optimization). They clearly know their team members well. Almost everyone at Seer is in their 20s, likely graduated from school recently, and perhaps still live at home. What a great strategy and tactic to win over the parents as amplifiers of meaning. How do you think Mom and Dad feel about his employer? Well, we immediately texted him a picture of the flowers with a "Wow." And, not to be outdone, I received a box of chocolate chip cookies in June, two days before Father's Day. We'll forever love Seer Interactive.

LIFE SKILLS FOR LIFE

If it's within your control, provide professional development opportunities that include life skills. The very best development experiences include ways to be more effective at home as well as work. For instance, learning emotional intelligence, listening skills, and patience can have not only a positive impact on employee performance but also a profound impact on the well-being of your family relationships. The Myers-Briggs Type Indicator has had a resurgence of interest because it does such a great job of speaking to people's strengths at work *and* at home. People crave respect; they want to be treated as a whole person, and not just a component that gets plugged in when they come to work. Some of the most heartfelt "thank-yous" I've received came from people who gained insights about family relationships while attending one of my leadership development workshops on the power of appreciation. They started practicing the skill at home, and according to them, "it completely changed my marriage." Another person told me they saved a relationship with an estranged adult child by remembering simply to stop being "right" and listen. She had attended a Listen Lab workshop several months prior. When the family sees your team members becoming better parents, partners, or spouses, it's not hard to imagine how much they value your investment into their loved one.

THE FAMILY AMPLIFIER PLAYBOOK

Get to know more about your employees' families. You can do this in a nonintrusive way by simply sharing your own family stories. Go first! People naturally play "ping-pong" exchanging family stories and experiences. If you know their families, then you'll be more aware of how the work they are doing is being reflected back to them, whether positively or negatively. You'll be in a better position to understand their motivations and consider adjustments that add meaning through the family amplifier. While it's essential to be transparent and treat all employees equally, learning about and showing genuine interest in their families exhibits thoughtfulness and lays a foundation to build trusting relationships and meaningful interactions.

This tactical playbook idea was inspired by one of my coworkers at QVC, Michelle Alexander. She was a director of customer service and had an enormous number of team members within her care at our San Antonio call center. She prided herself on knowing people's names and other key facts about them so she could strike up a rapport and build relationships. Michelle created a type of "baseball card" for her team members that captured the vitals of who they were, their strengths and style preferences, and even some family details. I witnessed how she built enormous mutual respect with people by connecting at a grassroots level. Michelle amplified meaning everywhere she went within QVC.

So, here's how you can leverage this concept. Use the template that follows to create your own version of a baseball card that captures vitals about team members and their families. You can do this for direct reports, peers, and your boss. If you choose not to capture the items listed here, perhaps consider using this as an awareness quiz. Give yourself a grade on how much you know about other people.

- Name of team member: _____
- Hometown they grew up in: _____
- Community they live in now: _____
- Birthday: _____
- Team member's parents' name(s) and status: _____

  _____

- Partner's name: _____
- Anniversary date if married: _____
- Kids' names, ages, and school district: _____

  _____

  _____

  _____

- Pets: _____
- Favorite family vacations: _____
- Favorite family activities: _____
- Family hobbies: _____
- Family holiday traditions: _____
- How the family gives back: _____
- Transcendent family goal: _____
- Transformative family goal(s): _____
- Any special needs: _____
- Fun or unique family fact: _____

It goes without saying that we need to be sensitive if others have had a bad family experience or gone through a painful separation. Sharing some of the items might be painful for them to relive their loss. But knowing that fact can be very helpful. You'll be aware how to fully empathize with them and their situation. As Stephen Covey explains, "The trust we have in people and in organizations comes, in part, from believing that they do care."[8]

5

The Work Partner Amplifier

If you are familiar with the breathtaking HBO miniseries called *Band of Brothers*, you would recall World War II medal of honor recipient Captain Dick Winters leading his men through harrowing experiences in Europe fighting the Nazis. One, in particular, was Easy Company's role in defending their position at the Battle of the Bulge in freezing temperatures under constant threat of artillery shelling. Dick Winters spoke to the bonding experience of having fought together through the most difficult challenges a team could endure. "I'm not sure that anybody who lived through that one hasn't carried with him, in some hidden ways, the scars. Perhaps that is the factor that helps keep Easy (Company) men bonded so unusually close together."[1]

What can we learn from the brave men, women, and war heroes who fought on our behalf and apply to our experience at work? We need to consider the powerful meaning that comes from bonding as we "survive" work challenges together, even if they are far less consequential in emotion and in terms of literally surviving. Fighting battles together at work creates bonding experiences that are not to be underestimated as an amplifier of purpose and meaning.

I know that work relationships have given me meaning and inspired me—and at times, a close partnership with a coworker was the only thing that kept me going.

In the golden age of direct mail, I worked for a direct response agency. The most important person in my survival chain at the agency was appropriately named Grace. She worked in the actual ground zero of the industry: the Hawthorne Advertising mail house for Colonial Penn Insurance. I didn't meet Grace in person until six months into the job, but we talked with each other every day on the phone multiple times—e-mail didn't exist. She was never my best friend (like the Gallup 12 survey question discussed later in the chapter) but actually was my best ally in a war to get the direct mail kits out the door to the right people and on time. I was like an artillery commander warning her when there was going to be incoming barrages of mail. Grace was like the forward observer describing what was happening on the ground in the mail house, and when they were being overrun with the workload. We cared for each other, and we had great empathy for each other's delicate emotional needs for the day. We always talked a little about personal stuff before getting down to business. It's what kept us human in a surreal world of endless names and addresses, and being the entity that flooded people with thousands of mail kits. Our relationship became the real meaning of work, not the dreaded project of mailing 500,000 mail kits to people over 50 years old with a boring insurance offer.

WHY WORK PARTNERS ARE IMPORTANT

Nearly everyone, no matter what his or her role, works with one or two key people elbow to elbow—figuratively, if not physically—every day. Even if we work within a large team, we have one or two people with whom we are inextricably linked to each other's success. That's how I define a "work partner." A work partner can play an important role as an amplifier of meaning since the relationship is so central to the experience of work itself. When we think about work, this person's face immediately comes to mind.

Work partnerships facilitate interaction, collaboration, and relationships. Research shows that belonging and feeling attached is a basic emotional need. The good news is that people can fulfill the need to belong by pairing because they interact and thus naturally build relationships. Top psychologists Roy Baumeister and Mark Leary say that employees may "experience the meaning of their work through maintaining 'lasting positive and significant interpersonal workplace relationships.'"[2]

Ideally, the work partner is the person who allows us to truly be ourselves. Work partners have a special bond that forms a foundation of psychological safety. We don't have to position or posture everything we say to each other. We accept our work partners for who they really are and like them any way, warts and all. We are each other's stress relief and sounding board to complain about the boss and other people, and we protect these shared opinions as we would protect something a good friend tells us in confidence.

Working pairs are often less formal and more intimate, and they are inclined to be more cooperative than teams, which tend to encounter greater conflict. People often develop personal ties in workplace pairs. They build camaraderie, alliances, and symbiotic relationships. Much like a friendship, pairs may develop affection, trust, and respect for one another as they discover commonalities. They become each other's mentors, learn new things about themselves, and gain a deeper level of empathy. In his book *On Becoming a Leader*, Warren Bennis writes, "We need true engagement; we need mentors and friends and groups of allied souls."[3]

Evidence shows that employees who have a work partner with whom to share assignments, responsibilities, and often workspace are more engaged at work. A work partner can make even mundane work more meaningful. The work has more meaning because employees are working not only for their own success or the success of the company but also for the success of their work partners. Two work partners can also push and support themselves to create something together that couldn't have been created alone.

The following are some search-for-meaning questions people ask themselves:

- Does my work partner "have my back" and support me even when I'm not with him or her?
- Do I have a bonded relationship at work that brings out the best in both of us?
- Do I have a work partner relationship in which we help each other learn and grow?
- Am I inspired to work with my work partner for the sake of interacting and achieving something together?
- Do I have a work partner who accepts me and respects me for who I am?
- Do I have a work partner I can confide in and trust to be my advocate?
- Do I have a work partner who will give me honest feedback and advice?
- Is my bond with my work partner strong enough to make me want to stay here?

One of the other questions we'll explore in this chapter is this: Does my manager enhance the relationship I have with my work partner? The answer to this question is all about creating the conditions for success that bring out the best in the relationship.

PARTNERS DON'T LET PARTNERS FAIL

An inspirational scene from the 2021 Tokyo Olympics went viral demonstrating how supportive a work partner can be when it matters most. And in this case, the work partner ends up receiving joy and fulfillment supporting his fellow Somali-born training partner in an epic marathon race.

Thirty-nine kilometers into the grueling 42-kilometer marathon, Bashir Abdi (running for Belgium) got a severe cramp in his right hamstring. He was in a pack of runners with fellow Somali training partner Abdi Nageeye (running for Holland). With one kilometer to go, Nageeye risks losing his position to wait for Abdi. He urges on Abdi, waving him forward, saying, "You must go!" Abdi responded, surging ahead in pain to take the bronze medal just behind his friend Nageeye.

When Abdi Nageeye was interviewed about the experience, he shared something revealing about the power of meaning as a work partner. "When you do something nice you get this flow, and get this nice feeling. I was just feeling very comfortable. It's a marathon, and it's a sprint. It's the Olympics. I don't even know how to explain why I did that. It happened so smoothly. I was more concentrated on him. I don't know, I had that feeling. I had a lot of confidence I would be number two. And I was just trying to help him so that he would finish number three. And then we did it. And then all the emotion came when you finish it together. We did it!"[4]

Even under the most intense pressure, he demonstrated how a partner bond is so meaningful, it surpassed his own self-interest in the moment for winning an Olympic medal. In the workplace, employees are not just motivated to work hard and succeed for themselves; they also don't let down their work partners, but instead do everything for the work partner to succeed as well.

Soldiers returning from the Vietnam War were asked why they continued to perform so well in the field even though the war was not supported at home. Evidence of violent protests were everywhere in the news, and the images made their way back to Vietnam. This was the first war covered on television. The soldiers understood what was happening at home and in the media, but they universally said they fought bravely in combat for the person to their left and their right on the line. There was no way they were going to let them down or leave them behind. The work partner can have that kind of presence and impact on the meaning of the work we do. They are worth fighting for when the relationship is strong.

SMALL PAYOFF? STILL WORTH IT WITH A PARTNER

A trusted work partner has the ability to elevate discretionary effort even on work that has a small reward or payoff. The simple emotional fulfillment of working together as a unit becomes the purpose that amplifies meaning. It's powerful enough on its own. I witnessed this directly from my wife, a professional copywriter with an ad agency. In 2021, for the second year in a row, she teamed up with her favorite artist at the agency to submit an entry for the company holiday card competition. The reward for winning was only $100, but they spent hours upon hours sweating out concepts on their own time until they were confident they had something great. I asked why it was such a big deal and worthy of going through that much effort. She said without hesitation, "It's not about the money at all. I love working through the challenge with Lynn. We have a great relationship and push each other creatively." For my wife Kara, her work partner amplifier was at full power because of the bonding relationship built on respect and pride. And as of this writing, they have won the prize together for the second year in a row!

EFFECTIVE PARTNERING DEPENDS ON RADICAL CANDOR

When I led the culture and brand development at QVC, I had a chance to work with my counterpart in London. We worked together in a roadshow of sorts traveling to each one of QVC's sites in the United Kingdom to teach "personal accountability." That's a very challenging subject for people, and it comes with sharp edges of opinions on what it really means. My counterpart Daniel and I had our own significant differences of opinion about accountability and what it really meant; however, we agreed on how to give each other open coaching and feedback, and during and after each roadshow workshop. We relentlessly worked through the issues raised in each workshop. Dan and I had radical candor in our relationship based on mutual respect. By the end of the two weeks, I felt like I was polished like a diamond from our honest and creative conversations. The whole effort never felt like work. It was like being on a purpose-driven mission together to deliver something great. All the while we were learning, growing, and feeding off each other through heated yet healthy debate. It was indeed hard work, but we came away inspired and committed to nailing it for the employees and for each other. Here's my conclusion from the experience: It isn't about winning with our individual point of view; meaning comes from creating something together as work partners that is far greater than anything we could ever do on our own.

YOUR BEST FRIEND AT WORK

Friendship is so important to the bottom line that Gallup includes it in their employee engagement survey. One of Gallup's survey questions is "Do you have a best friend at work?" Originally, I was never that keen on the "Do you have a best friend at work?" question because I thought it wasn't a factor that people can directly work on to improve. Admittedly, I scoffed at it until I looked deeper.

Gallup's research on engagement "has repeatedly shown a concrete link between having a best friend at work and the amount of effort employees expend in their job."[5] Gallup found that having a best friend at work is a "key trait of retention" and leads to better performance outcomes.[6] After recognizing these amazing outcomes and reflecting on my own experiences with friendships at work, I've changed my mind about the friendship question. Take a look at what Gallup discovered about the work experiences of workers with friends:

- They received recognition for their work in the last seven days.
- Someone encourages their development.
- They and their coworkers are committed to quality.
- Someone at work has talked to them about their progress.
- The mission of their company makes them feel their job is important.
- Their opinions seem to count at work.
- They have the opportunity to do what they do best every day.[7]

Gallup also notes, "The best employers recognize that people want to build meaningful connections."[8] According to Gallup, organizations that focus on friendships and inclusion could realize greater employee loyalty, fewer safety incidents, more engaged customers, and higher profits.[9]

NO GROUP, NO GROUPTHINK: ANOTHER REASON PARTNERSHIPS ARE STRONGER THAN TEAMS

We don't often think about it, but the relationship that pairs develop elicits a space of psychological safety—a space where partners share both the risks and the rewards. Pairs also form a psychological contract or open-ended agreement. It's almost an implicit license to critique without fracturing the relationship. Importantly, pairs differ from teams because partners are able to share knowledge, viewpoints, and ideas. And they do it with less ambivalence, apprehension, or fear of losing face. Pairs are also less susceptible to groupthink.

Work pairs don't experience the same pressure as cohesive teams where members tend to conform to the views and decisions of the group and go against their own better judgments. To get an idea of how destructive groupthink can be, it was responsible for the devastation and deaths that ensued during the invasion of the Bay of Pigs in the 1960s, the *Challenger* space shuttle explosion in the 1980s, and BP's Deepwater Horizon oil spill in 2010. The point is that we can stop the "yes, sir" thinking and avoid groupthink by working in pairs.

The bond that forms between work pairs can be synergistic and strong. People in pairs usually don't want to let their partner down. On a subconscious level, an obligation emerges that compels them to be accountable to each other. The interaction and interdependency that transpires between pairs confers a relationship that creates long-term value. This sustainable value transfers to something we all want—loyalty and commitment to an organization.

AMPLIFYING THE WORK PARTNER RELATIONSHIP

How do we begin amplifying meaning by creating the conditions for working partnerships to grow and develop?

Hiring for Partnerships

It is super smart to ensure the work partner relationship is healthy by making a good match in the first place. Include the future potential work partners in the interview process. It's vital to match a person's competency and experience with the job but more so to match the culture of their future work partners. You will hear important opinions from the work partner interviews as to whether they have a vision for the experience of working side by side with the candidate. Don't underestimate the importance of having good chemistry. People tend to pick up on chemistry right away, even in a brief interview. Listen closely to what they say because so much hangs in the balance of making a good match. If you make a great decision with their input, you have the potential of activating an amplifier of meaning that may last for decades.

Learn and Grow Together

It's a savvy move as a manager to seek more opportunities for work partners to develop friendships through shared learning and development. When people go through development experiences together (as opposed to solo e-learning), it unlocks an intimate knowledge of each other's strengths and weaknesses. This provides not only an opportunity for people to respect and appreciate what others on the team bring to the table but also reveals a viewpoint on their vulnerabilities. It sets up the permission and context for partners to coach each other in their quest to be more effective.

If you think about it, deep friendships are always rooted in trust. If you create the conditions through learning and development experiences for people to inevitably appreciate each other and coach each other, then you are increasing the odds of friendships to blossom. Pick a common learning and development goal between working partners and invest in them going through a workshop or program together. The common language they develop will streamline the coaching and support they need from each other to make it stick.

Learning from Each Other

Learning strengthens partnerships not only when work partners learn together but also when work partners learn from each other. Learning often inspires teaching, and CEO Richard Sheridan explains, "The hidden benefit of giving your team members the freedom to learn is that, eventually, they will embrace the idea of taking the time to teach." Sheridan says, "Knowledge isn't kept away in secret personal vaults like the crown jewels of little kingdoms."[10] How many times have you wished you had cross-trained your employees? How many times have you experienced the pains of losing that key individual who seems to be the only one who knows how to run a system or process? Work partners share their knowledge and become more valuable as employees—once again, leading to greater engagement and commitment.

Problem-solving and decision-making can be more effective because paired workers often approach tasks from different perspectives. Pairs provide the opportunity for individuals to learn, gain new skills, and leverage each other's strengths. A kind of cross-pollination occurs where individuals within the pair cross-train each other. They gain insights about the business, the task at hand, and new methodologies to solve problems. On top of this, rotating pairs have a larger pool of resources and network of alliances to draw from than an individual does.

Go Out of Bounds

Make the time to get people together outside of the boundaries of the work day and the office. What are the experiences in your area that are "all inclusive"? This is not a novel idea at its core. Bowling and softball leagues have been going on for decades. They have been immensely important to friendships and culture for businesses of all types. I think the shared beers after a softball game are likely even more important than the game itself. Now, however, you can get far more creative and be more inclusive in the process. And even though these events can involve a larger group, team, or even company, these events can lead to valuable, close relationships between work partners.

When I led the culture at Vynamic, our CEO was completely committed to building a community within the team. Our vision was "To Create the Healthiest Company in the World," and building a community within our culture was an essential step toward achieving this vision. He challenged the entire team to create, every other month, experiences after hours that had a signature creative flair. Some of the more memorable ones were the following:

- Mystery team scavenger event in historic old city Philadelphia
- Cooking lessons from a gourmet chef on a 150-year-old sailing ship called the *Moshulu*
- Chocolate-tasting event with wine pairings
- City bus tour of movie set locations within Philadelphia (climaxing with a race up the Philadelphia Art Museum steps à la Rocky Balboa)
- Tour and tasting at a community-sponsored agriculture setting out in the suburbs (complete with hayride)

Note: Don't put all the pressure on yourself as the manager to generate ideas for events or experiences. Rotate the challenge to teammates to discover or create events or experiences and plan them. Not only will they come up with incredible ideas that will excite the rest of the team (avoiding the boss nerd factor), but they will own the outcome. In other words, these events won't be considered "the boss's program" that people will complain about. They will be owned from within.

That said, as a leader you can identify clear, yet simple goals for the events:

- Have fun
- Get to know each other and learn something new
- Don't embarrass anyone
- Maximize participation and a feeling of inclusion
- Grow the culture and live the values

Having goals will give people creative constraints on designing the events. What would fit your culture and your values? By the way, not every event has to involve drinking. Let that evolve on its own, organically, after the official event. If people are having fun, they will always find ways to continue the fun together with or without adult beverages.

The friendships and other incredible bonding experiences that took place at Vynamic events created a culture that became zealous in a commitment to support each other. Vynamic was and still is a high-performance organization that delivers an amazing level of excellence in the health care industry. It takes guts and commitment to invest the time and money into these experiences, but I can tell you firsthand that it had an enormous return on investment.

Now that we understand that friendships at work amplify meaning, engagement, and productivity, we also understand that *we must create the conditions necessary to establish them*. Any of us can act to create the conditions for friendships to take root. It just takes a little creativity.

Meetings with Meaning

Meetings have always been the key touchpoint where culture lives or dies for teams and individual relationships. Meetings set the stage for work partner relationships to form and grow. It's obvious that so many people suffer through meetings and count the experience as time wasted. Ideally, it should be turnkey for a leader to completely change the dynamics and turn meetings into a high-value experience that people look forward to attending. The problem is that most leaders have never been taught how to create a meeting format that is inclusive in the way it invites active participation—the conditions for work partners to thrive.

With most meetings now going from in person to virtual with Zoom or Teams, the challenge to engage is even more difficult. Most of the best practices for running effective in-person meetings still apply to online, however, but we need to be extra creative in our approaches.

One of the excellent bosses at QVC modeled a simple, but highly effective technique to build rapport within our team. She *always* started every staff meeting by going around the table to hear from everyone. She began by asking an opinion question that required people to share something beyond the obvious that revealed their style and personality. She'd speak first to model the level of candor that was expected. Then, we'd go around the room with everyone participating. Often, others would jump in to add a humorous comment or ask a question out of curiosity for further clarity. This give-and-take had a natural, comfortable rhythm to it, which was a refreshing break for a team that was always over-the-top busy. Also, it didn't take up a lot of precious meeting time, yet yielded a super high value for both the employees and QVC. She was creating psychological safety for all of us even before we knew that to be a relevant term to describe the culture of our group.

In terms of friendships, we came to know each other so well that it paid off in our personal and professional working relationships. This simple act became the norm in our meetings. It set a precedent, because it established the value of rapport that carried over to our open culture and everything we did as a team. It became a clear expectation and a value unto itself.

I have lifelong friends from that team—and they started with rapport.

I have provided some meeting starter questions that you can use to facilitate rapport building. Please keep in mind that the key to keeping the rapport conversation genuine and authentic is to avoid digressing into a "status report" or getting lost in the weeds by getting off subject. It's vital to maintain control as the facilitator.

Meeting-Starter Rapport-Building Questions to Consider

Easy:
- What was the highlight of your weekend?
- What's something surprising that happened since our last meeting?
- What are you looking forward to this week? (It doesn't have to be work related.)

Moderate:
- What's a value you saw in action this past week?
- Who did you catch doing something right?
- What's your opinion on how people are reacting to . . . ? (Pick an initiative that has internal or external customer ramifications.)

Challenging:
- What do we need to be even more honest about?
- What did you take away from the town hall meeting?
- What's your sense on the state of our workplace culture this week?
- What's your reaction to the budget approval?
- What might we do as a team to rally together and get through our challenge?

MORE WAYS TO AMPLIFY WORK PARTNER AS THE MANAGER

1. Work Partner Design

- Customize pairing to fit the scope of the work and your team's needs.
- The scope could be a project, problem resolution, programming duos, or new hires.

- Define roles—ask your employees to help.
- Meet formally with your work partners monthly and check on individuals in the pair weekly.

2. Develop the Relationship

- Strengthen partner bonds. Managers often take work partner relationships for granted and don't supply additional nourishment.
- Give partners the opportunity to attend development sessions together that focus on important relationship-building subjects such as coaching, the Myers-Briggs Type Indicator (MBTI), emotional intelligence, and trust. These will nourish the good relationship that is already there plus create a solid foundation to help them work through the tough times together.

3. Create Co-ownership Opportunities

- Establish goals they can achieve together as a "unit."
- In addition to individual goals, give them a chance to "win" together in ways that build momentum and a history of success. Doing so will increase the mutual accountability and ownership that is essential to every great working relationship.

4. Meet with Employees as Work Partners

- Instead of just one-on-one or staff meetings, meet with work partner combinations. These can be powerful on-the-fly organic brainstorming sessions that help partners overcome frustrating barriers and serve as a catalyst of progress.
- Get in the trenches with your employees to demonstrate your advocacy for their mutual success. They will better know where you stand on what's important and be able to deliver on that together as a work partner team. Reduce the amount of translation and guess work on your expectations for what success looks like.

BUSTING THE MYTHS OF PARTNERSHIPS

In their book *Pair Programming Illuminated,* authors Laurie Williams and Robert Kessler describe three myths related to working partnerships between two people (or "pairs").[11] I'd like to share some of their findings with you so you can bust some common myths and combat resistance to change.

Myth 1

"It will work well only with the right partner."

Myth-buster: Williams and Kessler found that partnering two people together works well with most partners. They explain that one or two individuals will likely balk at the idea and never work well with others, but other than that, "people are able to work with almost anyone." They advise, however, not to pair an expert with a novice unless that expert is "willing to take on the mentor role."[12] The key is to rotate pairs each week, minimize pairing to a few hours per day, and at times allow employees to select partners they feel have the necessary skills.

Myth 2

"I'll never get credit for doing anything. I'll have to share all the recognition with my partner."

Myth-buster: Williams and Kessler admit that getting recognition is a little complicated but say that the myth is just not true. Paired individuals—along with your organization's performance appraisal structure that's based on individual success—may be even hairier. Williams and Kessler say, however, that things will run smoother if each person within the pair focuses on a specific task—although this is easier said than done. They suggest that a peer evaluation survey be developed. "Peer evaluation can provide valuable feedback to the manager on how helpful the engineers are as partners so the manager has a better idea on who to reward." Overall, as the manager it is up to you to instill the idea of team success, and as the authors state, "individual success means nothing without team success."[13]

Myth 3

"The only time I ever get any real work done is when I'm alone. Now I'll never get anything done!"

Myth-buster: Busted. In fact, two heads are better to get things done. Workers find they have a greater degree of mental flow and get more work accomplished in less time, with fewer distractions, and with less mistakes. Williams and Kessler say that pairs "explore more possibilities and revel in their joint successes. They know from minute to minute that they are achieving more together than they ever could alone, and this knowledge drives them deeper and deeper into flow."[14]

Williams and Kessler have discovered that pairs are more efficient at deferring interruptions. Like a dream come true, they say pairs "forward their phone to voicemail, turn off their email notifications, and don't take breaks to surf the web."[15]

SUMMARY OF WORK PARTNERSHIP BENEFITS

As shown already in this chapter, there are many benefits to helping employees identify and work closely with one or two work partners. As a summary, here in bullet-point form is a list of those benefits.

Benefits to Organization and Manager

- Boosts engagement, collaboration, morale, citizenship behavior, and productivity
- Delivers ongoing diversity program
- Reduces absenteeism and turnover
- Reduces personal internet usage and social media distractions
- Offers cross-training—provides continuous mentoring, growth, and development
- Facilitates collaborative, cohesive, and open culture
- Facilitates a workforce that works in the office instead of working from home
- Elevates leverage over competitors—ability to learn clients' domains quickly
- Makes the employee onboarding transition easier
- Avoids risks associated with knowledge hoarding
- Helps employees learn faster, become more creative, and work with more focus and intensity
- Helps employees accomplish more work in less time and with fewer mistakes

Benefits to Work Partners

- Creates meaningful work—builds quality partnerships and relationships
- Amplifies self-satisfaction, work satisfaction, and motivation

- Offers employee growth and development, as well as the ability for them to use their strengths
- Provides opportunity to learn from others, about the business, and the role they play in it
- Yields transferrable skills and improves internal and external career marketability
- Opens new opportunities for advancement and doubles chances of leadership opportunities
- Facilitates autonomy in the creation of interview questions, exercises, and hiring decisions

Additionally, employees sense that the company is investing in their future.

The New "Essential Workers"

I thought it was very emblematic that during the COVID-19 pandemic certain people were deemed as "essential workers" based on their job responsibility. Some of the obvious ones are first responders, grocery store workers, pharmacists, and of course, the heroic health care workers in hospitals treating patients. We gave them esteem and the accolades they deserved in the form of parades to honor their sacrifice to keep our world functioning. But who's essential now? Consider who keeps *you* going from day to day in your job. It's not a stretch to predict it's your work partner. Everyone has his or her own personal "essential worker" who amplifies meaning in an intrapersonal way.

BUILDING RADICAL CANDOR WITH BRAINSTORMING

Gallup confirms that managers should promote open communication and collaboration because they are "cornerstones of an inclusive culture, and provide a natural pathway to friendship."[16] One way to encourage employees to get to know one other and develop open communication channels is through brainstorming. Brainstorming is a turbocharger of energy, radical candor, and fun when done well. Leading "formal" brainstorming sessions will create a culture norm for sharing and building ideas that gets passed down to the informal organic work partner conversations that happen every day. It's creating the conditions for them to experience small wins together continuously in their relationship without you having to manage the process.

When you think of brainstorming, you might think of teams gathered in meeting rooms. Brainstorming, however, is a process, and the creative brainstorming process, like any other discipline, has its own set of rules that cause it to be successful. Once the rules are understood, brainstorming becomes an automatic process that doesn't need to take place in scheduled meetings. Work partners will switch into brainstorming mode whenever they are discussing a problem and searching for a solution. The rules of brainstorming are detailed in the "Customer Amplifier Playbook" in chapter 10.

When brainstorming is done well, the experience can be very satisfying. Think about your own positive experience of working together to solve a problem creatively, or to nail a great idea that capitalizes on an opportunity. Doing so galvanizes people with a special bond from indulging in the creative process—and the success that stems from it. This is a great way to create the conditions for work partners to communicate with curiosity and radical candor with each other.

THE WORK PARTNER AMPLIFIER PLAYBOOK: PROJECT HOP (HUDDLE ON PURPOSE)

We covered the value of work partners getting to know each other. What if you could take it to the next level and create the conditions where they proactively communicate with each other on a common purpose: to get incredible results together on a key project initiative? This is where the rubber meets the road at work and is the most directly relevant way to amplify meaning for them as partners.

I call my tactical design Project HOP. HOP is an acronym for Huddle on Purpose. The huddles occur at three distinct stages in the project or initiative time line (Kick-Off HOP, Halftime HOP, and Post-Game HOP). The templated format that follows works for project teams of all sizes but is especially powerful for work partners. You can facilitate the Project HOP discussion as the leader or let the partners work through it on their own depending on their level of rapport with each other.

Here are some tips to successfully implement Project HOP:

1. Use the Project HOP template for any significant project or initiative that work partners (or a team) conduct as a unit.
2. Prioritize the discipline of scheduling the three huddles (HOPs) with a firm commitment to participate from each team member.

3. Discuss and record answers to each of the items on the template together as a team.
4. Share the recorded Project HOP document with all participants and the manager of the team members. *Note:* This is key for setting up small wins with the ability to recognize and appreciate the progress being made.
5. Conduct check-ins leveraging the Project HOP documents for all key meetings related to the project.

Kick-Off HOP

Note: Schedule the Kick-Off HOP before getting fully engaged into the project work. The intent is to be mentally ready to perform as a galvanized team in the same way a winning sports team conducts their pregame preparation.

Project name:

Client:

Date of Kick-Off HOP:

Project stakeholders:

Project start date:

Project estimated end date:

Date set for Halftime HOP:

Project Purpose:

Why does this project matter
- To us as a work partner team?
- To our organization?
- To our company?
- To the customer?

If Stephen Covey is correct and "beginning with the end in mind" is a habit of highly successful people . . .

What would success look like for us?
How will we know if we are making progress?

What would our clients miss most if we dropped out in the middle of the
    project?
If we could "own" a single word in the mind of the client as a result of
    working on this project, what would we want it to be? (Examples: fast,
    efficient, smart, creative, etc.)
What values do we need to leverage to be highly successful?

Gamification Thinking

- In what ways is this project like chess?
- In what ways is this project like Twister?

What's in It for Us?

- When we are potentially drowning in stressful and difficult work related
  to this project, what's our lifeline that gives us a personal sense of purpose? (Why is it worth it?)

Apply Personality Assessment Research (Examples: MBTI, DiSC, or Strength Finders)

- In general, when we work together, we will likely have agreement and
  understanding about these aspects (perspectives and strengths we have
  in common):
- In general, when we work together, we may have a lack of understanding
  or conflict over these aspects (perspective and strengths we do not share):

Common Ground

- We will likely focus on these aspects and move through them quickly
  with easy agreement:

Uncommon Ground

We may encounter difficulties with these aspects (i.e., not being totally on the
same page, hesitant, or unlikely to compromise):

- How can we turn the difficulties from a potential conflict to a complement?
- What can we anticipate learning from each other?

Communication

- What does "being a great communicator" look like (to each person)?
- What is our preferred go-to communication method and media (face to face, Zoom, e-mail, text, phone)? Discuss the ramifications of each.
- What are our expectations on response time? How will we let each other know when it's not working?
- How will we remind each other to be on the same page regarding what needs to happen versus waiting? (i.e., progressive versus passive):
- What is highly ineffective and stressful (for each person)?

Coaching

- What is our level of coaching permission to one another?
- Who is the de facto lead regarding decision-making roles and timing?
- How should coaching be given (each person's preference)? Examples: right away in the moment, offer alternatives, let me think about it, make sure it's balanced, be brutally candid, give me examples, be private, be specific, be inspiring.
- What are the specific areas to be coached upon (each person's preference)? Examples: client interaction, communication style, clarity of direction, conflicting priorities, mixed messages, responsiveness, difference of opinion, asking versus telling.

Halftime HOP

Note: The Halftime HOP should be scheduled approximately halfway through the project time line, or after a significant milestone is achieved within the project scope.

Optional: Time Line Exercise

Note: If you can meet in person as a group, this exercise will capture all the major highlights that have transpired in the project so far.
Directions:

1. Post a super large butcher paper or whiteboard on the wall of a meeting room.
2. Create a time line that delineates a visual of when the project started and the time increments that elapsed since then.

3. Include room on the paper to include the time frame for completing the project.
4. Give markers to the participants and ask them to record on the time line all the major milestones that have occurred in the project.
5. Observe and discuss together what is worth celebrating as a team.

Feedback

What is going well that we need to do more of to finish the project with success?

What can we be more effective doing, and what can we adjust going forward?

What do we need to be even more honest about?

What grade would we give ourselves at this point regarding the following (1 is unacceptable; 10 is ideal):

1. Coaching each other:
2. Our dynamics (how we are leveraging our collaboration):
3. Creative/innovative approach:
4. Our unified brand image to the client:
5. Rapport with our client:
6. Quality of our work:
7. On-time delivery:

Re-vision the Purpose

• What does success look like now (with the vantage point of being halfway through the project)?

Post-Game HOP

Note: The Post-Game HOP should be scheduled once the project has been completed. The intent is to serve as a mea culpa look back at the project to bolster the relationship of work partners and improve performance for the next one.

Did we achieve the objective of the project? What would we rate it? (1 is failure; 10 is outstanding success):

How would our client rate our success? (1 = failure; 10 = outstanding success):

What went well that we should replicate for the next time we work together?

What was a struggle that we need to get better at for the next time we work together?

If we could do it all over again, what is the one thing you would change?

What came true that we identified in the Kick-Off HOP and/or the Half-time HOP?

- What occurred that wasn't anticipated at all that was a positive?
- What occurred that wasn't anticipated at all that was a negative?

What do you personally need advice or coaching on to be even more effective as a work partner for the next project? (Each person shares.)

What did our leader do especially well that was helpful in making progress?

What might our leader do better the next time to facilitate making progress?

What is a specific behavior of your work partner that you appreciate? (Each person shares.)

Overall, how meaningful was this project and the opportunity to work together? (Each person shares.)

6

The Team Amplifier

It's nearly impossible to find an organization that doesn't have teamwork listed as one of their corporate values. Everyone has experienced how essential it is to performance. People who have grown up playing sports often associate a sacred bond to winning as a team. There is power in the unity of the team especially when it rallies together to achieve a common purpose. When it comes to great teams, it's true that the whole is greater than the sum of the parts. It's no wonder that teamwork is a universal value and belonging to a team is a powerful amplifier of meaning.

The concept of being on a team and our ability as leaders to amplify meaning through the team has completely changed following the COVID-19 pandemic. Virtual and hybrid arrangements make it all the more challenging to galvanize people around the purpose of the team when members are physically separated. It has placed a burden on leaders to discover and implement both strategic and tactical approaches that engage the team in new ways that maximize their full potential. We will cover ideas in this chapter that can make the difference whether your team physically interacts with each other every day or is connected virtually.

The following are some search-for-meaning questions people ask themselves:

- Do I feel I belong as an accepted member of this team?
- Does my effort make a difference to the performance of the team?
- Do the people on my team support me and value my ideas?
- Do I believe in what this team stands for?
- Does our team have a bond that motivates us to accomplish things together?

TEAMWORK BEGINS WITH BELONGING

Being assigned to a team means nothing if an individual feels that he or she doesn't belong on the team or is not accepted by the team. Forcing individuals into a constant battle to be something they are not or having to flex their style to fit in is not sustainable in the long term. It just won't work. People will end up checking out, or leaving the team altogether. Have you ever gone to a party where you felt you didn't belong? How long was it before you made a hasty exit? People must be confident that others on the team accept them for who they are.

One tactical method that directly impacts a sense of belonging and inclusion involves how you start team meetings. In addition to building rapport (which we will cover in detail in this chapter's playbook), "team-sourcing" the agenda is a high-impact practice you can easily add into your repertoire as the leader. It gives everyone a chance to participate and influence the focus of the team right from the beginning. Here's how it works:

- Come prepared to the meeting with your own key personal agenda items, but don't be the first to share with the team.
- Ask team members to build the agenda. Say, "What do we need to put on our agenda that would help you make progress? I'd like to hear from everyone."
- Capture the items team members offer. If you're in person, do it on a whiteboard or flipchart. If you're virtual or projecting slides, then type them onto a slide or into your chat feature.
- Add to the list, if necessary, after everyone has had a chance to contribute.
- Ask the team to prioritize the list together by qualifying the agenda items into one of these categories: A = must cover, B = good to cover, C = bonus to cover. Mark them accordingly and proceed to cover the As.

This method should be used consistently for nearly every meeting. It's smart to let people know ahead of time that you expect them to come to the meeting with agenda items. If they come prepared, they will also feel included as an integral member of the team.

There is great comfort in being included. Thought leader and social scientist Simon Sinek describes it this way: "The most basic human desire is to feel like you belong. Fitting in is important." People question (and often doubt) whether they belong, especially in the early stages of their team experience.

It's hard to be patient, but after going through the necessary and painful steps of "forming and storming," people gain, at long last, emotional equity for belonging on the team. By then, they've also earned the scar tissue and callouses that give them grace and mercy among teammates to be capable of "norming and performing." In other words, teammates give them a greater latitude for occasionally messing up or at least not being perfect.

Confidence in the Leader

If you're new as the leader of a team, or have new team members, there's no doubt you'll experience growing pains. Every team goes through a progression of team development stages to reach peak performance. Forming, storming, norming, and performing are the stages identified in 1965 by psychologist Bruce Tuckman, whose simple model describes what a team experiences as it moves through its developmental stages.[1] Becoming aware of your team's stage will allow you to take proactive action steps to help the team progress through *forming, storming, norming,* and *performing.* Taking proactive action is key because team members want to have confidence in their leader. A leader willing to take action to move the team forward as they progress in their capabilities of performing together will gain the team's confidence.

I've created a leader guide, based on Tuckman's four stages, that identifies key symptoms of each stage and the action steps to progress forward as a team:

Forming Stage

Key identifiers:

- There is a feeling that everything is "yet to be determined."
- Team members desire to be accepted and liked by others.
- Everyone would like to know more information on what this is all about.
- People may say to themselves: "I'm not sure who the real leader of the team is yet, and what they'll want from me."
- Everyone seems to be overly polite with each other.
- People are feeling each other out about who has the power and authority.
- Team members are trying to determine what they have in common to build a bond.
- People probe for expectations on outcomes.
- Some communication is in the form of signals—both overt and subliminal.

Action steps to create/strengthen a sense of belonging:

- Create a sense of belonging and psychological safety for the team.
- Make the experience of group interaction relatively predictable.
- Take time in meetings to build rapport with introductions.
- Create order by using an agenda and clearly stated goal(s) for the team.
- Ask for input on the general strategy to meet the goal. Include all team players.
- Support team members' attempts to participate.
- Discuss task requirements before designating individual assignments.
- Make the callout that the team is likely in the *forming* stage (and that it's OK and common).

Storming Stage

Key identifiers:

- Team members are airing differences of opinion.
- There is obvious disagreement on approaches people are taking.
- Emotions have come into play—both good and bad.
- People feel stressed at these meetings because they need to work through so many various conflicts.
- Some people are getting their feeling hurt and seem to check out of the process for a while.
- Everyone is focused on *how* the team is going to do things.
- The flow and general attitude of team meetings seems unpredictable.
- The real leader(s) of the team are beginning to emerge.
- Team members may wonder if others on the team still respect them.
- The range of behaviors runs the gamut from being hostile to being intimidated.
- Blaming the leaders is a popular thing to do.

Action steps to create/strengthen a sense of belonging:

- Build trust by setting goals and ground rules on operational procedures to flush out conflict. (Gain clarity.)
- Realize and acknowledge that it is good for people to feel "safe" to express their opinions and disagreements.
- Develop and gain agreement on a decision-making process.

- Allow people to revisit and think through initial decisions involving complicated goals and tasks to determine if it still makes sense.
- Continue to ensure that the team agrees with and understands the goal(s).
- Establish norms that allow people to provide honest feedback to each other.

Norming Stage

Key identifiers:

- People are clear about the overall goal and reach consensus more readily.
- Team members seem willing to flex on roles and task assignments to meet the goal.
- Overall there is a focus on task achievement and a team structure that will meet the goal.
- Although coalitions and subgroups are still evident, people are more tolerant of this fact.
- Trust in each other, cohesion, and cooperation has increased.
- There is still conflict at times, but the team works through it more effectively.
- The division of labor is allocated more evenly across the team.
- People are less "territorial" as the focus on tasks increases.
- Communication is more open and task oriented.

Action steps to create/strengthen a sense of belonging:

- Take a more consultative role as the leader but be ready to offer direction when the situation warrants it.
- Ensure the team's two-way communication with other departments is solid by having more than one person share the burden.
- Notice the norms of participation that have been established; allow people to conform to their own natural style, even if it is different from the norm of the team.
- Allow team members to ask for help and support from each other (on assignments and in meetings).
- Ask for feedback and seek ways to take the team to the next level (including your role as leader).
- Meet with people individually to get their take on the performance of the team; brainstorm how their personal ownership role in the team's performance could be enhanced.

Performing Stage

Key identifiers:

- The quality and quantity of work achieved has increased significantly.
- Team goals are clear and agreed upon.
- Team members are clear about their roles.
- Assignments of roles match well with people's strengths, abilities, and interests.
- Feedback is readily given and accepted about the overall performance of the team and the individuals on the team.
- Leadership comes from an increased "delegation with empowerment" style.
- The team plans how it will solve problems and make decisions.
- Problems that arise are defined; appropriate solution-oriented decisions are made.
- The decision-making process is highly participatory.
- People have accepted their individual role and the contribution of others.
- Adequate time is given to discuss problems and potential resolutions.

Action steps to create/strengthen a sense of belonging:

- Discuss together what a high-performance and high-quality outcome would look like.
- Encourage innovation by identifying and appreciating the creative and accountable work people are doing.
- Help people work through their strong desires to succeed by ensuring deadlines are reasonable and doable.
- Realize people are focused on high quality and will want to check all the details twice.
- As challenges arise, define what the real problem is before trying to solve it.
- To make tough decisions that involve other teams, do fact-finding with them to learn the scope of your potential decision(s).
- Intervene quickly and stay focused on the tasks at hand when conflicts arise.
- Take the time to do process checks to ensure clarity and that everyone has been heard.
- Get feedback from others outside of the team.

SYMPTOMS OF TOXIC TEAM CULTURE

Leaders need to be continuously vigilant in guiding their teams through the four stages. In many ways, a team is like a garden. You may work hard to make your garden pristine in spring, planting a gorgeous burst of beautiful plants with vibrant colors. Leave the garden untended, however, and by August, your garden will be unkempt and overgrown. Likewise, no matter how well you lead the team in the forming stage, if you then leave the team to fend on its own, it will potentially devolve into a toxic culture.

In toxic cultures without accountability, the goal is to leave the meeting with zero action items on your plate. People are operating at the minimum requirements line of discretionary effort.

In toxic cultures, you hear team members say, "I'm confused. Just tell me what to do." This is code for "I'm too unengaged to want to think about it for myself. And, if you tell me what to do and I do it, then I can blame you when it doesn't work out." This passive-aggressive thinking mode is unaccountable.

Toxic cultures that fear for their own security and are prone to CYA (cover your ass) syndrome do not take risks that are germane to innovation practices. The opportunistic nature of collaboration always feels a little risky because you are moving into unknown territory.

In toxic cultures, it is easier for people to blame others when things go poorly because their first instinct is to protect themselves. It's easy to point a finger, fain confusion, or complain about lack of clarity. The opposite is having the emotional intelligence to immediately ask questions to get back on the same page and clarify expectations.

In toxic cultures where feedback is not given, practiced, welcomed, asked for, or appreciated, it's nearly impossible to make real-time adjustments. You lose the ability to roll with the punches of the project and improve performance in the moment it's needed most. Honesty and candor must be established as an overt expectation.

MAKING A MEANINGFUL CONTRIBUTION

The magic of being on an engaged, high-performance team is that every player will go to great lengths to support each other. They never let each other down. There is a bond of loyalty and commitment that forms causing people to do heroic things for the sake of the team. Everyone wants to feel they are doing their part. When team members have a clear vision for the impact of their contribution, it encourages them to do even more.

As managers, we amplify meaning by reminding team members about the difference they are making. We serve as an extra set of eyes and ears, helping them become more aware and confident in their value as a team player. Again, it's about thinking of your role to be all about "catching people doing things right." It's remarkably easy for people to lose sight of the impact they're making. Team members too often get lost in the weeds of their work and can't see it. We must take it upon ourselves as leaders to call out the positive effects we're seeing. When we scale the "catch people doing things right" approach across an entire set of team members, it results in a team with an inseparable bond and a commitment to making a difference. As leaders, we become a catalyst of progress and performance in the process. We become the eyes and ears of progress. We also clearly delineate what is truly valued in terms of effective behavior for all team members.

If you practice this "master level" team leader competency, then you will set yourself apart as the person everyone wants to work for. Everyone else in your organization will also notice the performance advantage you've achieved.

ROCKING PERFORMANCE AS A TEAM

Learning how to play an instrument is a lonely and often miserable endeavor. Many a kid has been held hostage by their parents until they practiced their little fingers off. Getting over the hump of being completely incompetent and awkward takes a lot of hard work and perseverance. Most of us went down that path as kids, and only a few of us survived to play a single note that meant anything of significance beyond a too-tense-for-words recital that our parents dutifully attended. An enormous number of kids give up their instrument before they ever get to play a pleasant note. Even in school programs where 100 percent of students begin an instrument, more than 50 percent of the students quit within one or two years.[2]

So is there a secret that causes the rare musical instrument survivors to get over the hump and begin to play for the joy of it? Many of us—and yes, I'm one of them—say upon reflection that their breakthrough came when they started playing with others in a band. You see, at that point, you aren't just practicing for yourself, you're playing your part for the bigger success of the team. That's a lot to live up to. It's a motivating factor to simply do things to avoid letting others down. That's one of the key things the team amplifier acknowledges.

The School of Rock capitalizes on the team amplifier to get amazing results. Kids go into the School of Rock as three-chord hacks and come out as proverbial rock stars. They learn to play their instrument at an accelerated rate by being immersed into the process of creating music with others. They are assigned to a team (i.e., band) to perform in a meaningful concert-formatted recital. The stimuli of playing an instrument in the context of a group performance is highly motivating. The experience puts a white-hot spotlight on your role and contribution as a bandmate. An emotional bond forms from the interpersonal dynamics of having to listen deeply and play off of each other. Once you experience the magical feeling of being a musician (not in a vacuum, but part of something bigger and greater than yourself), then you're hooked. The feeling from playing together with audience feedback in a successful public performance amplifies the meaning even more. The School of Rock's format for learning is really *The Progress Principle*[3] (noted in chapter 1) in action. By the way, some of us old farts who have experienced the magical experience of playing in a band chase that feeling for the rest of our lives. I know a lot of other musicians who say playing in their band in its heyday was the greatest time of their lives. Ian Anderson of Jethro Tull got it right with his lyric, "You're never too old to rock 'n' roll."

THE POWER OF SMALL WINS AS A TEAM

> The goal is not to be perfect by the end. The goal is to be better today.
>
> —Simon Sinek

One of the things that blew me away when I read *The Progress Principle* was that small wins have nearly as much impact on engagement as major achievements. Authors Teresa Amabile and Steven Kramer identify why small wins are so potent by pointing to self-efficacy as the emotional response. They say, "*Progress* motivates people to accept difficult challenges more readily and to persist longer. If people feel capable, then they see difficult problems as positive challenges and opportunities to succeed."[4] This is great news because it gives us a whole new set of tools to amplify meaning that are frequent, relevant, and timely. It's small wins. We don't have to wait to get the emotional payback only at the end of a massive undertaking.

Throughout the years, I've observed one of the coolest nuances of teamwork that delivers visible proof of the power of winning together. In our Culturology workshop based on the Progress Principle, I created a scenario where small teams of five or six people are challenged to play a simple nursery rhyme song like "Twinkle, Twinkle Little Star" or "Row, Row, Row Your Boat." Here's the catch: The team is given a set of Boomwhacker musical tubes that represent an entire octave of notes, but they have no idea what note starts the song, and there is only one way it can be played correctly. The team must engage in a rapid-prototyping style of problem-solving to figure it out, one note at a time. It's an intense, high-energy exercise of unlocking the answer and then having to perform it as a team.

Each time the team discovers the next note in the sequence of the song, they spontaneously shout for joy and whoop it up as a group. It happens every time. They experience the emotional power of small wins on their way to achieving the greater purpose of performing the song. It's a *live* example of the Progress Principle in action. Yes, the transactional purpose of being able to perform the complete song in front of the group is motivating, but the small wins and breakthroughs they experience as they work through the creative process amplify meaning each step along the way.

I always challenge the teams following the exercise to think through what they experienced. Here's the major insight I ask them to reflect upon: "If you were that highly engaged and joyful for accomplishing something as trivial as discovering a correct note with a Boomwhacker, then imagine how you and others must feel at work when you achieve a win—especially together as a team." Once people experience this powerful dynamic firsthand, it causes them to reprioritize what they're willing to do as a leader to influence small wins at work. The small-win focus becomes their new go-to engagement and performance strategy. It opens up a whole new set of creative options on how to create the conditions for small wins to take place and be recognized.

Creating Small Wins

Here are several effective approaches that create the conditions for small wins to happen more frequently and in ways that team members receive a sense of meaningful accomplishment.

1. **Priority management basic training:** I'm always amazed when I ask participants in our workshops whether they use a basic "to-do" list. It's unusual if more than half the hands go up. That means that almost 50 percent of the participants are simply "winging it" and have no reliable record of what to do next, or if they are "winning" anything. I'm not sure how people have succeeded to navigate through their career without a

to-do list as a basic rudiment for conducting business. Besides organizing and prioritizing the workload, a to-do list is essential for creating small wins. The research shows that every time we finish something and check the box on our list our brain releases endorphins and serotonin. It explains why many of us complete a task and then write it down on our list in order to check it off. What might seem crazy actually has merits for keeping us happy, motivated, and mentally sharp. So, if you have not given your team the training to implement an effective to-do-list-based methodology, then you're missing out on perhaps the lowest-hanging-fruit technique for leveraging small wins. It's well worth making it a mandatory practice for all.

2. **Highlighting milestones:** Milestones are markers of progress leading toward a goal. The idea here is to make the milestones just as noteworthy as the goal itself because there are a lot more of them, thus multiplying the small-win opportunities along the way. Breaking down a project or an initiative into the smallest incremental milestone steps (tasks) is great project management 101. Take the time to be aware of the next milestone in the sequence so you can be the one to recognize the small win when it takes place. Because most people are at full capacity, they won't likely call it out themselves, or be aware it even happened, unless they were working on it directly. This is especially true if most of your team is working remotely. You can create milestone small wins by using time frames as a marker. For example, identify what you want to have the team accomplish before lunch, by the end of the day, or by Wednesday at 5 p.m.

3. **High visibility:** It's far more motivating to accomplish a goal if you can see it. For example, if you're a martial arts student, you can look around the room at other students and instantly recognize their levels of proficiency by the color belts they wear. Boy Scouts and Girl Scouts have badges that lead to becoming an Eagle Scout or earning a Girl Scout Gold Award. The local bank conducting a United Way campaign has the contribution thermometer out in front of the bank. All of these motivate by visibly showing the next level to achieve (i.e., "win"). So, what is it for you? What can you visibly display that demonstrates your commitment to getting the work done? If your team is remote, you'll need to do it electronically or build it into your communication platform whether it's Slack, Teams, or Google Workspace. Visibly answer these questions for your team. Where are we now? What's next? How will we know when we get there?

4. **Hurdle-hopping brainstorms:** When the team has reached a hurdle in their work, it's an opportunity to have them overcome it by rallying their tenacity as problem solvers. Quickly gather the team physically or virtually to define the problem and proceed to facilitate a brainstorming session that sparks potential solutions. The key to success is speed. Demonstrate the ability to rapid prototype as your hurdle-hopping tactic. Leverage the rules of brainstorming that we covered in the "Work Partner Amplifier" chapter (chapter 5). I've provided a format for conducting a tightly facilitated, one-hour brainstorming session in the "Department Amplifier" chapter (chapter 8). Remember that winning together to solve problems is galvanizing and deeply meaningful. Choosing not to act causes frustration and a loss of engagement.

TEAM MEMBERS SUPPORT AND VALUE EACH OTHER

Hall of fame hockey coach Fred Shero was nicknamed "The Fog" because of his deeply philosophical and often enigmatic quotes that he would post on the locker room blackboard. One of the most enduring quotes was "Win today, and we walk together forever." This was on the Philadelphia Flyers' blackboard prior to game six of the Stanley Cup finals in 1973. The underdog Flyers, affectionately called the Broad Street Bullies, hoisted the cup that night by beating the mighty Boston Bruins led by Bobby Orr. Clearly the former champion Bruins had a more talented team, but Shero leveraged the ultimate amplifier to propel the gritty Flyers over the top. It's incredibly special when a team wins with shear grit, will, and teamwork.

The Flyers had literally fought for each other all year to get to the Stanley Cup finals. No one dared mess with a Philadelphia Flyer without another teammate jumping in to inflict pain for their provocation. The Broad Street Bullies had so many games erupt into famous bench-clearing brawls that the league changed the fighting rules to regain control (and some dignity). As a longtime Flyers fan, I knew the players weren't fighting for fighting sake but, instead, fighting for each other. Their loyalty and bond was so strong that it became compelling for fans like me to tune in to every game.

Fred Shero's vision of "walking together forever" amplified the deep meaning the Flyers already possessed as a team. Who wouldn't want to carry that feeling forward and, in a sense, immortalize the emotional connection of playing on a team with that type of unwavering loyalty? It's been a long time since the Flyers have won the Stanley Cup, but we can look back now and confirm that Fred Shero's amplifier quote did come true. No hockey franchise has had a stronger alumni connection than the Flyers, and of all the Philadelphia sports teams, the 1974 Flyers stand atop of the pinnacle as the most beloved team in the city's history.

What, then, is the opportunity in front of you that you can identify for your team? What would cause them to "walk together forever"? What could they accomplish together as a team that would stand the test of time? Whether you have an old-fashioned blackboard, a whiteboard, or smart board, what could you communicate to amplify the meaning of the team in your organization?

Who on your team needs your support? Great teams and bosses pick people up when they are down, and they don't hold it against the team member if they are not at the top of their game in every instance. We need to be aware of this dynamic and be proactive in communicating how committed we are to the individual's success on the team. Doing so helps them answer positively to the question about being accepted. Acceptance gives meaning a chance to be felt within the team context. Making a commitment to achieve psychological safety for the team and with the team is a worthy goal with enormously positive implications.

When Google conducted their extensive research to determine what their highest-performing teams had in common, they identified psychological safety as the number one factor. They defined psychological safety as the belief you won't be punished for making a mistake and the ability to freely speak your mind, including admitting vulnerabilities. The belief of psychological safety led to performance in the form of moderate risk-taking, greater collaboration, and creative solutions.[5] At a time when every team needs to innovate more effectively, this is exactly the behavior that leads to breakthroughs.

How do we lead for psychological safety? Here are a few tips:

1. Immediately address the inevitable team conflicts that arise by putting the focus back on what you want to achieve together. The question to ask is, "How might we achieve a mutually desirable outcome?"
2. Take blame off the table and replace it with forward-looking accountability and curiosity. Blame always looks backward. Accountability always looks to the future. The question to ask is, "What are the possibilities we might explore to move this challenge forward as a team?"
3. Be a role model of the vulnerable and transparent behavior you want to see in your team members. Asking for feedback puts you and the entire team into that mind-set. The question to ask is this: "How might I be more effective leading this team through this challenge?"

The study concluded that if you create this sense of psychological safety on your team starting now, you can expect to see higher levels of engagement, increased motivation to tackle difficult problems, more learning and development opportunities, and better performance.[6]

A Thousand Miles of Support

To demonstrate the immense power of a supportive team, think of the way Canada geese work together. The leader of the flock creates a draft making it easier for each subsequent bird in the line of their V-formation to cut through the air. When the lead bird gets tired, he or she falls back to the end of the line, and another goose becomes the new leader. This innate coordination is one of the most stunning examples of collaboration in the animal kingdom. They can travel hundreds of miles together efficiently as a team because that have literally reduced the friction (technically "drag") of working together. I also find this to be amazing as a bonus. Did you ever notice that geese "honk" continuously to each other the entire time in flight, even at high altitude? Animal behaviorists claim they honk to provide immediate feedback to their exact location to synch up the formation, plus, to encourage each other to keep up the hard work of flying together. Don't great teams exhibit some of these exact characteristics?

VALUES UNIFY THE TEAM

Golf probably doesn't come to mind when you think about a team sport. On Sundays we see the highlights of an individual hoisting a trophy on the 18th green after winning. But golf has one standout event that may be the most intense team sporting competition you can experience. It's the Ryder Cup, and it is played every other year between the United States and Europe. Underdog European teams have beaten their talent-loaded Team USA counterparts many times. Everyone points to this anomaly as a result of the Europeans' special team bond. Team USA almost always has far more superstars on paper, yet Team Europe finds a way to win against all odds. But something magical happened for Team USA in 2021 at the Ryder Cup held at Whistling Straits in Wisconsin. Team USA finally played together as a galvanized team and won the cup. When they interviewed superstar Rory McIlroy from the European team, he explained, with tears flowing, how much the event means to him and how much he loves and respects his teammates. He was weeping for his team members in the loss because they too had a deep bond, and he so desperately wanted them to experience the joy of winning together. Keep in mind that players typically earn more than $1 million for winning a tournament, but they don't receive prize money for the Ryder Cup. The competition only provides charity money donated on behalf of their teams. It's another example demonstrating that it's not about extrinsic rewards. It's the pride for their team and the countries they represent that brings performance intensity.

To be fully engaged, team members need to feel their own personal values are in alignment with their team and its mission. Values are formed based on deeply held beliefs. If people value something, it's because they believe it gives them a return on investment. At work, that comes from both emotional and extrinsic factors. Individuals on a team constantly seek confirmation that their values are being lived out through the team's work. As a leader, you can help people confirm the connection and show them how their investment has meaning.

The behaviors that have a return on investment become the foundation for building shared values. In the team context, the investment being made comes from the time, energy, and literal cost of doing business together. A healthy, high-performing team constantly seeks the best return on investment for the effort they exert. Obviously, when the team discovers the best return, they want to replicate it. This is the genesis of team and organizational culture.

When the shared values of the team are in harmony with the values of the individuals, then everyone is on the "same page" in terms of unwritten rules of engagement. As a result, the way people communicate, coach, and make decisions happens naturally and in alignment with what is valued. From a team culture perspective, being in alignment reduces the transaction "cost" of working together. In other words, the flow of getting things done has a minimum amount of emotional friction and consternation—all those things that slow down the process and turn great decisions into politically expedient, mediocre compromises. Doesn't it feel phenomenal when we are free of these business barnacles? People often use the term *flow mode* to describe being at the top of their game. The term is appropriate for teams that are aligned in their thinking process, values, and purpose. It may be rare, but if you've experienced working on a team in flow mode, then you know alignment is well worth pursuing.

THE POWER OF A TEAM BOND

When the New England Patriots came out of the tunnel for the traditional player introductions at the start of Super Bowl XXXVI in 2002, they stunned everyone by coming out as one team. No one had ever done that before. It had always been one player at a time doing their special dance or celebration in an individual moment of glory in front of millions of viewers. Coming out as a team all at once was a clear demonstration of unity. That bond helped propel them to victory over the highly favored St. Louis Rams. The Rams probably had better players, but the Patriots won as a better team that day. People really took notice of what happened, and it set a trend. Every team since that Super Bowl has chosen to be introduced as a team. Here's a gut check to consider: If the people on your team came out of the proverbial "tunnel," would they come out as individuals or a team?

Meaningful Meetings

The virtual work phenomenon has taught us there's no substitute for time spent together. The time the team is physically together must be viewed as a significant opportunity to be leveraged. You can't treat "days in the office" as just another day of making the doughnuts. Look at your calendar for the upcoming days the team will be in the office and prioritize them as key events to lead as a catalyst of progress.

Your ability to plan and execute effective meetings that make coming together productive and meaningful is vital for engagement. I think a lot of well-intentioned leaders (and parents) believe that "quality" time will suffice for "quantity" time. In reality, both are necessary and highly desired to amplify meaning. It's up to you make it a positive experience for the people on your team.

The question, then, is this: How might you be more intentional about spending time with the team as a team? Let's review meetings from four different time-factor lenses as creative constraints: (1) daily, (2) weekly, (3) quarterly, and (4) yearly. Here are suggestions to get your creative juices flowing. By the way, don't feel you must be the sole creator of team get-together strategy. It's far smarter to ask team members for their ideas so they are at least somewhat bought into the concept.

Daily

It has become a standard practice in healthy high-performance cultures to have team huddles. These are daily, quick-hitting, stand-up meetings to communicate headlines and build rapport. They are highly effective and so easy to execute. Huddles work especially well in rapid-collaboration cultures because they are fast and can be implemented organically anytime besides the normally scheduled huddle time. Huddles are sometimes called "scrums" in the software development industry. They are so effective that they named an entire methodology "Scrum" to symbolize its most important feature.

Here's what you do. Pick an appropriate meeting location, and pick a time when most people are in the office. Depending on the size of your team, let each person give a shout-out about what they are focused on today. As the leader, be sure to include what you're doing, and consider adding anything else that you know from your higher perspective to dial people into the big picture of the organization. Don't forget the opportunity to do shout-outs of appreciation for great work.

Warning: Do not let the huddle evolve into a status report meeting! Effective huddles must be short and sweet (like a tweet). That's one of the reasons to make it a stand-up-only meeting. Also, don't allow huddles to become a political grandstand of self-promotion. If you see that beginning to happen, nip it in the bud. Huddles are about gaining clarity with rapid communication, not a forum for people to prove how "busy" or "important" they are.

Here's a tip: Designate your huddle time at a unique time like 9:10 a.m., or 11:50 a.m., to make the huddle meeting instantly memorable. The huddle time will create its own brand simply because the unique time will become its signature name.

Weekly

If the practicality of doing a daily huddle doesn't work for your team, then at least do it on a weekly basis. Better yet, create something altogether different. Set up a team lunch once a week on the same consistent day of the week. I recommend Monday (shake off the blues and reminisce about the weekend events) or Wednesday. Wednesday is called "hump day" for a reason. It's the halftime of the week. It's a good time to get recalibrated and refreshed to finish the week strong. Or select Friday because it's everyone's favorite uplifting day. End the week on a positive note together.

Keep weekly meetings simple but mix them up a bit to keep it fresh. Go to different places, occasionally do a potluck, and don't forget to treat every now and then. Some organizations always pay for lunch on the weekly lunch day. Don't do that unless you are committed to do it forever. It's hard to extract a perceived entitlement. Part of the key to success of these meaning amplifier lunch meetings is *not* adding to your team's already crammed work schedule. Everyone takes a lunch, and you can assume that you're not borrowing against other hot-priority work time.

Quarterly

Quarterly meetings are fantastic milestone markers for making progress toward big goals. If you're not leveraging quarterly meetings, then you are missing a great opportunity to be strategic as a team. I recommend committing to at least a half day for the quarterly meeting. Celebrate the last quarter's successes, be transparent if things fell short, conduct strategic planning, set goals for the next quarter, and take some time to develop the team. Consider bringing in an outside speaker, or have a leadership development pro facilitate team building such as the MBTI (Myers-Briggs Type Indicator), DiSC, or StrengthsFinder. These are just a few of the many great tools out there that allow people on the team to understand each other and discover ways to improve their relationships.

Yearly

Do you have a big yearly event that people look forward to? What might you do to demonstrate that working on your team is a special experience? Yearly meetings can be a golden opportunity to galvanize the resolve of the team and make working together truly meaningful.

Think of the potential content of the meeting from two directions: looking back and looking forward. This is called the Janus effect. It is symbolized by the two-headed lion that you often see above elaborate gates or entrances. It points out the importance of acknowledging both the past and future as you walk through a "threshold" together.

Team Meeting Communication Plan for Looking Back

1. What has happened over the course of the year that you can celebrate?
2. What milestones did you hit? What goals did you achieve?
3. What sacrifices were made? How did the team go the extra mile?
4. What were the challenges that fell short?
5. What is the impact the team made in the bigger picture of doing business?
6. What did the team accomplish together that could *not* have been achieved as individuals?
7. What do you personally appreciate about the team's attitude or performance?

Team Meeting Communication Plan for Looking Forward

1. What should people anticipate in the coming year?
2. What are the clear goals?
3. What are your expectations?
4. What will it take to achieve the new goals?
5. What does "great" look like for the coming year?
6. What does it mean to be a member of this team?
7. What are you personally willing to do to support the team going forward?

Note: If you cover these items, you will be the rare minstrel of vision and clarity as a leader.

Take at least a half day for this yearly event. A full day would be even better. Plan to have the meeting out of the office, if possible, to let people relax by changing the scene. And just like the quarterly meeting, design a blend of business, social, and development within the flow of the meeting.

Note: In unhealthy cultures, I've seen leaders back away from taking their team on retreats, and even half days out of the office for development or fun-time bonding. It's a huge, short-sighted mistake. Don't cave into the politics of your organization and make it an excuse based upon fear of looking "frivolous" or "soft." Team members easily pick up on the vibe of what's going on, and they will trust less in your commitment to do what's right as their advocate. If you're a confident leader and are convinced that getting together will make a difference in team engagement, then what do you have to fear? If you can't boldly explain your good reasons to anyone who would challenge you, then you need to get out of that toxic culture.

Also, don't let the snarky sarcastic eye rolls of cynical people sway you when the term *team building* comes up. Never manage to the least common denominator. Don't be too hard on them, though. It's likely they have never experienced effective team building and only know the awkwardness of it when it is done poorly.

Think about it. If you're not "building" your team, then by default you are willing to let it fall apart. Be the leader who is known for team building. You'll set yourself apart as someone special and make them jealous. Frank Sinatra once said, "The best revenge is massive success." That's you! But only if you amplify meaning for your team by making the commitment to get together for time well spent.

Clarifying Team as a Purpose

The logic is inescapable. Beliefs always drive behavior. If people believe in the team's ultimate purpose, then they will go into autopilot mode to behave in ways that help the team perform. So the real opportunity to influence performance is by relentlessly articulating why the team's work is important. If the team's work changes every day, then you even have to express it daily.

You might be asking yourself, "But what if the purpose of our team is not compelling?" Purpose is there, but it might not be for the reason you'd first imagine. For example, how would a team of sanitation workers connect to a higher purpose of working together? If we look at the literal output of their work, then of course it's not something anyone would find motivating. It's a tough, physical, stinky job. You'd think that someone doing that work would automatically put forth the absolute minimum amount of discretionary effort just to get by and survive the day. If you make that assumption, you are missing the true amplifier of meaning for teamwork. The team's ultimate purpose is not necessarily the output of the work or the nature of the work. The ultimate purpose and the meaning we derive comes from being part of the team in and of itself.

Yes, teamwork is a meaning amplifier even in a vacuum. Have you ever noticed how hard a team of sanitation workers works? They hustle and do their job well for each other. Teammates are the *why* of their hard work. It has nothing to do with the garbage or some far-flung, pie-in-the-sky reason like "cleaning up planet Earth." They seem to consistently create a culture of high work ethic that is self-governing. At the end of the day, they respect each other as much as a team of elite athletes who perform together.

You amplify meaning through the team by focusing on the purpose of being a team. Here are three questions for you to answer. These are examples of what you should articulate directly to your team:

1. What is the team able to accomplish together that would be impossible as individuals?
2. How does the team benefit from being successful together in the work?
3. Why is it important that we work together as a high-performance team?

When I made the decision to launch out on my own with my consulting and speaking practice, the one thing I missed the most was the dynamics of teamwork. It had been part of my everyday experience for more than 25 years. Being on my own felt odd without a team to huddle with, cry with, laugh with, and win with. I had no idea how much teamwork meant to me. I had to crank up some of the other amplifiers of meaning to compensate for that void. As a consultant, clients can become your team in a way, but I have to admit, it's not quite the same.

How about you? What was the most inspiring team you've ever been on? Looking back, if it's not your current team, what did that feel like? How much did you love the total experience of being on that team? Now, compare that to your individual output or performance. It's not a wild guess to assume it was likely the high point of your entire work experience so far. This is why if any of us, as leaders and motivators, underrate the team amplifier, it will be to our own peril.

TEAM AMPLIFIER PLAYBOOK

The COVID-19 pandemic had an immediate impact on people feeling disconnected with each other. The reality of working remotely meant that people would lose the personal touch of getting to know each other at a deeper level from the spontaneous rapport that occurs in the office. In fact, loneliness has become a chronic symptom of virtual separation. Remote work became an enigma for many leaders, causing them to feel powerless to make an impact on the relationship-building basics that build trust for themselves and within the team.

I developed a tool for leaders to be intentional about reconnecting people even if they work exclusively by remote. I call it the "Virtual Team Playbook," and of course, it can also be effective for in-person meetings. The purpose is to build rapport, trust, and clarity of expectations. It allows team members to share genuine, authentic, and transparent thoughts about their style and preferences in working effectively. The playbook goes far beyond doing a trivial "ice breaker" with the team. The questions that I developed are focused on relevant factors for working together that elevate everyone's awareness and empathy. Use the Virtual Team Playbook consistently, and you will see results as the team builds rapport and connection with each other. Here's how it works:

Directions

Invite reflection: Select one question at the start of each meeting. Send it out prior to the meeting to give people time to reflect.

Go first: Share your answer with the team as the leader. Model the amount of time and detail you'd expect to hear from others.

Be curious: Invite participation from everyone. Ask follow-up questions as appropriate to probe for clarity and understanding.

Go deep: Consider holding a specific team meeting to cover all the questions within a specific category (e.g., personal style, personal preferences, personal perspectives).

Personal Style

• I would describe my leadership style as _____.
• My leadership style works for me because it brings out my strength of

  _____. For example,

  you'd likely see that in action when _____.
• My favorite way to communicate is _____.
• My least favorite way to communicate is _____.
• On a scale of 1 to 10, my sense of humor at work is a _____. I would

  describe it as _____.
• You may notice that I'm stressed when you see me _____

  _____.

• When it comes to responding and participating in group discussions, I'm more likely to . . .

  a) Speak what's on the top of my mind, and be one of the first people to contribute.
  b) Listen in order to process the information first and wait to contribute if there is something more to share.

Personal Preferences

• I'm most passionate about _____ in the work I do.
• My best time of day when I'm highly productive and energized is _____

  _____.

• The thing that zaps my energy the most at work is _____

  _____.

- The super strength I rely on most is _____
  _____.

- When it comes to decision-making, I prefer to . . .

  a) Make decisions quickly and reach closure to get it done, and here's why

  _____.

  b) Process the creative possibilities and remain open to the best potential options, and here's why _____.

- I tend to do my very best work when other people or my manager _____
  _____.

- I love when team members _____.

- Sometimes I get annoyed when people _____.

- To help me become even more effective, I would welcome feedback from others specifically on _____.

Personal Perspectives

1. The most influential experience I've had that shapes my approach toward work and people is _____.

2. The one value I've formed as a result of growing up in my hometown is
   _____.

3. I'm working to be even better at _____.

4. Outside of work, I'm extremely happy when I'm _____
   _____.

5. The reason I work so hard and want to be successful is _____
   _____.

6. When it comes to teamwork, I think we are at our very best when we
   _____.

7. The one misperception people may have about me is _____

_____.

8. The one aspect of work that is most meaningful to me is _____

_____.

9. In my life or career, I was originally planning to become a _____

_____.

10. The one thing I've learned from someone at work that I will never forget is

_____.

7

The Manager Amplifier

> People leave managers, not companies.
>
> —Jack Altman, CEO of Lattice[1]

Everyone has heard the refrain, "People don't quit the company. They quit their boss!" All the evidence from engagement and retention measurement firms confirms this is quite true. A Gallup study of more than 7,200 U.S. adults "revealed that one in two had left their job to get away from their manager to improve their overall life at some point in their career."[2] It makes sense that the pandemic-driven "Great Resignation" was fueled in part by the epidemic of poor leadership.

The manager or "boss" (the short-cut title still used by most people) who amplifies meaning engenders loyalty through good times and bad. Yet many managers don't consider themselves as a source of meaning. Too many just see themselves as administrators of the work process without the responsibility to engage others. I'm hoping to provide new insights that help you acknowledge how important the "boss" relationship is on its own as an amplifier of meaning.

It's very sobering, but as the manager, you are a "filter" through which the majority of a person's work experience is viewed and judged. Think of your past jobs. Was your overall experience at those places positive, neutral, or negative? Now, think of your manager and your relationship at each of those jobs.

I'd bet the quality of your experience is in sync with the relationship you had with your manager. I know they have almost always been that way for me. The proverbial cocktail party test will also bear this out. If someone at

119

said party asks you, "So, how was it working for XYZ Company?" chances are very good that you'll first respond with a crack about the incompetent boss you worked for, or you'll be proud to tell them how much you liked it there because you worked for a really good leader.

What attributes, attitudes, and behaviors put a manager in a position to be a meaning amplifier? The following search-for-meaning questions people ask themselves will help with the answer:

- Is my manager *for* me or *against* me? Is my manager my advocate or my antagonist? (Am I a plus or a minus in his or her mind?)
- Does my manager respect me and the work I do by giving me meaningful recognition?
- Is my manager willing to do what it takes to support me and the work I am doing?
- Does my manager show me respect by coaching me to be accountable for my work, allowing me to gain a sense of ownership in what I do?
- Does my manager make a deliberate effort to develop an open, personal relationship with me that includes clear, timely, and (whenever possible) face-to-face communication?
- Can I count on my manager to help move the work forward and make progress? (Is my manager a catalyst or inhibitor of progress?)

WHAT ADVOCACY LOOKS LIKE

Let's start out with a gut check and reflection to get us calibrated with the manager amplifier. Can people look you in the eye as their leader and truly know, without a doubt, that you are absolutely their advocate? Think of the managers you've had in your career that you'd describe, without hesitation, as your advocate. Did your confidence in their advocacy translate into performance? I'd be stunned if your relationship and your performance were anything less than "you at your very best."

So if this was true for you, why would it be different for anyone else who now reports to you? Please don't underestimate the importance here. Everything in this book is meant to put you firmly on the advocacy side of the relationship equation. Have you been blessed to have an advocate in your life? How about a boss who became a role model for how to treat and inspire others? I can write this chapter only because I've been so fortunate. During my first stint with QVC, Terry Harmon was my boss and advocate.

I was a regional manager in the Affiliate Sales and Marketing Department, and Terry was my director. Like clockwork every day around 3 p.m., Terry would come walking through the maze of cubicles whistling a very distinguishable, repetitive, and happy little tune. I'm convinced he subconsciously knew that his whistle provided a type of empathetic warning—a warning that "the boss" was coming, and he was about to pop into my cube. He had that measure of grace. This kind gesture always gave me a split-second chance to look busy and get my act together. Terry would peek around the corner of my cube, and if I wasn't on the phone, he'd proceed to sit in my guest chair and put his feet up on my desk. The next thing he'd always say was, "Van Valin, where're we hung up?" He'd say this with his Ohio country boy inflection and tone that was immediately disarming. These five words were emblematic of everything Terry Harmon stood for as my advocate. Here's why it was so meaningful to me.

You might think, "Where're we hung up?" is a jarring or aggressive question. But it was the exact opposite. The word *we* was the game changer, and it defines advocacy. Terry was clearly rooting for me because, in the end, my success was *our* success. It was never about putting me on the spot or making me feel incompetent. Instead, it was a vote of confidence. *We* are going to make progress. *We* are going to solve the "hung up" issue of the day, together. His approach was that simple, and it was deeply meaningful.

Terry putting his feet on my desk might also seem intimidating, but instead, it conveyed that "I'm hangin' here, I'm committed to stay for a while, and I'm comfortable with you; let's chat." I didn't know the terminology at the time, but Terry gifted me the psychological safety to be myself. When anyone in this world gives us the gift of freedom to belong, to be ourselves, it comes wrapped in a bow of respect. That is one of the factors for why the unorthodox act of putting his feet up would seem immediately positive to me. It's important to note that Terry had already made significant deposits into my emotional bank account as my boss. A meaningful relationship, like the one Terry developed with me, takes an investment of consistency over time.

There's an amazing payoff for being an advocate. Working for Terry, I exceeded my sales goals and had the highest performance among the regional managers even with the second-smallest territory. There was something magical about the chemistry of advocacy that put me over the top. Each of us has our own unique manifestation of strengths. When I'm at my best, I'm creative, open minded, curious, and candid. Terry brought that out in me, and it translated into the motivation to perform—to put my strengths into action. It gave me yet another clear purpose in my work. I wanted to succeed as much for Terry as I did for myself.

So where does this leadership attribute come from? Are we born with it, or do we learn it along the way? The wise-guy answer is yes. In the case of Terry Harmon, he didn't graduate from Harvard Business School with an advanced degree in human psychology. Instead, he had spent 12 years playing in "the show": major league baseball with the Philadelphia Phillies. I have his baseball card as a personal treasure to prove it. When you consider what it takes to be an elite athlete competing in a team sport, there's no doubt that God-given talent and hard work is essential. But confidence and drive are the intangible ingredients that take players over the top as individuals and teammates. Terry experienced the power of motivation up close and personal from some of the best in baseball, including Greg Luzinski, Mike Schmidt, and Larry Bowa. Terry's informal dugout-style banter combined with the competitive intensity to be the best carried over into the corporate world by giving me a clear purpose: to live up to his advocacy. He was the most meaningful boss I've ever experienced, and it seemed completely natural and genuine coming from Terry Harmon.

A Commitment to Advocacy

It takes a mind-set of commitment to become an unquestionable advocate to people's success. The payoff is enormous for both of you since your employee's success equates to your inevitable success as a manager. If you demonstrate that you are fully committed to solving problems *with* them, they will view you as a trusted ally. As a result, you will hear more of the unfiltered truth about situations and be able to apply your energy to where it matters most, facilitating progress instead of stagnation. In return, they will want to perform and deliver for you because satisfying "the boss" now means something far more than staying out of trouble. It's about clearly demonstrating that you are in the battle together. Your relationship becomes a positive partnership. You can become their catalyst of progress and nourisher of meaning if you are committed.

Phil Mickelson is one of the top 10 greatest golfers of all time. He's legendary for an aggressive "go for it" style of golf that has produced an endless highlight reel of jaw-dropping shots from seemingly impossible scenarios. Phil has also had his share of heartbreaking near-misses along the way. The only major tournament that stands in the way of him earning the elusive career grand slam is the U.S. Open. He has come excruciatingly close, and he has the dubious record of six second-place finishes. You might think that a golf pro would be a lonely solo practitioner, but nothing could be further from the truth. For 25 years, Phil has had one of the best partners with him every step of the way in his caddie Jim "Bones" Mackay. Although Michelson was the boss, Bones served as technician, director of reconnaissance, coach, psychologist, and decision-making partner. It was a unique role, and it is a relationship that is emblematic of advocates working together. Mickelson trusted Bones so much that he gave him veto power over decisions made on shot choices. Although rarely used, it was the very act of giving that kind of respect and trust that leads to great, confident, and committed mutual decision-making. They were truly in it together. At post-round press conferences, Phil talked about "we" when describing his performance. Bones is now considered as one of the greatest caddies of all time with 42 PGA tour wins and five major titles while being "on the bag" with Phil as a super-talented golfer and advocate boss.

Asking Advocacy Questions

If you want to directly show your team members that you are there to help, support, and remove roadblocks, then ask advocacy questions. In the next section, there is a list of basic questions that facilitate progress and leverage your authority. People view you as the trump card to either get things done or get in the way. It's the extreme reality that comes with the title of "Boss." The questions you ask will determine how committed you are to helping versus hindering. I have listed the most useful questions in the ways you can amplify meaning as a manager. All these questions avoid blame. They are intended to hold you accountable as a leader and demonstrate your ownership of the issue. Accepting the responsibility to facilitate progress encourages empowerment. How might you be brutally obvious in your attitude that you are *all* in this together?

Advocacy Questions

- How best can I lead you?
- How best do you like to receive constructive feedback?
- How best do you receive coaching?
- What have past leaders done that drove you crazy?
- What could I do to get the most out of you?
- What obstacles can I remove to help you do your job better?
- What's getting in the way?
- What's stuck that needs to get moving?
- What additional resources or training would help you with your career or personal advancement that I might be able to provide?
- How do you plan on providing constructive feedback to me?
- What's keeping you up at night?

- What's the biggest decision you have in front of you, and how might I support you in getting it right?
- What does success look like?
- What are you hoping to accomplish today?
- What's the next step *we* need to take?

Advocating Up with Grace

Our general culture seems so on edge and at odds with each other these days. Grace is in short supply yet so badly needed. Grace is a wonderful symptom of advocacy and the ultimate outcome of psychological safety. When grace is our filter, we accept the nuances and foibles of each other at work. Some people set themselves up as victims expecting their managers (and coworkers) to be perfect. They have prewired their thinking that the boss is their antagonist and go on autopilot with that assumption. Sadly, this self-fulfilling prophecy often comes true. The bigger truth is that we are all struggling to do our best, and that includes the boss, who has the extra pressure that comes from leading others. In terms of accountability, the answer to the chicken-and-egg question when it comes to grace has only one solution. It must start with *you*. Anyone, whether a direct report, peer, or boss, has the power to be the first one to extend grace. I encourage you as the leader to be the first, and then watch grace come right back to you and applied in abundance.

RECOGNITION ON PURPOSE

> The act of recognition also sends messages to other employees about what success looks like. In this way, recognition is both a tool for personal reward and an opportunity to reinforce the desired behavior to other employees.
>
> —Annamarie Mann and Nate Dvorak[3]

While 50 percent of employees leave their job because of poor management, the positive perspective is that people will *stay* with your company longer, plus do incredible work for a respected boss. Gallup confirms that employees who receive adequate recognition are more likely to remain at their jobs over the next year than those who do not receive adequate recognition.

Let's take just one consistent driver of engagement, for example, employee recognition. We covered the best way to communicate recognition and appreciation in the "Self-Satisfaction Amplifier" chapter (chapter 3). But let's look at it here in the context of the manager amplifier. The role a leader plays in recognition is often just as important—if not more important—as the work process itself in the processes getting done efficiently. That is, giving employee recognition amplifies meaning, connecting purpose to work.

My wife came home one night after working very late for the third night in a row. It was only Wednesday, but I could tell it was already a brutally long week for her. As we were winding down after a quick dinner, she said with a flicker of hope in her voice that she got a note from her new boss. The note said, "Hey, I just wanted to tell you I think you're doing a great job." I can only begin to tell you how much that one-sentence email meant to her. I could see on her face and hear in her voice that it made her hard work and sacrifice matter. It was so simple but so powerful. Her boss, with one empathetic note, turned on the amplifier of purpose that made her hard work have meaning. You have that impact as the boss. It's so critical to realize people are starving for your approval. My wife Kara went to work the next morning ready to take it on with vigor.

Amplify the meaning of your people's work by simply acknowledging the energy, talent, and care they put into it. Use the definition for the term *engagement* provided in chapter 2 so you know exactly what to look for as you "catch them doing things right." Beyond the actual words you use, the delivery of your feedback is also important. For example, face-to-face recognition given in front of a team or other employees amplifies meaning because it not only boosts self-esteem and sense of accomplishment but also sets an example for others to follow. You set a positive precedent within your circle of influence every time you give it.

Be Specific

Including specific details in your recognition can make the recognition even more powerful. In his classic book *How to Win Friends and Influence People*, Dale Carnegie tells the story of a printer who, according to his supervisors, had a bad attitude but whose work impressed the boss. His employer, a Mr. Roper, went to the young man and expressed his appreciation for the printer's work. Carnegie explains:

> What Mr. Roper did was not just flatter the young printer and say "You're good." He specifically pointed out how his work was superior. Because he had singled out a specific accomplishment, rather than just making general flattering remarks, his praise became much more meaningful to the person to whom it was given.[4]

Saying "great job" will go a long way. But being more specific will have an even greater impact. Carnegie notes that the young printer's attitude changed completely after his conversation with Mr. Roper.

Gallup provides three effective ways to provide personalized recognition and praise:

1. Learn how employees like to be recognized.
2. Praise people for doing good work and achieving their goals while emphasizing why the recognized act was important.
3. Promote a recognition-rich environment with praise coming from multiple sources at multiple times.[5]

Their Purpose: To Please You

It's easy to put on the blinders and not see how much people try to please you. Yet your people are putting forth hard work and discretionary effort to make you happy, driven by a simple conclusion: "When the boss is happy, I'm happy. Therefore, I'm going to make darn sure to do everything I can to make the boss happy." This plays out every minute of every day in your world at work. But are you able to take advantage of it?

The emotionally intelligent boss leverages the "I'm happy = you'll be happy" equation by taking the high road. Instead of attempting to motivate out of obligation or anxiety, they provide opportunities for their people to please the boss—even to surprise and delight the boss. The easiest way to give them this opportunity is not only to clarify your expectations on deliverables but also to share your vision for what "great" looks like to you.

In other words, share with them the ultimate potential stemming from the work they are doing. This requires a little imagination and serves as a compelling stretch goal for people. Then give them the autonomy and freedom to go for it. Allow them to activate their creativity and discretionary effort to supersede your expectations. They will be cranking up an amplifier of meaning in the process, and you'll have something remarkable to appreciate about them.

One of the most powerful ways to activate the manager amplifier is to be disciplined and diligent to communicate your vision over and over, then recognizing and acknowledging the effort people are making to make that vision come true. Rinse and repeat for success!

"That's Why We Pay Them"

Engagement largely comes down to whether people have a manager who cares about them, grows them and appreciates them.

—Mark Crowley[6]

Some managers have a "Well, that's why we give them a paycheck" mentality toward appreciation. If you are one of those managers, you'll never turn on the manager amplifier. Sadly, you're missing out on a huge opportunity. You need to realize that the manager amplifier is the only amplifier you have complete control over. If you want to have the quickest results, and a direct return on your investment of time, this is the amplifier to work on—and recognition and appreciation is the manager's most effective amplifier tool.

ACCOUNTABILITY AS A PURPOSE

Here's how I define the term *accountability*: "Accountability is an attitude of ownership—a mind-set that seeks to discover and act upon the ideal outcome."

You can amplify accountability as a purpose unto itself. Imagine your entire team operating with this mind-set on the challenges they face—*wow*!

One of the most powerful actions you can take as a leader is to make the definition of accountability clear to your team members in words and deeds. Demonstrate to them how accountability is your expectation. It is the purposeful mind-set you are looking for in the way people work together. Doing so will shape your immediate culture with unstoppable power to rapidly solve problems and innovate valuable breakthroughs.

While it might seem like only semantics, avoid the trap of using the expression "I'm going to hold people accountable." That inadvertently defines accountability as something negative. For example, why would anyone choose to be accountable if the expression is translated as "I'm going to *blame* you if this doesn't work out"?

Being "held accountable" is basically a threat. If that's what "accountability" already sounds like in your culture, then you have work to do. You have the power to make an impact by repositioning the meaning through a communication strategy accompanied by training.

Stay true to the positive definition of the term *accountability*. An attitude of ownership is not something you can impose on someone. People must internalize and apply it for themselves. Accountability comes from within. When you see people holding *themselves* accountable, then you can be confident you've created a winning hallmark attribute within your culture. It starts one person at a time.

For this to happen, accountability must translate as having a positive payoff. In other words, people need clarity on "What's in it for me?" Accountability has significant ramifications on an individual being personally successful in driving results. Author Denise Breaux suggests that when leaders "blame failures on their subordinates, subordinates are likely, over time, to no longer see a relationship between work outcomes and their own efforts and abilities."[7] Healthy high-performance cultures always possess accountability as a positive hallmark. Realize it's a battle for hearts and minds. It's worth fighting for. Instead of a "threat," accountability needs to be viewed as a winning attitude and competitive advantage.

It's crucial to make the expectations of accountability exceedingly clear and apply them equally among employees. Let's get "back to the egg" on what you really want to accomplish:

- You want people to act *accountably* because they see the merit and the upside for doing so. Tell them, "Here's what's in it for you."
- You want them to act *accountably* and with consistency in the long term. Their positive belief about accountability will drive behavior on its own without your prompting. Tell them, "I'm anticipating and expecting accountability."
- You want them to act *accountably* when you're not there to make sure they exhibit discretionary effort. Tell them, "Here's what success looks like, and this is why it matters."
- The attitude of ownership is often organic, fluid, and spontaneous. Of course, it's challenging to fully determine and anticipate how accountability can be applied to all circumstances. That's the nature of work. Therefore, it's important to train people on the attitude, so they are empowered to apply it on their own.

Outstanding leaders incorporate accountability into their everyday dialogue beyond that of formal corporate policy. It's part of the psychological contract that emerges between leader and follower. Leaders who communicate this level of clarity on the tangible and intangible rewards and ramifications get results.

MAKE IT PERSONAL

If you create an environment where the people truly participate, you don't need control. They know what needs to be done and they do it. And the more that people devote themselves to your cause on a voluntary basis, a willing basis, the fewer hierarchies and control mechanisms you need.

—Herb Kelleher, former CEO of Southwest Airlines

Great leaders make a deliberate effort to build personal relationships that amplify meaning. Many leaders insist that they have rejected the old command-and-control type of leadership yet believe that issuing clear orders is all they need to demonstrate their leadership. No matter where you stand in the hierarchy of the organization, those at lower levels should feel that they have an open, personal relationship with you—a relationship that not only allows them to be candid with you but also assures them that you will always empower and support them.

Randy Ronning was the executive vice president of QVC's merchandising and dot-com division. It's a huge job with a lot of very intense people to manage. Yet, Randy kept an open lunch calendar every day with an invitation to anyone in the department to meet with him for lunch. Levels didn't matter. I'd see him in the North Fork Café at QVC every day with someone different. Sometimes it was a vice president; sometimes it was an intern. That was no surprise since the invite was open to anyone smart enough to take Randy up on his generous offer of time. By the end of his first year, he had developed personal relationships with hundreds of people.

Here are three takeaways from Randy Ronning's example:

1. *Open access:* Everyone says they have an open-door policy. That's a bunch of baloney if viewed from the perspective of subordinates. Most people would rather visit the Wizard of Oz than have a meeting with you if you're way up on the organization chart. Yes, it's that intimidating. What can you do to get down to their level and meet them in their space? Randy leveraged the lunch hour, and the friendly confines of the North Fork Café to build relationships, mutual respect, and a culture of openness that paid off in a myriad of ways.
2. *Relationship equity:* When high-level leaders express a genuine interest in knowing their people personally, they want to reciprocate by living up to the high esteem that has been given to them. Randy even had the amazing ability to remember the names of his employees' kids. As a result,

when he'd ask them to do something that seemed impossible, they'd do it without hesitation. Instead of operating out of fear or obligation, it was a chance for them to delight someone they viewed as their advocate. I experienced that feeling of reciprocity firsthand. Randy built equity, reciprocated loyalty, and amplified meaning one lunch date at a time. It's no surprise that his organization consistently produced breakthrough results through hard work.

3. *Insider intelligence:* This is the bonus. Imagine the cultural reconnaissance data Randy would gather every day on the state of his workforce from people in the trenches. You couldn't possibly conduct a formal survey that could even come close to the value of learning directly from people in the trenches. He had the inside scoop that allowed him to clarify his message and speak truth to power on the health of his culture.

Show Up

One of the most significant leadership challenges that sprung from the seismic COVID-19 pandemic shift is the virtual work void. The separation it caused was both physical and emotional. Communicating spontaneously, generating organic ideas, and simply building relationships became virtually impossible (pun intended). Let's face it: Hallway conversations and watercooler talk don't happen effectively over Zoom or Teams meetings. There are effective techniques to rebuild the connection that we covered in the last chapter, but let's consider one truth that doesn't change whether you are virtual or in person: Great leaders are in touch.

We don't have to victimize ourselves as leaders by being tethered to our devices or resigned to Zoom and Teams. Even if most of your people work virtually, there are still days where people come together in the office. Savvy leaders recognize the in-office days as key opportunities to build relationships and galvanize purpose. To leverage these prized days, they return to one of the early breakthrough concepts of effective leadership: managing by walking around. In these remote times, deliberately seeking out spontaneous face-to-face conversations to hear what people are working on and offer ideas on how you can support them is crucial to maintaining relationships and helping your people succeed.

Remember, it's almost guaranteed that people feel they never get enough time with you as their manager. Walking around gives them that time, helps drive progress, and is a huge demonstration of respect. It gives you an edge to be able to be in the know, solve problems on the spot, and hear firsthand what your team is really working on. I've heard other thought-leaders describe face-to-face personal conversations as a new-fangled technology called High-Speed Instantaneous Vocal Technology! Whatever you end up calling it, it's highly effective.

If you're already running the excuse through your mind that you're too busy to implement this idea, then consider this: Who could possibly be busier than a Silicon Valley start-up leader? Busyness didn't stop the CEO of Intel, Andy Grove, from leading by walking around. Andy made a huge statement to his team by foregoing a cushy office. He worked out of a normal cube among the team to demonstrate how important spontaneous interaction was to driving results. On a regular basis, he would get out of his cube to walk the floor. When Andy would come up to people he'd ask, "What are your 1-2-3's?" In other words, "What's hot? What are you working on?" Andy did it in a respectful and curious way that didn't come across as a threat or test of competence. Asking people this question surfaced the underlying transactional purposes of the day. He was there to remove obstacles and give support. This is one of the most effective techniques I've come across for creating small wins that spark the emotional reward of work feeling meaningful.

Intel is legendary for having a fabulous culture of collaboration. Andy Grove must have cast that shadow every day. He was motivated to help people train their brains on prioritization but, more important, to unlock glitches in real time. He became the ultimate catalyst that drove success at Intel by being in the trenches every day with people at all levels. If a busy tech legend can do it, then, why can't we?

What are your 1-2-3's for putting this idea into place at your organization?

1. _____

2. _____

3. _____

The Communication App

Building personal relationships is about communication. Face-to-face communication is best, but communicating effectively through technology is also important—especially in the digital age.

If you want to be more effective as a communicator, then emulate how people engage with social media. Social media has established a new pattern for communicating and consuming information. It has become an intimidating high bar for managers. It's also a significant opportunity to set yourself apart as someone who understands there is a whole new level of expectation on speed, relevance, and customization in the way people communicate.

In addition to being digital natives who grew up in the smartphone revolution, millennials and Generation Z have become extra savvy at personalizing their desired media through apps. Mobile is fresh, relevant, and immediately available. They know how to enable mobile to get what they want, when they want it. You can assume that most millennials and Gen Zers want and need that same mode of communication at work. Are you delivering on their expectations? Are they getting the information they want from you when they want it?

This is the new general expectation for the way you should communicate as a leader. That's a very high bar to live up to, isn't it? It almost sounds like a full-time job. A lot of leaders feel like they're really trying hard but never seem to satisfy the voracious appetite for information and feedback of their new generation teammates. It's frustrating for everyone.

Is there an app for that? The answer is yes. *You* are the app! You can make a couple of immediate changes to leverage this important communication dynamic. Think of it this way: You must *push* the information to your team that they want. How do you know what they want? Ask them! Become their app store.

Asking them will help you gain emotional intelligence. And be ready to communicate with speed. Be relentless and communicate *live* real-time all the time.

Make your communications quick, easy, and digestible. Go for quantity of frequency, not quantity of words. Check in with them on how it's going. What's working and not working? What obstacles are they encountering, and how can we work together to remove those obstacles? Be willing to make adjustments. They will tell you if there are things you're communicating that they'd like to "unsubscribe" from. The first thing on their list will likely be your boring weekly status report meeting. Don't take it personally.

If you listen and communicate well in short and frequent bites, there is a greater chance that everyone on your team, especially millennials and Gen Zers, will value and respect you as a leader.

THE ULTIMATE LEADER GUT CHECK

Ask yourself these questions in any given decision-making scenario: "Am I acting to benefit others or myself?"

Peter Drucker, who is considered the father of modern management because his insights and pioneering ideas transformed the way we conduct business, said the following:

A leader, any leader, must act for the benefit of others and not for oneself.

The aspect that makes leadership so rare is that we are wired to act for our own benefit first. It takes huge discipline and emotional intelligence to think and act with empathy.

The wonderful irony to this equation comes from the fact that benefiting others always and inevitably benefits us in ways that are even more rewarding. The sense of satisfaction and meaning we receive transcends any of the risk we take by advocating for others.

ARE YOU AN AWESOME BOSS?

Awesome bosses are leaders because others are willing to follow them. They inspire and bring out the best in people because they are *advocates* for their team members and enable them to be successful. They show respect for their people by publicly *recognizing* their performance. They model *accountability*, driving ownership of results. They show respect by developing *personal relationships* with their people, and thus earn that respect in return. Open communication, either face to face or through technology, is a key component of those relationships.

Awesome bosses recognize that their success depends on the success of their people. As a result, every action they take is first and foremost to benefit others and not themselves.

In sum, an awesome boss taps into the wisdom and energy of the team by creating an atmosphere of collaboration and a desire to improve. The awesome boss is someone people want to work with, learn from, and emulate.

Do the people on your team think of you as the awesome boss? What's standing in the way of making it happen?

YOUR PURPOSE AS A MANAGER

There's no doubt the role of manager is fraught with challenges, frustrations, and stress. It doesn't have to be that way. The managers I've encountered who achieve fulfillment view their role differently. They see the impact they have on the well-being of others and turn it into their purpose for leading. Here are suggestions on how to gain the positive perspective of converting your role into a purpose. Make a commitment to think through the impact of your role as a purpose and consider whether these purpose statements apply to you.

- To create a path for others to follow beyond me.
- To bring out the best in others.
- To bring joy, harmony, and fulfillment to my team members.
- To allow others to be satisfied and successful in raising their family or living their best life.
- To be a model of advocacy leadership worth emulating.
- To lead in ways so that people feel connected and have a sense of belonging.
- To lead with an open, curious, and creative spirit.

THE MANAGER AMPLIFIER PLAYBOOK

In the first chapter, I introduced the incredible study that revealed the genesis of motivation at work. *The Progress Principle* research from Harvard Business School discovered that *making progress in meaningful work* was the number one driver of engagement. The study also proved that managers have the greatest control over events that facilitate or undermine progress.

If engagement is won or lost based on the relationship between managers and their direct reports, then it comes down to the one-to-one, everyday events that make the difference. The battle for engagement is won or lost in the trenches, by the granular choices taking place throughout the day—choices a manager influences to make progress in meaningful work.

The playbook for this chapter is called the Progress Playbook[8] because, through deliberate planning at the beginning each day, you can ensure that your people will make smooth and productive progress that day and every day.

As a result, implementation of the Progress Playbook has the potential to give you stunning results as you work to improve engagement. One of my clients, from a Fortune 500 management software firm, literally put the Progress Playbook on her office wall right next to her laptop. It was a reminder to use it every time she had a virtual call with her team members who were scattered throughout North and South America. She was a senior vice president and had the lowest engagement scores of any division within the global HR business unit of the company. In the next engagement survey, after using the Progress Playbook consistently for three months, her division went from having the lowest scores in HR to the highest, and they had the greatest incremental improvement across the entire 100,000-plus employee global enterprise. She attributed the impressive achievement to using the Progress Playbook with discipline on every call.

Purpose of the Progress Playbook

The Progress Playbook is designed to give you specific action items to plan and implement every day to jump-start progress in meaningful work.

- **Catalysts** are the key actions you can take to facilitate progress in meaningful work.
- **Nourishers** are the key relationship-oriented actions you can take to boost engagement through emotional support and team connection.

Executing the Progress Playbook

- Review each catalyst and nourisher question (see figures 7.1 and 7.2) at the same time you "plan" your day. In other words, have your planning list/device out at the same time you review the questions.
- Take time to reflect on the answers to the questions. Transfer action items onto your to-do list.
- Focus specifically on what you will do *today*. The questions are meant to spark ideas and raise awareness.
- Use the Progress Playbook *every* day as a discipline.

Progress Playbook

Your daily engagement guide to facilitate progress in meaningful work.

CATALYSTS
Take action to facilitate progress

Communication:

☐ What are the clear, meaningful work goals (short- and long-range) I can share today?

☐ What information can I obtain and communicate to the team to facilitate progress? What should they know?

☐ What can the team and I learn from yesterday's successes or failures? How can I facilitate that learning?

Coordination:

☐ What can I delegate (or let go from my to-do list) to increase autonomy and ownership?

☐ What pending decisions allow me to involve teammates today (without slowing down the process)?

☐ What critical resources can I obtain to allow the team to make progress today? What do they need?

Consideration for people and ideas:

☐ What can I do to ensure the perceived time pressure on the team is at the optimal level today?

☐ Who may need my help today? How will I schedule time with them to be their consultant?

☐ How might I be a catalyst of ideas to help the team reach solutions today? How can I tap their creativity?

☐ How might I encourage teammates to collaborate today to spark a breakthrough in their work?

Figure 7.1 Progress Playbook catalysts.

NOURISHERS
Take action to enhance the meaning of the work

Respect:

☐ What contributions can I recognize today that are making a difference towards progress?

☐ What are the ideas I can champion today to eliminate barriers and bureaucracy for the team?

☐ What can I be even more open and honest about today to show my team respect?

Encouragement:

☐ What can I do to encourage the team in their efforts today (especially the tough challenges)?

☐ How might I best express my enthusiasm and confidence in the team?

Support:

☐ Who may need emotional support on the team? How will I schedule time with them today?

☐ What is my specific plan to interact directly (face-to-face) with teammates today?

Affiliation:

☐ Why is today's work meaningful? How might I communicate that to galvanize the team?

☐ What am I personally working on that I can share with the team today?

☐ How might I bring teammates together today to build a bond of rapport and camaraderie?

Figure 7.2 Progress Playbook nourishers.

8

The Department Amplifier

The legendary politician Tip O'Neill from Massachusetts once coined the phrase "All politics is local." In other words, no matter how big the issue, whether it was Vietnam, Watergate, or the Cold War, he recognized the importance of how it played on the streets of Boston and Hyannis Port. Tip O'Neill, a Democrat, was the Speaker of the House, and he became an effective working partner with Republican president Ronald Reagan. They were like the odd couple together but negotiated as good-faith partners to help lift the United States out of the economic malaise of the 1970s.

Speaker O'Neill's brilliant insight on the significance of empathizing with people at the local level gives us a perspective to emulate. I borrowed and modified O'Neill's insight to apply to corporate culture. I've witnessed (and now recognize) that *all culture is local*, too, and so should you if you want to amplify meaning through your department or business unit.

Most employees are dialed in to what's happening within their department far more than what's happening in the larger organization. It's simply a factor of relevance and proximity. This reveals the opportunity to amplify meaning through our department, especially if it feels beyond our ability to champion the company purpose. Many organizations have become more business unit driven, and have greater autonomy to chart their own course, especially since the COVID-19 pandemic. The purpose of the department has come into clearer focus for the savvy leaders willing to amplify it.

The other variable to recognize is the difference between the health and performance of the culture at the department level compared to the entire company. I've seen a double-digit disparity on engagement scores not only among departments but also among departments and the cumulative company score.

This works both ways. Within an average company culture, a business department can be remarkable—or toxic. Departments can be safe islands in the middle of a company storm, or they can be toxic anomalies within a utopian culture. This provides us with encouraging news. Leaders have more control to influence culture at the department level and make the high-impact decisions that amplify meaning. They don't have to feel trapped or powerless within a company culture that is missing the mark.

The following are some search-for-meaning questions people ask themselves:

- Do I clearly understand how my work impacts the goals of the department?
- Is the purpose and vision of this department motivating me to perform at my very best? (Am I connected to the meaningful purpose of our department's work?)
- Do I trust the leadership of the department and feel confident in the direction they have set?
- Do I feel I can grow my reputation and career aspirations by working within this department?
- Are we making progress as a business unit toward a meaningful purpose?
- Am I inspired and motivated by a clear rally cry for the mission of our department's work?

The *department* amplifier gives us the platform to become the leader everyone wants to work for. I've seen so many outstanding leaders build a reputation of being the best of the best in the way they shaped a successful business unit. I've watched them influence by creating a department culture that is the living example for what is possible, and what the values look like in action. In some cases, they've even set a high bar for the rest of the company to model. A department's culture is often a direct reflection of the strong characteristics and attitudes of an individual leader who is compelling and authentic. Some people might even call it a cult of personality if it's distinctly unique. What is the shadow you would want to cast and see reflected in others?

CASTING A MEANINGFUL SHADOW

You never know who is watching and the impact of your "shadow." Back in the start-up days at QVC, our culture had an "all hands on deck" expectation that we'd do whatever is necessary to survive and support the business. Imagine the daunting challenge of launching from scratch something as interdependently complex as a live television shopping network. Many times, after a weekend of great sales, a mild panic would set in as we thought, "How are we going to ship out all these orders in time?" That's the ultimate good/bad problem for a start-up. Sure enough, the word would go out to everyone at all levels to head down to the warehouse to pack up items and get them out the door as soon as possible. As I mentioned before, I was in the Affiliate Relations Department. We wore suits and ties to work and didn't really feel in our element in a hot warehouse with packing peanuts, tape guns, and endless orders to put into cardboard boxes, but we did the best we could.

One particular time, I remember being quite annoyed because, for the fourth day in a row, we were called down from the air-conditioned comfort of our cubical maze on the executive floor to pack boxes, yet again. I spent the first 30 minutes complaining loudly to my team members, until I observed something that transformed my attitude. Across the warehouse, I saw the executive vice president of customer fulfillment, who was also in a shirt and tie, collapsing huge boxes and stacking them up into piles. He would then pick up the cardboard piles and dutifully walk them over to a gigantic compacting unit, toss them inside, and activate the loud hydraulic mechanism to compress them for recycling. He did it over and over again all by himself. I realized at that moment that QVC was destined to become successful. If someone at that level was willing to do whatever it takes, then who was I to complain? All of a sudden, the humbling work of packing orders had new *meaning*. We were all in it together. It took just one accountable act of a leader to amplify, and I'm sure he had no idea that I saw the shadow he was casting on our entire department.

Note: Fast-forward 20 years to my second time working at QVC as part of the culture-shaping team out of HR, I had the good fortune to work with the senior executive team of the Customer Fulfillment Division to craft their purpose statement. Based on my own personal experience from that hot day in the warehouse all those years ago, it felt very appropriate to express their department's statement as: "Delivering a Promise in Every Box." I knew exactly what that meant. We lived it and brought it to life. The shadow had stayed with me for 20 years.

The line from Led Zeppelin's epic song "Stairway to Heaven" warns us that "our shadow's taller than our soul." This metaphor is appropriate given the influence we have as high-profile leaders. There's no doubt the expectations of others become more intense the higher up we go in our organizations. Casting a poor shadow can be amplified in a negative way. Consider what staffers for the U.S. vice president once said about their boss, Kamala Harris:

"With Kamala you have to put up with a constant amount of soul-destroying criticism," one staffer told the *Washington Post*. "It's clear that you're not working with somebody who is willing to do the prep and the work."[1] It's a good reminder that people are sensitized to authority and will react positively or negatively to the shadow you're casting. Here's a quote from Brené Brown as a gut check for leaders at all levels:

> Connection is the energy that is created between people when they feel seen, heard and valued; when they can give and receive without judgment.[2]

THE PURPOSE OF CLEAR GOALS

One of the powerful ways to amplify meaning through the department is by clarifying goals. Goals at the department level are often more relevant for team members because they see a direct connection to their own ability to influence the outcome. It is also easier to communicate and track department-level progress than it is to do the same for company goals. Goals act as a collaboration catalyst for department teams by aligning them on a clear outcome. *The Progress Principle*[3] research from Harvard Business School called out "clear goals" as the top catalyst for making progress in meaningful work.

The Vision of Clear Goals

It was a beautiful night to fly out of Philadelphia. The view of the setting sun from my window in the 737 had me mesmerized and reflective for most of the trip. As we descended into Memphis, I'll never forget seeing the lights of thousands of houses below extending for miles out from the city, as far as the eye could see. This was a highly meaningful moment. It hit me that the deal I had done with the Memphis cable system would instantly bring QVC into all those living rooms the next day. I admit it was a slightly stunning moment as well because each light flickering below represented a family that would have QVC in their cable lineup and become a potential customer. With my one deal, inked with the cable system that served most of Memphis, I hit my sales goal for the year and put our department over the top of our total subscriber goal. As you can imagine, it was an amazing feeling of accomplishment to know that I had contributed to our total win as a business unit by launching the entire new market of Memphis with one flip of a switch. Mission accomplished.

THE MISSION OF YOUR MESSAGE

Your department's purpose is essentially the capability to move your key strategic initiatives forward through a set of clear execution goals. I believe it's appropriate to call your key strategic initiatives "missions." Missions are defined by having a clear, specific objective and a stated time frame to carry it out. I use the term *mission* for business in the same context as a military mission because they are far more useful and practical as a communication tool in that context. True missions are very definitive as opposed to some lofty statement that people must interpret emotionally for themselves. If the mission is, "The 2nd Company Rangers will take Hill #206 by removing the enemy positions by zero–nine hundred," then there are number of steps the lower-level commanders are empowered to execute to successfully achieve the mission. Clarity of the execution goals for the mission creates the opportunities for small wins and enormous wins to be targeted and achieved. And each of those wins at the department level is another opportunity to leverage the department amplifier.

Is it any wonder that our American armed services are considered the most effective in the entire world? In large part, it is because they are highly engaged and committed. That comes from the leadership discipline of communicating the mission with clarity. The rare times in which the U.S. military has failed, it has been because the mission was unclear or tangled up in a political web of unaligned messaging.

Clarify and Amplify Your Message

- Q: Are the people in your department dialed in and aligned to your department's key strategic initiatives (missions) and associated goals? A: Review your potential messaging platforms to create a media plan. Present them with clarity. Rinse and repeat.
- Q: Are people aware of the impact they can make by accomplishing the mission? A: Ask and empathize how they see their role playing out.
- Q: Are they fortunate enough to be able to visualize what success looks like when they achieve it? A: Ask and emphasize what they see as a symbol of success.
- Q: What is the company mission that the department has the most direct impact toward achieving? A: Make the connection back to your department and communicate the critical outcome of the work.
- Q: How will you plan to tell people where they are making progress as they pursue the goals? A: Review and plan your opportunities to communicate the progress achieved using a combination of media vehicles (i.e., low tech and high tech) that reach your audience.

These questions shape your messaging content and delivery vehicles. The answers must be shared repeatedly to create a foundation of beliefs that galvanize resolve. You can look forward to seeing engaged and high-discretionary behaviors as a result.

ACTIVATING YOUR DEPARTMENT'S HIGH-PERFORMANCE HALLMARK

In the "Manager Amplifier" chapter (chapter 7), we reviewed the performance advantage of accountability and the way it should be defined: Accountability is an attitude of ownership—a mind-set that seeks to discover and act upon the ideal outcome. Let's look at accountability in the context of your entire department culture.

When accountability becomes a clear expectation as a value within your department, it is a game changer to your culture and ability to succeed. Whether you're leading a small team, or the entire business unit, accountability is a worthy hallmark to emphasize and measure. I've witnessed the transformative power accountability plays in the high-performance capacity of a department.

Here are two tactic approaches to consider if you want to build a foundation of department accountability:

1. **Apply accountability to "live out" other specific values.** For example, if you had the company value "Create a Learning Environment," then identify the role accountability would play in bringing this value to life. Instead of people waiting for others to teach them, they should look inward to see what they could do to share knowledge with others. They need to own it. Let's make it even more relevant by making it a specific expectation. Here is what it might sound like: "When a person comes back from attending a workshop, trade conference, or certification class, it is an expectation they will own the 'Create a Learning Environment' value by scheduling time to teach others what they learned." By the way, there is a great payback in doing so. Research from the National Training Laboratories shows the highest learning retention rate (90 percent) comes from teaching others.[4] Accountability is always more attractive to people when they can see "what's in it for them." If you make this act an accountable expectation, you will not only establish accountability as a department hallmark but also elevate an important corporate value in the process.

2. **Inspect what you expect.** One certain way to help anchor the positive belief and expectation for accountability is to measure and discuss its practical application. I developed a practical tool to put accountability at the center of the table for discussion. It is called the Accountability Gap Assessment (see figure 8.1). The idea is to challenge team members to identify the attitudes and behavior they are seeing in themselves and/or the collective team. The powerless victim-oriented expressions are listed on the left, and the corresponding positive accountable expressions are listed on the right. Ask people to consider the blend of what they are seeing from both of the columns and correlate that to a number on the scale that represents the range of people's mind-sets. Essentially, by averaging everyone's number, you establish an Accountability Gap Assessment score that you can track over time. Perhaps even more important, the scores provide an opportunity to openly discuss what needs to happen to raise the score. For example, if team members feel that 6 represents what they are experiencing, then the next questions should be (a) "What are you seeing that makes us a 6 on the scale?" and (b) "What might we do to get to become an 8 on the scale?" The ensuing conversation invites participation on ideas and action items to be even more accountable. This can be implemented at every level, including an entire department, as a pulse check done electronically with Survey Monkey or even live during town halls using phones to activate the Poll Everywhere app, for example.

What do you see in action

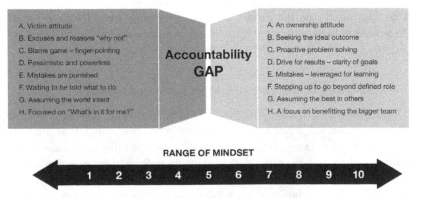

A. Victim attitude	A. An ownership attitude
B. Excuses and reasons "why not"	B. Seeking the ideal outcome
C. Blame game – finger-pointing	C. Proactive problem solving
D. Pessimistic and powerless	D. Drive for results – clarity of goals
E. Mistakes are punished	E. Mistakes – leveraged for learning
F. Waiting to be told what to do	F. Stepping up to go beyond defined role
G. Assuming the worst intent	G. Assuming the best in others
H. Focused on "What's in it for me?"	H. A focus on benefitting the bigger team

Accountability GAP

RANGE OF MINDSET

1 2 3 4 5 6 7 8 9 10

Figure 8.1 Accountability Gap.

THE AMPLIFICATION TIPPING POINT

When I work with organizations specifically on engagement, my advice always focuses on the tipping point: "If you want to once and for all increase employee engagement, address it where it is won or lost. It's your *supervisors*." They are the front line of engagement for every organization. The most effective approach to making a deep and meaningful impact falls within the scope of the department. This worthy pursuit is in the department sweet spot because the effort can be laser focused and aligned to your department culture and missions.

It's hard to escape any engagement survey analysis that doesn't clearly point to a person's manager/supervisor as the key driver that makes the difference. A person's boss plays the most crucial role in shaping the daily events that impact the way people feel about their work experience. For better or worse, supervisor competence is the tipping point for bringing meaning to work for employees at the department level.

The Beliefs of Supervisors Can Destroy Meaning and Purpose

If you are a department leader, then you must overcome the killer beliefs that paralyze supervisors and their efforts to influence engagement and instill purpose and meaning for the employees they supervise. This is your best opportunity to move the engagement needle. It requires a focus and commitment to get real with how most supervisors think.

Raise your awareness by *listening* for the unaccountable killer beliefs supervisors have toward engagement. What supervisors say out loud reveals what they believe on the inside. These self-defeating inside beliefs manifest themselves as behaviors that end up killing engagement. You can change their beliefs—but only if you understand them first.

Seven Supervisor Beliefs That Kill the Department Amplifier

Killer belief #1: "I shouldn't have to motivate them. That's why we give them a paycheck." When is it finally going to be universally known that extrinsic motivation (a paycheck) is not a sufficient motivator, other than to get people to show up? We covered this from the individual's perspective in the "Self-Satisfaction Amplifier" chapter (chapter 3). Giving people a paycheck is the price of doing business in exchange for their contribution. A paycheck clearly has very little to do with what that "contribution" looks like.

The Corporate Leadership Council research discovered that intrinsic factors are four times more powerful as a motivator than extrinsic factors. These are factors like, feeling respected, communicated unto, empowered, appreciated, encouraged, clear on goals, supported, and part of something bigger. The only one that has direct control on providing these intrinsic factors is a person's supervisor.[5]

Killer belief #2: "I couldn't motivate them if I tried. They're only here for the paycheck." This is a self-defeating, prophetic assumption that reeks of a victim mind-set. The truth is that nearly everyone comes to work to do a good job. They seek respect—not just the paycheck. Your supervisors are someone's boss, which means they are the number one factor and filter through which employees view their total work experience. This plays out at every level in an organization. The accountability starts with supervisors to create the conditions for their employees to be successful doing good work. That is the most basic expression of respect that people require of their supervisor. Indeed, some people will not make a good choice to be engaged no matter what, and the supervisor must have the courage to send them packing to the competition as soon as possible. I've heard people with this attitude described with as CAVE dwellers (Consistently against Virtually Anything). It's a sad place to be stuck.

Killer belief #3: "I don't have time to get them engaged." Supervisors can't afford *not* to get their people engaged. Everyone is chasing their own tail at work these days. If your hair is on fire, welcome to the club. But engaged people get more done. That means supervisors will have more time. Engagement isn't the ole chicken-and-the-egg enigma. Supervisors must be the ones to take the first step to engage. They need to make the time. Engagement is a "give to get" equation. *The Progress Principle* revealed that the more rigorous leaders become in the quest for results in a highly respectful, collaborative manner, the more effective they will be at engaging their team. That's the great news that should be comforting to all; engaging their people is built into the supervisor role as a leader—not something separate and different that they must add into their already jam-packed personal agenda.

Killer belief #4: "If we just manage people, and the process better, then we won't have to motivate them." People aren't robots, or component parts that get plugged into a predictable system at work. They are flesh and blood and driven by emotions just like you. Unless people do nothing but rote-linear tasks all day long, work is mostly organic, unpredictable, and change saturated. People earn their money by thinking and responding as problem solvers and opportunists. Processes can minimize predictable variables, but they become cumbersome when change occurs and frustrating when emotions are in play. There is no substitute for supervisors rolling up their sleeves along with their people and solving real-time problems together as a unified team to give and gain respect. Respect trumps process every time.

Killer belief #5: "I don't know how to motivate them. I don't have a PhD in psychology." It's not necessary to parse people's psyches and manage through a gauntlet of emotional nuance in order to engage people. Again, the research from *The Progress Principle* shows that if supervisors facilitate progress in meaningful work, they will be tapping the number one driver of engagement every day through the very basic fundamentals of great supervision. It's about creating the conditions for success. Every day, supervisors should ask themselves, "What can I do *today* to knock down the barriers that are frustrating people and facilitate progress on meaningful work for my team?" Answering that question is the most powerful thing supervisors can possibly do to engage. No advanced degree required.

Killer belief #6: "I'm not motivated myself. How can I motivate them?" We've all heard this safety announcement every time we board a jet: "Should the cabin lose pressure, the oxygen masks will drop down. Extend the elastic band over your head. Secure your own oxygen mask before placing masks on small children or infants." The health of the helper is always vital whether it's an emergency or a boring day at work in which a supervisor needs to engage his or her team. But the research from *The Progress Principle* study revealed that engaging others was a key factor in managers feeling deeply satisfied and fully engaged. So, where does it start? Supervisors can put on their own "oxygen mask" of engagement by unlocking the conditions for success for their team. They can use their people's uptick in engagement as a springboard to propel their own motivation and passion for leading people.

Killer belief "7: "If I motivate them this time, they'll expect it every time in the future." That's right, and they should! If it works this time, why wouldn't supervisors do it every time? It feels great to be engaged. Work gets done, the day goes faster, and it's something to feel proud of. A supervisor is in a position of leadership to get results. If turbocharging their team's performance by engaging them makes the difference (and it most assuredly will), then supervisors will be hungry and motivated themselves to make sparking engagement a regular part of how they lead. It's a natural. This isn't about tricking people or pulling one over on them. It's about a supervisor being genuine and authentic in a way that is transparent. People immediately know the difference and will respond appropriately. You don't have to be perfect; you just need to show you care and respect them.

STOP MANAGING AND START ENGAGING

How many people do you know who had some career epiphany along the way that sounded like, "Gee, someday I'd really like to be managed by someone"? Obviously, no one! And, on the other side of the same coin, few people want to actually "manage" people. It's typically an unwanted burden that comes as an obligation for being promoted. We take fantastic individual contributors and assume they can apply their magic formula of success to others who now report to them. The results are shockingly disappointing most of the time.

Engagement is a personal choice, and it's a choice that can be influenced. Remember that we defined engagement in chapter 2 as "the extent to which a person *chooses* to apply their *energy, talent,* and *care.*" Supervisors at all levels have the most influence on the choice people are making to be engaged at work. The effective department leader raises the awareness of supervisors on the vital influence of their role. Acknowledging and addressing the seven killers of engagement can be the most effective initiative any organization can take to spark a higher level of engagement and performance.

My summary of the killer beliefs might seem harsh, yet I've witnessed these consistently for years in workshops and through the engagement survey diagnosis processes I've led. I'm sure you've seen many of these beliefs for yourself through your role. I don't recommend shying away from addressing them head-on, but you do need to do it with tact and positive intent. Your approach must leverage the psychological safety factors we reviewed previously that spark conversation and a willingness to change. I believe this expression from Alan Mulally, the former high-impact CEO of Ford Motor Company, is the perfect way to begin your messaging to the supervisors in your department. He is noted for saying it this way: "You're not the problem; you have a problem. If you can tell me the problem, we can all rally together to fix it." Alan Mulally captured a wonderful expression of accountable advocacy that begins the improvement journey.

CULTURE KRYPTONITE: PERFORMANCE MANAGEMENT SYSTEMS AND THE DREADED REVIEW

Think of the irony: HR departments in nearly every organization have instituted complicated people-management practices like lemmings ignoring the basic tenets of Human Psychology 101 and what has worked all along. We have explored the most effective approach revealed by *The Progress Principle.*

Instead of "managing people," great leaders consistently create the conditions for people to be successful. If you lead a department or business unit, it's vital you are aware of the negative impact performance-management systems have on your specific team members. Nothing can kill their sense of purpose and meaning in work more than the shambles of performance management that exists today.

Here's what has happened. Well-intended HR professionals have inflicted a bureaucratic nightmare upon managers in the spirit of codifying proper leadership behavior. This misguided effort has led to the creation of systems that have inadvertently turned down the amplifiers of meaning at work and, at the same time, reduced the manager and worker to see their role as a commodity that feeds the cold, unfeeling corporate machine. Managers in your department have been given this "tool" to help them structure performance reviews, yet it has shoved managers into an unpainted corner with a system that inevitably crushes their workload, fuels anxiety, hurts their relationships, and consistently disappoints the very people they want to engage.

The Bad Actors

It's curious how this megatrend started in the 1990s when consulting firms saw an easy way to weasel their way into the culture business by trying to turn it into a predictable system and a process that nonbelievers of culture would buy off on as "strategic." I view it as a sellout for those who were stuck in their old paradigm thinking that being values centric was allegedly "soft management" and not strategic. Too many HR people lacked vision and confidence that values could stick. Many still seem to underestimate the profound difference values can make to shape a healthy culture.

What we have witnessed throughout the years is that applying a rigid system with Orwellian HR language has sucked the word *human* right out of the equation. For the most part, the process discounts a person's natural and organic style of meaningful leadership that leads to engagement and performance of their team.

One Shining Moment

If there is an aspect to this megatrend that has been worthwhile, it's been the process some organizations and departments have implemented to identify the unique attributes that make someone stand out as a fit within the culture. This at the very least has helped personify the values that buoy their brand and culture. If there is nothing unique that is identified, then all the competency descriptors seem to fall into the soup bowl of sameness and have little value.

A few savvy culture-centric departments have taken full advantage of what sets them apart by breaking the mold on how performance is evaluated. In other words, they use their brand attributes and values to drive the creative process for what the system should look like. They can identify the very specific behaviors that create an amazing brand experience. This is so much more compelling for people. Plus, it ensures alignment and perpetuation of the company's unique and differentiating cultural advantages.

An HR Reputation Killer

I feel the one-size-fits-all performance-management systems, coupled with overly detailed competencies, have had little or no effect on changing behavior. Instead, in many cases they have also inadvertently alienated the HR professional from having a further influence and credibility as a consultative partner in the organization. Why? Because HR is now seen as an out-of-touch stumbling block instead of a true advocate and partner. It's reduced HR to an administrator in chief of a process that 9 out of 10 people loathe—instead of a culture-shaping leadership role.

If you doubt what I'm saying, consider the many leaders who have risen to significant prominence in your organization. How many of them would look back and cite their personal experience with a performance-management program as their "turning point" or "prime catalyst" that led to their success as a leader? It would be extremely rare.

Why is it, then, that so many organizations and departments continue like lemmings to follow a performance-management system down a one-way path of no return? For many, too much time and treasure have been invested to risk pulling the plug. You are left perfuming the pig with incremental changes that only strip some of the scales of complexity and bureaucracy from the system. That's downright depressing and a waste of precious talent.

I am making these statements with confidence because I've personally lived it as a leader and have been party to the design and delivery system firsthand. I realize you may be cringing if you're in the leadership development field and believe I'm speaking heresy. My guess is I've struck a nerve—either since you disagree because your organization's system is so uniquely clear and logical, or you realize what I'm saying is true yet are stuck in the proverbial spider web that cannot be undone.

Get Real, Fast

These programs are often so big, and have so many stakeholders, it's nearly impossible to retract them. My best advice is to rip off the Band-Aid quickly and decisively. Replace it with a format that leverages your brand and inspires the humans you serve internally. Get "back to the egg" on what the original intent is for the process in the first place. Isn't it about creating the conditions for people to be successful? And isn't the intent to create a fair way to surface the high-level talent who live your values and drive performance? Think about how a new format could add to the meaning of the work experience and not take away from it by the negative emotions that will forever be linked to per-formance reviews.

The opportunity to get creative and match your review process with your brand and values can be a game changer for your entire culture.

THE DEPARTMENT AMPLIFIER PLAYBOOK

There is a tactical and practical way to amplify meaning by rallying the depart-ment to solve problems that stand in the way of achieving your high-stake mis-sions. Patrick Lencioni, the legendary consultant and thought leader, notes in his book *The Advantage* the value of a "Rally Cry" in pulling people together and engaging them in the pursuit of a core mission.[6]

Here's how you can use a rally cry at the department level. Look for the opportunities and moments that would galvanize resolve to work out a sig-nificant issue together. Your department rally cry should sound like, "Here's what we need to all come together for, *right now*, to solve and execute!" In other words, "We need all hands on deck to brainstorm a solution and a plan to get it done."

I experienced the power of using a rally cry to energize and engage a highly diverse department at QVC. We'd gather together to rapid-collaborate breakthroughs to grow the QVC business. The savvy senior team of the new QVC Interactive Division created a culture that had a clear expectation for supporting each other. We also worked very hard to establish a deep un-derstanding and appreciation for the creative process. It made the rally cry gatherings highly energized and productive. Some of the low-hanging fruit ideas we generated together increased sales by more than $1 million in less than a week on QVC.com. Having that type of reinforcement from winning together raised everyone's confidence and tenacity to go for even bigger wins every time we got together. The feeling from the collective creative buzz was palpable and viral.

Here is a list of the five key rally cry ingredients for successful department rapid collaboration:

1. Clear definition of the problem/opportunity
2. Speed (time pressure serves as a creative catalyst)
3. Optimism and confidence (clarity for why our effort will have a meaningful impact)
4. Discipline to work through the creative process
5. Accountability to follow through with executable action steps

The template shown in figure 8.2 is a meeting plan that represents the design of the rally cry meetings but condensed to a one-hour time frame. If you wish to have a two-hour or three-hour meeting, simply lengthen the time frames on the clock accordingly, except for the "Get Settled" stage. Most of the rally cry meetings we facilitated at QVC were three hours long because the opportunities we were addressing were new and significant in our mission to build the QVC.com business.

With so many people working remotely, it's important to note this format is perfect for using during Zoom or Teams calls. No matter what, it is vital to maintain very strict time adherence or the meeting will not cover all the steps. I recommend designating a person to be the timekeeper to call out the time remaining and when to move on to the next phase. A person should also be designated to record ideas and action steps at the same time participants use chat features to communicate their ideas.

It may take some practice before people understand and appreciate the "rules" of the process, but they will inevitably enjoy the game-like challenge of working through it together. If you are the leader of the meeting, then take charge firmly to guide people through the stages. Be sure to show them the meeting plan (template) from figure 8.2 as a "map" for how the agenda will flow.

If you use this problem-solver format, your rally cry efforts will amplify meaning to your entire department with the confidence you can achieve nearly anything together.

The 1- hour Virtual Problem-Solver

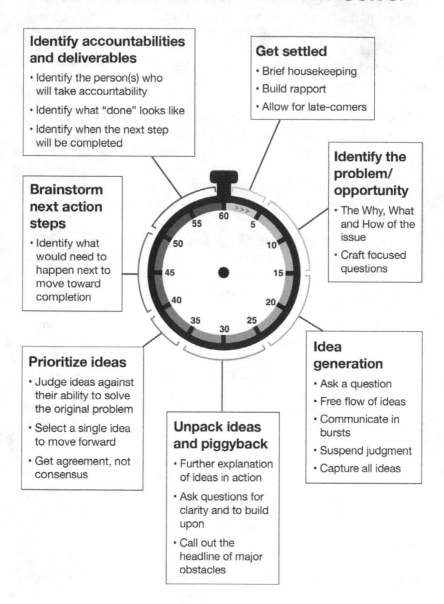

Identify accountabilities and deliverables
- Identify the person(s) who will take accountability
- Identify what "done" looks like
- Identify when the next step will be completed

Get settled
- Brief housekeeping
- Build rapport
- Allow for late-comers

Brainstorm next action steps
- Identify what would need to happen next to move toward completion

Identify the problem/ opportunity
- The Why, What and How of the issue
- Craft focused questions

Prioritize ideas
- Judge ideas against their ability to solve the original problem
- Select a single idea to move forward
- Get agreement, not consensus

Unpack ideas and piggyback
- Further explanation of ideas in action
- Ask questions for clarity and to build upon
- Call out the headline of major obstacles

Idea generation
- Ask a question
- Free flow of ideas
- Communicate in bursts
- Suspend judgment
- Capture all ideas

Figure 8.2 The 1-hour virtual problem solver.

9

The Company Amplifier

When meaning directly informs a company's real-world behavior in every step of the way, the result isn't a siloed culture and fragmentation where value gets compartmentalized; it's unity of character and purpose.

—Dr. Martina Olbertova, founder and CEO of Meaning Global[1]

If you asked most leaders to consider a strategy for amplifying the meaning of work, the *company* amplifier is likely the first option they would choose. More and more organizations are now amplifying purpose as the cornerstone of their entire strategy. The pressure to articulate a higher purpose has dramatically increased as more leaders have become aware of the positive impact of such a purpose. The COVID-19 pandemic exacerbated the trend: Employees were leaving companies that lacked purpose in droves, as they searched to fill the void. Company purpose has become elevated as the ultimate recruiting tool for the elusive high-performing talent and engaged workers seeking meaning at work.

When you consider the change saturation every one of us faces in every aspect of our respective businesses, it makes *purpose* even more vital as a tethering point to help us stay focused. Purpose galvanizes the resolve to remain together, as a unified company through change—good or bad.

The company amplifier should also come with a warning, however. I've seen too many leadership teams make the mistake of putting 100 percent of their energy and attention exclusively on a company purpose at the expense of the other amplifiers of meaning. We reviewed in chapter 2 that employee engagement and performance is driven from multiple sources of purpose. There are so many amplifiers to leverage—so many ways to give meaning to the work. That said, there is a huge upside in crafting a company purpose that is clear and compelling, because it will enable and activate all the other amplifiers.

The following are some search-for-meaning questions people ask themselves:

- Do I know what this company stands for and our purpose for being in business?
- Does my work make a difference to the success of the company?
- Does the company culture allow me to be at my best and thrive?
- Do I value the same things that the company values?
- Am I proud to say I work for my company?

CULTURE IS THE UNIVERSAL COMPANY PURPOSE

As we asked in the opening chapter, what if your company doesn't seem to have an obvious purpose that is dramatic or game changing? Does that mean you've reached a dead end, and you won't be able to connect your employees to a meaningful company purpose? Fortunately, that's not the case. The one universal aspect every company possesses that is worthy of centering your purpose on is your culture. In this chapter, we will examine the leading principles that define your "culture narrative" and their ability to amplify meaning. It will give you a game plan for crafting a culture narrative that has a profound impact on workers feeling their work truly matters.

The two most obvious examples of putting culture front and center as a core purpose are Southwest Airlines and Zappos. They set the bar for leveraging culture as their primary point of differentiation. While the stories of Southwest and Zappos are familiar, many people may not fully realize the stunning breakthrough performance that makes these two companies among the most respected brands in the world. In a field of sameness and commoditized service, both companies discovered the way to the top leads through their culture.

Why am I so confident about culture as a universal *purpose* anchoring point? Consider this: culture impacts every single person in your organization, as well as your stakeholders. Culture is as strategically significant as your technology, sales pipeline, or equity position. Your culture is the only unique point of differentiation over which you have the ultimate control. It is the one thing that a competitor can't replicate by either building or buying. Your culture is worthy of focus, at all levels, as the driver of your company purpose. If you can tell a compelling story that clarifies why you do what you do, then people will engage in the spirit of your culture as a purpose. They will see how their work matters to the success of the company. You will also unleash a creative tsunami of people working to achieve your most important strategic imperative: the one that allows everyone to thrive as they shape a culture that grows your business. Here's how you do it.

CULTURE NARRATIVE: THE MOST IMPORTANT STORY YOUR ORGANIZATION WILL EVER TELL

When people have great clarity on your culture story, they become personally invested in making it come true. Are you getting the total buy-in you need to drive performance in your organization?

People will see themselves and their role as highly meaningful in unfolding the story. Scaling that commitment across a critical mass of employees builds awesome power and momentum coming from within your culture. A culture narrative becomes a sustainable core strategy of engagement that shapes a high-performance culture.

Narrative; Now Trending

You hear the buzzword *narrative* all the time these days. For example, it's used as an overt strategy in every successful political campaign. A narrative is essentially a plan for communicating a story, an account of events, or an experience. Narratives are highly effective in stimulating our right-brain imagination with a story and creative flow that sticks in our memory.

How might you use a culture narrative strategy to break through the clutter to shape a purpose-driven culture?

Winning the Hearts and Minds

To be a savvy culture shaper, you must realize that a narrative strategy is highly effective as a belief-changing discipline. Branding professionals have been using narrative strategies for years to make their messages stick in the minds of consumers by shaping beliefs that drive desired behavior.

Culture shaping has the exact same dynamics at work in the hearts and minds of your employees. The beliefs employees have about your organization drive the behaviors that bring your unique culture to life.

Your culture narrative consists of the stories that are repeated formally by leaders, and organically around the watercooler. Those stories create shared expectations. Are you being intentional about creating high-impact stories?

The Questions Are the Answer

Here's how you can leverage a culture narrative framework to tell the complete story of your culture in a meaning-rich way. Imagine being able to define quickly and succinctly the *who, where, why, what, when,* and *how* of your culture story in the form of "leading principles." Leading principles are your *brand, vision, purpose, values,* and *mission(s).*

The model shown in figure 9.1 defines and illustrates how to articulate the five Ws and the H of your organization by connecting them to your leading principles.

Simplicity, consistency, and rigor in telling your culture narrative is the key to success in making it stick. The companies that have become cultural icons like Southwest, Zappos, and Ritz-Carlton communicate their story through every touchpoint experience whether it's internal or external.

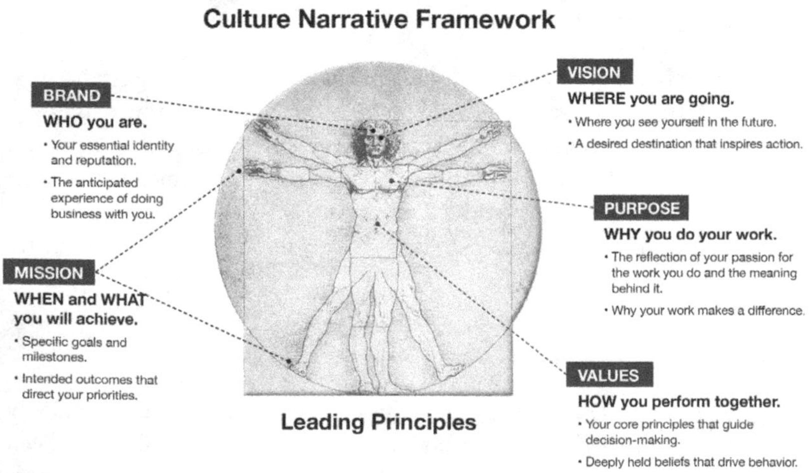

Culture Narrative Framework

BRAND
WHO you are.
• Your essential identity and reputation.
• The anticipated experience of doing business with you.

MISSION
WHEN and WHAT you will achieve.
• Specific goals and milestones.
• Intended outcomes that direct your priorities.

Leading Principles

VISION
WHERE you are going.
• Where you see yourself in the future.
• A desired destination that inspires action.

PURPOSE
WHY you do your work.
• The reflection of your passion for the work you do and the meaning behind it.
• Why your work makes a difference.

VALUES
HOW you perform together.
• Your core principles that guide decision-making.
• Deeply held beliefs that drive behavior.

Figure 9.1 Culture Narrative Framework.

Here are 10 high-impact opportunities to apply your culture narrative:

1. *Engagement strategy:* Amplify purpose and meaning by connecting people to the short-term goals and long-term vision of the organization. The narrative provides the core repertoire for every leader communication effort designed to increase a sense of belonging and inclusion within your culture.

2. *Recruiting:* Tell your story to attract top talent and show off the substance of your culture.

3. *Hiring criteria filter:* Probe for alignment to your leading principles and ask for examples of how candidates have demonstrated these attributes in the past.

4. *Onboarding:* Connect your fired-up new employees right up front to what is expected within your culture. Clarifying expectations right from the start promotes psychological safety and accelerates their ability to collaborate and contribute.

5. *Leadership development:* Center all leadership competencies within the context of your leading principles. Measure performance based on how they drive your culture narrative.

6. *Energize every meeting:* Establish the ritual of starting every meeting with a focused discussion on how your values apply to the work that is in front of the team today. Use it as brainstorming stimuli for aligning actions that drive your brand. Get specific on the fundamental behaviors you want to see in action.

7. *Grow motivation:* Allow people to see their own growth potential in the context of pursuing your culture narrative goals. That vision gives them the confidence they are in the best place to learn, grow, and advance in their career—a key factor for engagement and retention.

8. *Decision-making:* Get on the same page by leveraging your leading principles as guideposts for aligned decision-making. Use them as a filter for all significant decisions.

9. *Rewards and recognition:* Use the framework to create your categories for recognition and appreciation. Leverage the winning stories to build a legacy that exemplifies great performance.

10. *Build your brand:* The expression of your employment brand and external brand should be centered on your culture narrative. External customers care about your purposeful commitment to culture because it has a high impact on their experience of doing business with you. Show it off with pride.

Innovation Fuel

The culture narrative empowers your creative thinkers to be purposeful and act upon ideas and solutions that move the story forward. Creativity depends on envisioning possibilities. Turn the disrupters loose in your organization by framing innovation challenges within the context of your culture narrative. Each challenge comes with its own purpose that amplifies meaning as people make progress.

Your Culture Story Continues

Keep in mind that your culture narrative is a living and breathing entity. It's as fresh as the question "What happened today?"—which introduces the story of "how it impacts tomorrow." Your ability to update, refresh, and reinforce the events that bolster your culture narrative keeps it alive and relevant. Your culture narrative isn't the story of yesterday, it's the story that helps people positively anticipate what's next. Your culture narrative framework provides the essential context to continue the next chapter of your success story. It's a super-strong purpose unto itself for every company.

But you must reckon with it for yourself. Is the full story of your culture worthy enough to be the theme of your company purpose? There are far too many payoffs to not have a well-crafted culture narrative be among the most significant considerations for your purpose. Let's take a deeper look at each of the leading principles to reveal the ideas and opportunities to strengthen your culture narrative in ways that amplify meaning.

THE PURPOSE OF *BRAND*

I walked into my client's office, and the first thing she said was, "Steve, you're going to see something special today! There's a fly-over at 12 noon." I'm thinking, "A what?" Then I remember she had told me about a phenomenon that could only happen at Boeing in Philadelphia. The most engaging event for employees was going up to the roof of their humongous office building and experiencing a helicopter squadron flyover. My client was Boeing, and they built military helicopters at their high-tech manufacturing plant next to Philadelphia International Airport. When the brand-new helicopters would fly out together on their maiden voyage to "the customer," the U.S. military, the Boeing leaders organized and coordinated the fly-over events for all employees to experience their brand up close and personal. Ironically, I was there that day to do workshops on employee engagement for the Accounting Division. So, I experienced accounting professionals cheering, smiling, and even misty eyed from the emotional tug in seeing their collective effort in action and on their way to support our troops. Purpose achieved. The helicopters roared overhead, and the thunderous concussions from their rotors felt like a Metallica concert. The people told me it never gets old. They love it every time. Those helicopters were the embodiment of the Boeing brand for the Philadelphia-based engineers, accountants, and staff at every level. It was so cool to see and experience meaning being amplified through the Boeing brand.

Do you have a similar opportunity with your brand? Let's get on the same page with *brand* and how it can be leveraged to bring meaning to your culture.

Your brand answers the *who* question. It's who you are. It's your essential identity and reputation as a company. It's the anticipated experience for doing business with you that you intentionally create to cut through the noise of the competition. I like to think of it as "the promise you make, and the promise you must keep." For Boeing, the helicopters were the promise and purpose of their work. The experience of seeing them off on the journey to the customer verified it was a promise kept. When an organization does that consistently, they end up owning mental real estate in the minds of their customers and, in Boeing's case, their employees, too. That's a piece of property that earns a priceless return on investment.

It should be noted that branding and culture shaping are inextricably linked and work together using the same underlying principle. Both are about influencing decision-making and are based on the immutable human behavior principle that "beliefs drive behavior." Once you change people's beliefs in a positive way, winning behaviors follow. It takes rigor and discipline to communicate consistently enough to make an impact. But the most important factor is living out your brand with integrity and authenticity. When you demonstrate how your brand strategy drives your most important decisions that impact your customers, people begin to believe it. It must be internalized.

If you influence the deeply held beliefs and attitudes employees
have toward their work experience, then they will act in
ways that reflect and support those beliefs.

Brand positioning guru Denise Lee Yohn identifies the connection this way, "If you want to produce the kinds of specific outcomes that will allow you to differentiate your company, you need to define a unique culture that cultivates the necessary kinds of employee attitudes and behaviors. Companies that do this well also identify a desired brand identity. If your company culture is aligned and integrated with that identity, your employees are more likely to make decisions and take actions that deliver on your brand promise."[2] I believe aligning culture with your brand identity is fundamentally important because it empowers people to be creative in delivering something remarkable. Nothing could be more engaging.

Your culture delivers your brand experience. If people internalize the purpose behind your brand, then they will transfer a sense of meaning to customers. Dr. Martina Olbertova, the founder and CEO of Meaning Global, says it this way: "It's meaning that people consume in brands, not brands alone—it's what they represent that matters to us. It's how they connect to the fabric of our own human values, mindsets and behaviors, how they strengthen our identities that's important."[3] Alignment has never been more important.

At QVC, I experienced working within a culture and brand that felt perfectly aligned. We had a metaphoric statement for the brand experience we wanted to create: "To be a trusted neighbor over the backyard fence." Picture the great relationship you have with a trusted neighbor and how they treat you. Recreating that experience applied to everything we did with our customers—and internally to the way we wanted to treat each other. As a brand, it meant we presented our products in a helpful, low-pressure way using stories to sell instead of hype about the price. As a culture, it meant we treated each other with openness and trust, and we had each other's backs. That's what a trusted neighbor would do to support their neighbors if they needed help. No questions asked. When we defined our values at QVC, they became a natural extension of our core brand experience. We called the values "The QVC Difference" as a permanent reminder of the strategic imperative to live out our values so that we could deliver our differentiated brand experience. Even though we also had a higher purpose at QVC "to change the way the world shops," our trusted neighbor brand and values became the down-to-earth purpose we sought to achieve every day. We had created the conditions for success that were deeply meaningful and motivating. Our engagement scores were always benchmarked in the top five percentile across the board.

What is a metaphor or analogy that describes *who* you want to be in the mind of your customer? Capture it here:

THE PURPOSE OF *VISION*

When you walk up the stairway leading to the offices of Franklin Electric Company in Moorestown, New Jersey, you're greeted with an impressive spectacle. Extending from the bottom floor all the way to the top is a beautiful mural of a tree painted in a way that wraps around the three walls of the stairway, giving you a feeling of enclosure as if you climbed right into it. The work of art is called the Vision Tree, and within the various branches, Franklin Electric has listed its values. Toward the top is the company's business philosophy, summed up as, "We create relationships, not transactions." Franklin Electric Company had many choices for what to identify as its vision. It is a distributor of electrical supplies for construction, maintenance, and original equipment manufacturers, and the company could have easily picked something related to inventory, price, or speed of delivery. But, instead, there is no doubt Franklin Electric is in the business of relationships and works to shape a culture that creates relationships as a differentiator. The impression of the Vision Tree is a constant daily reminder to team members of their purpose in working together. Bill Walker, the CEO, explained to me that when candidates came into the office, their interview started in the stairway. They can easily determine whether candidates have the potential to be a culture fit based on the connection they make with the Vision Tree.

A compelling vision is one of the five leading principles. It answers the *where* question for your organization. It describes an end state or destination that is worth pursuing. Jim Collins, the author of *Built to Last*, describes its importance this way: "A visionary company creates a total environment that envelops employees, bombarding them with a set of signals so consistent and mutually reinforcing that it's virtually impossible to misunderstand the company's ideology and ambitions."[4] A vision can be that compelling if done well.

I've spent a lot of time working with leaders and teams to craft vision statements. I admit it's very difficult for most leaders to think creatively in the future-focused abstract mode that is required to articulate a vision. The thing that makes the exercise so challenging is that a vision needs to be visual. In other words, you must be able to "see it" for the statement to be effective and to be accurately called a vision. Many times, I see so-called vision statements missing the mark. Inadvertently, organizations often end up simply re-expressing their purpose with slightly different words. But if you can't "see it," it falls flat.

Yes, a vision statement must be aligned to your intended purpose, but again, it must also be visual to be effective. Think of it this way: *A vision, in its ideal form, is a visual hyperbole of your purpose being fulfilled.* For example, if your personal purpose is to run a marathon, then the vision might be: "Cheers and smiles from my family and friends as I cross the finish line exhausted but with my arms raised high." That specific vision might become the motivational force that keeps you going when you hit the proverbial wall in the race. Remember when Rocky Balboa acted out his famous scene on the steps of the Philadelphia Art Museum? As moviegoers we immediately saw that his emotional commitment to fight for his dignity (and Adrian) was going to carry him through.

Here are some of the rare examples of vision statements that bring purpose to life:

A computer on every desk and in every home.—Bill Gates, founder of Microsoft

This vision brought to life the purpose of designing a software system that was so easy and practical to use that everyone would need and want a computer. Ironically, Microsoft didn't even build computers at the time. It was so successful with the Windows software that we literally have computers in every pocket now.

I have a dream that all men will be judged by the merit of their character, not by the color of their skin.—Martin Luther King Jr.

There are many reasons why Martin Luther King Jr. captivated our spirit to live out his dream. In large part, it had to do with the way he literally showed us all what equality and justice looked like. We are all still engaged in the purpose of pursuing the dream he described in the summer of 1963. Most people would agree that it is among the most powerful speeches ever given.

I believe this nation should commit itself to achieving the goal, before the decade is out, of landing a man on the moon and returning him safely to Earth.—President John F. Kennedy

President John F. Kennedy shocked the world with this statement to Congress in 1961. This proclamation was a vision, purpose, and mission rolled into one. The deeper purpose, conveyed by President Kennedy, was to bolster the technological and psychological prowess of the United

States while we were engaged in the height of the Cold War with the Soviet Union. We needed confidence as a nation. Kennedy allowed us to see in our mind's eye the monumental achievement of a "man on the moon." If our nation could do that, we could do anything. Putting a man on the moon was the ultimate visual hyperbole that has never been equaled.

A chicken in every pot, and two cars in every garage.—Herbert Hoover

This is another vision from a politician that communicated the purpose of his candidacy for president. Herbert Hoover successfully ran for president on an economic platform that would bring back basic prosperity for all citizens. It worked. He became the 31st president in 1928.

I saw an angel in the stone and carved to set it free.—Michelangelo

Michelangelo used this vision to express his purpose and the motivation that kept him going through the excruciatingly difficult work to create the statue *David*. Anyone who has ever seen this stunning work of art would say his vision came true indeed.

Most of these examples are famous for all the right reasons. They had enormous impact and have become widely admired as stunning achievements; however, I don't want to set the bar so high that a vision seems unattainable for your business. One of my clients is Burns Mechanical. They are a high-performance building systems partner that installs and maintains the infrastructure in some of Philadelphia's most impressive and complex buildings. In a strategy session with the senior team, we were grinding away on identifying the ultimate difference maker in its work. It was clear to everyone that Burns had a unique capacity to be a creative partner with its clients and not just a low-cost bidder of the work. Burns Mechanical president Dan Kerr described a future where the team would be at the strategy table with clients to replicate the success they had achieved as creative collaborators. Once we heard that described by Dan, their vision came into view: *"To earn a seat of influence at the strategy table."* Everyone could see that. Our work to articulate the other Burns Mechanical leading principles was anchored in this clear vision.

What's your vision that brings your purpose to life? What is the visual proof that will become symbolic of achieving your purpose? Can you literally picture *where* you are going?

Capture your vision here: _____

_____

_____

As a gut check, if you struggle to picture anything, then chances are your purpose may be too obscure. For example, if your stated purpose is very broad, as in, "To make the world a better place," then your opportunity to make it relevant comes by identifying what that "better place" looks like, specifically within your business's sphere of influence. Give it another attempt with that in mind—using your mind's eye. You'll know it when you see it.

THE PURPOSE OF *PURPOSE*

> Defining a corporate WHY and making sure it guides decisions and operations has become a cornerstone of doing business.
>
> —Hubert Joly, former Best Buy CEO and
> author of *The Heart of Business*[5]

As a leading principle, a *purpose* identifies the *why* of your work. It should reflect the passion and meaning behind it. Ultimately, it points to why your work makes a difference. Anatomically, I like to think of it as the heart and soul of your business. When people see the connection for how their work impacts your purpose, then the conditions for meaning are created.

In his fabulous book *The Heart of Business*, former Best Buy CEO Hubert Joly shares his experience transforming the company to be purpose centered. He defines the term *purpose* this way: "It is the ultimate goal of the business, the essential reason *why* it exists, and how it contributes to the common good. Best Buy's purpose has been central to the way the company has grown and evolved—and continues to be. It's what helped inspire previously discouraged and anxious employees and boosted the company's share price about tenfold since 2012." Joly adds, "Best Buy's purpose would be to *enrich its customers' lives through technology*. We would do this by addressing their human needs in the key areas of entertainment, productivity, communication, and even food, security, and health and wellness."[6] The impact of Best Buy's purpose can be felt when you ask any one of its team members for help. As a retail experience, these employees have upped their game with impressive results.

In a 2020 *McKinsey* survey, 82 percent of U.S. workers said that it's important for companies to have a purpose; however, only 42 percent reported that their company's stated purpose had real impact.[7] That's a sobering statistic, especially when you consider how much work and effort it may have taken leaders to author and communicate their company's purpose. What a waste. What is going wrong?

Most of the recommendations in this book are focused on the execution steps to make your purpose real and relevant. In the end, taking action is the most important factor for amplifying the company purpose as well. But here are cautions and remedies on the front end related to how you state your company purpose. Specifically, I've noted the faulty assumptions that cause a stated company purpose to fall short and have little impact. I do want to encourage you, though. It's not easy, but if your organization gets the expression right, then everything else you do to execute your purpose will be anchored on a statement that connects emotionally for your employees. It's worth the effort.

Failing on *Purpose*: The 10 Faulty Assumptions

1. **Assuming purpose has to be a "cause."** Aaron Hurst, CEO of Imperative and author of *The Purpose Economy*, calls this out by saying, "We may assume or put Purpose in a box as a cause. But Purpose is really a verb that invites action."[8] Don't force a cause that's not an authentic connection for your company.

2. **Assuming the purpose statement is authentic to your audience.** You need the credibility of "street language" surfaced through a listening tour with employees. People will disconnect if it sounds like an HR fabrication or idealistic platitudes that came from an overpriced consultant. Always field test vital communication language with the diverse audience of your culture before finalizing.

3. **Assuming you must say it all.** We've all seen cringe-worthy kitchen sink descriptions that sound like they're selling a Swiss army knife. Think Dunder Mifflin from *The Office*. The mumbo-jumbo of trying to cover too much buries the headline. Commit, and then stay focused.

4. **Assuming a "one and done" is all people need to get it.** A statement is especially prone to failure if it is too esoteric and/or broad. Even so, if you "roll it out" and do nothing more, it will never stick. If your purpose is to become meaningful, it must be fully internalized and integrated into your culture. Give people the opportunity to make it meaningful through dedicated training.

5. **Assuming people see the relevance.** Even if it seems obvious, you must communicate the connection between purpose and your other leading principles. Demonstrate how they work dynamically together to grow the company and the opportunities that will create for people.

6. **Assuming one well-crafted purpose for the company is the only purpose at play in people's lives at work.** Avoid overemphasizing and investing into just one purpose at the expense of ignoring all other potential amplifiers. As humans, we are far more complex and have the capacity to multitask when it comes to having purpose impact our lives. The highest level of fulfillment comes when all amplifiers are turned up.

7. **Assuming people see the progress being made toward fulfilling the purpose.** Identifying and communicating progress must be integral to your plan to engage people into your purpose. Progress toward purpose amplifies meaning.

8. **Assuming people feel connected and empowered to bring the purpose to life.** Be proactive to connect and empower people to work on making the purpose come to life. Ask them what they might need, and how you can support them.

9. **Leaders assuming their personal perspective of the purpose doesn't matter.** Don't expect people to be any more enthused about your company purpose than what leaders are willing to express. Leaders need to communicate their own personal perspective for how the purpose impacts them. This encourages others to reflect for themselves and internalize it. That is how they discover what's in it for them.

10. **Assuming you can perfume the pig and people will believe you.** If you have a toxic culture, then the hypocritical statement of your purpose has zero shot of success, unless you use it as a launching pad for a high-integrity total makeover. This is risky because if leaders continue to *not* walk the talk, they will sabotage your effort even further. People must see positive change immediately.

So, what does an effective purpose statement sound like? I've listed a few below, categorized by what they focus on and how companies align their priorities. Note that some of these might be labeled as "mission" or "vision" statements by their organization, but I believe they are more in line with how we defined purpose in the Leading Principles model.

Purpose Statement Examples

Culture at the core . . .

- Virgin Atlantic: To grow a profitable airline, where people love to fly and where people love to work.
- Sony: To establish a place of work where engineers can feel the joy of technological innovation, be aware of their mission to society, and work to their heart's content.

- Mary Kay: To give unlimited opportunity to women.
- Boeing: People working together as one global enterprise for aerospace leadership.
- LUCK Companies: We will ignite human potential through Values-Based Leadership and positively impact the lives of others around the world.
- Marine Corps: The few, the proud, the Marines.

All about the customer . . .

- Best Buy: To enrich its customers' lives through technology.
- Walmart: To give ordinary folk the chance to buy the same things as rich people.
- Nike: To bring inspiration and innovation to every athlete in the world. If you have a body, you are an athlete.
- KPMG: To help clients inspire confidence and empower change.
- The Hankin Group: Designing, developing, and managing environments with integrity that inspire people to lead richer, more fulfilled lives.

Transcendent change . . .

- Tesla: To accelerate the world's transition to sustainable energy.
- Apple: To make a contribution to the world by making tools for the mind that advance humankind.
- Shire: We enable people with life-altering conditions to lead better lives.
- QVC: Changing the way the world shops.
- Netflix: Entertaining the world.

Going for *the* Ultimate Expression

Is it possible to create an expression that is so powerful that it serves a combined function of brand, vision, purpose, and values all in one? Yes, I'm officially crowning Ritz-Carlton's expression as the GOAT (Greatest of All Time), at least so far. They have articulated the ultimate expression that gives meaning to everything they do. They call it their motto:

We are Ladies and Gentlemen serving Ladies and Gentlemen.

When they say "We are Ladies and Gentlemen serving Ladies and Gentlemen," it begs a creative and empowering question in the minds of employees at all levels. How would a lady or gentleman act in a given situation if they are serving another lady or gentleman? The question reveals all sorts of creative possibilities that lead their entire customer philosophy of meeting the "unexpressed" needs of guests. They've even taken it further by identifying the

"Ritz-Carlton Basics": 20 specific behaviors that are symbolic of their motto in action. They invoke the discipline to review their "Basic" behaviors on a daily basis to ensure it is ultimately clear and aligned across the culture. As a result, Ritz-Carlton has become clearly established as the premium service provider within their industry, and the company has created a standard that all others can only hope to chase at this point. Even if you can't come up with something as brilliant, brainstorming with your leaders on what your purpose might be is a priceless investment in alignment.

Identify your purpose here. Be certain to include *why* the work of your company makes a difference.

_____

_____

THE PURPOSE OF *VALUES*

Think of your culture as a garden. Your leading principles not only tell you what to plant but also show you how to grow healthy plants and keep the weeds tended. A garden left on its own will quickly devolve into an ugly, intimidating mess.

Culture shaping is also a "forever" effort. I have seen so many organizations assume that once they've cracked the code and created the proverbial poster with a vision statement and a set of values, then they can sit back and reap the harvest. With culture, it's not just what you sow, it's *how* you tend to people and their beliefs that determines what you reap.

Your values answer the "*how* you must perform together" question. They serve as guideposts for decision-making and represent the core beliefs that drive positive behaviors. Anatomically, they are the "guts" of your organization. Consider values this way: They are called values because you value them. Why? Because acting on them delivers a return on investment. The return can be both a tangible result and/or an emotional response that amplifies meaning.

When values are articulated well, they focus everyone on what matters to be effective. I've never met a person who didn't desire that clarity. Everyone wants to be in an environment where they can thrive and grow. The clarity of knowing what is valued sets up the conditions for small wins to take place in the form of recognition and appreciation. That reinforcement gives people confidence in how to work together.

Culturology Values

When I launched my consulting firm Culturology, the first thing I did with my founding partner, Dr. Mike Brenner, was to articulate our values. We didn't want to use meaningless, generic words. So instead, we created a pattern that lists an action-oriented "value" phrase, followed by a "belief" statement that describes why it's important, and then a "behavior" statement that brings the value to life. I've listed my Culturology values here as an example for your creative consideration in crafting your own statements.

Be Curious First

- Creativity begins with an open-minded, positive attitude that unlocks possibilities.
- Ask the extra question, learn a fresh perspective, and discover new answers.

Think Breakthrough

- Imagination and the power of great ideas change the world.
- If you are not a little nervous, be bolder.

Create an Experience

- Profound growth takes place when we are moved mentally, physically, and emotionally.
- Cultivate a thriving environment that nurtures new thinking and personal insights.

Be Authentic

- We owe each other the candid truth given with respect and positive intent.
- Share the "real" you—the sum of many foibles and the priceless lessons learned.

Incite Serious Fun

- True passion blurs the line between work and play and inspires the best of both.
- Be at the top of your game—doing what you love and loving what you do.

Live It

- Our right to guide others comes with the commitment to serve as role models first.
- Teach others continuously, using words if necessary.

Why do we *value* our values? Simply stated, the Culturology values represent what is most important to us. They serve as guideposts for our decision-making and highlight *how* we operate at the top of our game individually and as a team. Without a doubt, if we are doing a great job of living our values, then clients should feel the difference in the experience we create with them. We invite our clients to give us feedback along the way to ensure we are delivering upon our commitment.

A Fundamental Difference Maker

Let's examine the fundamentals of getting clear with your values. I don't believe it's adequate to simply use broad and cliché terms to identify your values—for example, stand-alone words like *teamwork, customer focus, integrity, excellence, respect,* and *collaboration.* These terms have become generic for a reason in so much as every organization requires these attributes to simply stay in business. I consider them to be what I call "greens-fee" values: the obvious, no-brainer, absolute must-have values. The question is, do they tell people specifically what the expectations are for working at your unique company? Only in general. The more specific you get, the more aligned and proactive people will be in living up to the winning behaviors you identify. The goal is making it clear how a value translates to decision-making and discretionary effort.

David Friedman, the founder and CEO of High Performing Culture, has been instrumental in helping organizations crack the code on behaviors that are actionable. I've learned directly from David and been inspired by his focused and disciplined approach. He has helped hundreds of companies identify what he calls "Fundamentals." Instead of using broad, general terms for values, such as *customer focus,* a Fundamental-formatted description of customer focus might sound like this:

> *Deliver Legendary Customer Service. Do the little things, as well as the big things, that blow people away. Create extraordinary experiences they'll tell others about. Mere customer satisfaction is for lesser companies. Create customer loyalty by doing the unexpected.*

Do you see the clarity this Fundamental brings to the expectation of "customer focus"? It's written in more of a street language format that paints a vision for what the behavior looks like when acted upon. Here's the other very important tactical approach in using David Friedman's Fundamental technique. Instead of trying to trim down a list of values to a small number that can be arbitrarily memorized, it has far more impact to have a significant number of Fundamentals—as many as 20 to 30—that have direct application to the actual challenge of the work. For example, imagine having 26 highly descriptive Fundamentals. You can assign one of them one at a time to be the "Fundamental of the week." All the focus and energy of applying that Fundamental for an entire week would come around twice a year. That has far greater potency for application and impact than people being able to recite a nebulous list of "no-brainer assumption" values.

Whether you use a Fundamental format to articulate your values, or create a hybrid version, the key to application and relevance comes through rituals. The concept of rituals to influence the winning behavior mirrors the impact of developing a habit. A habit, like brushing your teeth, is something you do automatically. As a result, it becomes a sustainable and repeatable practice that lasts over time. Imagine the impact of creating a ritual or habit to review a specific Fundamental every day at work. Connecting the Fundamental to the application of the work at hand is highly relevant and valuable to team members.

David Friedman talks about rituals in the business context as the meetings in which you routinely put the Fundamental on the agenda as the first item to review together. If the team spends 5 to 10 minutes reviewing the Fundamental as it applies to the actual work of the day, then it will be a catalyst for new ideas, performance, and clarity of purpose. I have seen it used firsthand to solve problems by getting everyone focused on what matters . . . *now*. The format is so effective, people look forward to the discussions. The conversations create psychological safety as a team—and a feeling of belonging to a winning company.

Here is a format I created to help managers lead meetings to discuss the Fundamental technique or values with their team. The practice of this ritual is core to institutionalizing the behavior of your values.

Fundamental Questions to Apply at Team Rituals

Time-focused questions:

1. (Past recognition): What has happened that is an example of this Value/ Fundamental in action?

2. (Present acknowledgment): What are we planning to do in today's work that models this Value/Fundamental?
3. (Future focus potential): What might we do differently today to live this Value/Fundamental?

Additional questions for consideration:

- If we gave ourselves a rating on this Value/Fundamental, what would it be (1–10 scale)? How might we move toward it being a 10?
- What might we do as a team to be a "10" with this Value/Fundamental today?
- How might this Value/Fundamental make a *difference* in our work (with clients and each other) today?
- What do you need to know in order to be more effective today? (This is the ultimate proactive/accountable communication request question.)
- What might we need to share in order to get on the same page with what's most important today? (This is an invitation to communicate priorities as they see it.)
- Who has been an example of this Value/Fundamental in action? Who did we catch doing something right? (It could be an individual or a team.)
- Which of the behaviors pertaining to this Value/Fundamental do we need to advance and expand to be more effective as a team?
- How is this Value/Fundamental relevant to you? (This is a great way to mine for personal stories/connections.)
- What do we need to be more honest about right now? (This is great for a staff meeting and for the leader to model going first.)

The ritual of covering values or "Fundamentals" in this way never gets stale because the work it applies to always changes. Plus, the Value/Fundamental and questions change but are always directly relevant to the challenge at hand. Again, if we think of culture as a garden, then using rituals is the equivalent of adding organic fertilizer on a daily basis. You will grow a healthy, thriving culture.

THE PURPOSE OF *MISSION*

Of all the leading principles, *mission* is the one term that many organizations use and abuse most often. When leaders say they want a mission statement, they almost always end up realizing they need a purpose statement instead.

Mission is achievement oriented in the same way a military mission is defined by a time frame goal. It's likely your company has several missions at play all at once, not just a solitary one. Each mission has its own unique purpose built into it and, therefore, has the capacity to amplify meaning.

Mission answers both the *what* and *when* questions linked to your key strategic initiatives. It identifies intended outcomes. These are priorities to be executed usually within a six-month to two-year time frame. Anatomically, a mission is the equivalent of the body's moving parts—the arms and legs of the organization.

When I rejoined QVC for the second time, I was immediately engaged in QVC's two-year mission to build the largest live television studios in the world. It was a massive undertaking, a big gamble, and a strategic move. The intended outcome was to establish a barrier of entry to the live shopping genre. Any competitor who wanted to get into the game would have to come up with untold millions in capital to match our live production prowess at QVC.

Our mission was a total success, and we created Studio Park, QVC's world headquarters in West Chester, Pennsylvania. QVC became the undisputed leader in electronic retailing and bought out its biggest rival, Home Shopping Network, about 20 years later.

A mission amplifies meaning significantly when people see their role in achieving the objective. The time frame factor for a mission sets up the conditions for not just small wins along the way but also a big win when completed. Many of these are worthy of huge celebrations and fanfare. Large or small, they always need to include employee recognition and appreciation. People see these as so meaningful, they chronicle taking part in specific missions on their resume. Each one is its own impressive story to be told for the experience of living through it, scar tissue and all.

Here are some options to consider for framing your missions. Remember, these answer the *what* question for your company and should include a *when*:

- Launching a new product or service
- Creating a new market
- Achieving a monetary goal
- Expanding the size of the company, such as number of customers, employees, or stores
- Improving the benchmark ranking of your product(s) or service
- Elevating employee engagement scores
- Increasing the number of people promoted
- Growing the number of people trained or certified

- Refreshing the brand image
- Implementing a new CRM (customer relations management) model
- Attaining a give-back or charitable cause goal
- Realizing a green or sustainability company goal

None of these will become a motivational factor for people unless they are communicated regularly to engage people into the *what* and the *when*. Missions give you the best opportunity to activate the Progress Principle[9] at the company level. Do that by tracking and communicating progress against milestones and by recognizing the effort and sacrifices of people who are working hard to achieve them.

One of our most charismatic and respected leaders at QVC was our chief financial officer (CFO). He had a reputation for being a very tough character and often intimidated people with his intensity and no-nonsense style of candor. Our team in HR was always aware he'd challenge the money we were investing in training and our culture. It was a nervous moment presenting anything to him for approval; I must admit, it was like visiting the Wizard of Oz. You could easily assume he didn't see himself as a rah-rah "culture champion," but in reality, he had as much of a positive impact as anyone whether he intended to or not.

Here's what he did. Every year, the CFO presented one of the most mind-blowing explanations of how our business really worked financially behind the curtain. Every employee in the organization was invited to one of several large rock concert–like events set up in our studios or warehouses. He talked about QVC's sales numbers for the year, and what made us profitable. He'd use sarcasm and humor to talk about some of our mistakes along the way, and what we were doing to make our goal of double-digit EBITDA growth. Realize that anyone outside of finance or the accounting department had never even heard of the term *EBITDA* before coming to one of his presentations. It stands for "earnings before interest, taxes, depreciation, and amortization." This was always a little awkward at first, but he would make everyone stand up and recite in unison what EBITDA stood for. It was funny, it was gutsy, and it was always the best lecture on finance you could ever want to hear. Hundreds of diverse employees from all areas of the company rallying together around the mission of double-digit EBITDA growth at a finance presentation—who could imagine? But here's the other way he made the company's financial status powerful and meaningful: He connected it to our other growth mission. The way the math works, if you have double-digit EBITDA growth for five years, then you will double the size of your business. So, our other high-profile mission was "to double the business every five years." And we did that many times over. The CFO's yearly EBITDA presentation had the enormous impact of getting us on the same page and galvanizing our resolve at QVC.

Never underestimate the impact of dialing in your culture to the missions of your company. You may need to be bold and dramatic to make them stick. Each mission needs its own communication plan built into the process. Think bigger. Every person in your culture is a stakeholder in your missions. They should be fully included to make missions meaningful.

What are the missions your culture can rally behind? Identify them here and be certain they contain a *what* and a *when*.

———————————————————————————————————————

———————————————————————————————————————

———————————————————————————————————————

COMPANY AMPLIFIER PLAYBOOK

Sneezers: How to Activate a Positively Viral Force to Transform Your Culture

This playbook is designed to give you the most powerful way to integrate your culture narrative and the purpose they possess into the beliefs of your employees.

I've got great news for you. Lurking underneath the surface of your culture is one of the most powerful forces to transform your culture. It's a highly underrated and untapped resource that can jump-start your culture breakthrough from the inside out: a select group of culture heroes are ready to be activated. Before the pandemic, I used to call them "Sneezers" because these amazing people are positively viral influencers. They represent the very best of your culture. The term *sneezers* has become wildly inappropriate for obvious reasons, but I hope it at least conveys the sentiment for their potential influence. You can call them your own unique name that mirrors your brand culture. Just don't call them something boring and bureaucratic like a "committee." This group of unique individuals is more like a "council" or "skunk-works" team.

Defining Attributes of a Sneezer

Sneezers are people who raise the game of everyone around them. Sneezers typically operate at every level and in every department.

- *On the outside*, they are advocates for your brand and deliver the experience that fulfills your promise to the customer. You wish you could have all your best customers interact with them directly.
- *On the inside*, they are champions for accountability and respect. You likely see them acting as a catalyst for creative collaboration to solve problems and drive ideas forward.

Identifying Your Sneezers

In my experience, a leader typically can answer the following questions with confidence in under 10 seconds. These are easy, no-brainer questions because every organization has Sneezers. Again, just to be clear, Sneezers are *positively* viral. Their attitude and approach to work are emblematic of the very best of your culture.

Questions to Surface the Sneezers in Your Organization

1. Who are the people in your organization who are indispensable examples of your culture at your very best?
2. Who are the people who are "poster-child" worthy to represent your values?
3. Who are your absolute most valuable "go-to" team members that you can't afford to lose because of *how* they work?
4. Who do you wish you could clone for every position because of their attitude and purpose-driven orientation?
5. Who is worthy of investment for development as an incentive to stay with your organization because of their leadership potential and positive influence?

Isn't it obvious who they are in your organization? I bet you had no problem picturing their faces. They stand out that much as being unique and special. By the way, if people must think too long to answer the sneezer ID questions, then they are lacking a true Sneezer. Conduct this exercise as a type of Rohrschach test. It should be that simple and clear to you and to others on your leadership team.

Imagine what you could accomplish if everyone shared the character and work ethic of your Sneezers. So, why wouldn't that be possible? You have an opportunity to transform your culture if you apply some discipline by following proven action steps to get there.

Activating Your Sneezers

Sustainable culture change always happens from the inside out. A strong top-down leadership commitment is essential, but it is not enough on its own. You must build support from within to influence at all levels. Sneezers have a circle of influence that can be expanded to impact a critical mass of people that will also reflect and "own" the best aspects of your culture. Here's your strategic and tactical guide for reaching your culture change tipping point faster, and with a method that sticks.

Phase 1: Identification and Charter

1. Gather your senior team together for a meeting to launch the Sneezer initiative.
2. Clarify your goals for your culture with the senior team. Set the stage for context and perspective. Cover these items:

   - What's at stake in your strategic plan that is dependent upon your culture to initiate and execute? What key initiatives might live or die depending on the way people work together to execute?
   - What are the measurements in place that reveal the "health" of your culture? Include retention data, engagement scores, and ability to recruit top talent. What do you want them to be? Create a gap analysis.
   - What is the current challenge in recruiting top talent? What's at stake if you can't get the right people on board?
   - What is your current challenge with retention? Share what you know about why people might be leaving the organization from exit interview data. What are the ramifications?

3. Identify the Sneezers with senior team input and buy-in.

   - Define the purpose in creating a special team that can address the issues listed in item 2. Although not the panacea, the Sneezer team has the capacity to have an enormous impact.
   - Define the attributes and characteristics of a Sneezer (share the "Questions to Surface the Sneezers" listed earlier to frame their answers).
   - Ask each person to "nominate" their best choices for Sneezers. You can also take the extra step to give them time to ask team members directly for their feedback. Oftentimes leaders at the top only have impressions of people that can be different from the reality of how that person works day to day.

Note: Discuss nominations as necessary to confirm around the table. The stories or rationale for selecting people is inspiring and a highly positive experience. Remember, you are identifying the "best of" your culture. This process will help galvanize your team on what culture success looks like in action.

4. Clarify the future role of the Sneezer team with a written scope document that lists intended actions and outcomes. The charter is dependent on how in-depth you want to go with the Sneezer team. The charter you create will avoid future scope-creep and make the effort feel more official for the Sneezer participants.

   Note: For the first year, I would recommend a limited scope to build small win–style momentum and to gain a feel for dynamics of the Sneezers when they get together. You can then make adjustments accordingly to be as aggressive as you wish with bold and audacious goals.

Phase 2: Change-Agent Activation

Culture change is about elevating shared expectations. Activate your Sneezers as a powerful team to drive culture change from the inside out.

1. Invite your Sneezers to attend a kick-off meeting.
2. In the meeting, explain to them the criteria for which they were chosen. Be certain to provide a congratulatory tone on being nominated. This is a big deal, and they should receive appreciation for representing themselves and the organization in the positive way that was worthy of being nominated.

   Note: Again, you don't need to call the group "Sneezers." The term was only used as an internal expression at the outset of the program to make the point to the senior team about these employees being "positively viral." Other terms for the team could be *Culture Team, Culture Catalysts, Difference Makers, Culture Crew,* and so on. Again, use what feels right within your culture. Alternatively, you can ask the team to come up with their own name. This is a great first assignment to gain their buy-in and break the ice.

3. Consider having the CEO or CHRO (chief human resources officer) kick off the meeting to share a culture "state of the union." It's also vital to make the connection on why culture is a competitive advantage, and to present a vision for the future expectation for what the culture will look like.

4. Explore with the team the creative opportunities to influence culture at your most vital touchpoints where culture is won or lost. Make this a lively brainstorming discussion.
5. Discuss the future talent plan and your goals for hiring people. Cover the impact and importance of hiring people who will enhance the culture (in the same way the Sneezers enhance the culture).
6. Ask the Sneezers what they need from you in terms of support and development to be effective and successful. Record their ideas and commit to getting back to them with answers on next steps.

   Note: Give them the opportunity to decline participation in the group even though it's highly unlikely. You want them to understand their special role is completely voluntary. Being a Sneezer is an honor, not a burden.

Ways to Leverage the Sneezer Team

Recruiters Extraordinaire

If you only use your Sneezers for this role, it will all still be well worth the effort. Here's what you say to them: "We want new hires who approach work with your type of attitude. In other words, if we could replicate you and your attitude and values, we'd gain a huge advantage in the way we work together." Ask them whom they know who is similar in attitude and values, and whom they would be proud to bring in for an interview. Remember, it's not just about style or skill set—it's about mind-set. You want to replicate their mind-set. Ask them to set a SMART (specific, measurable, achievable, relevant, and time-bound) goal pertaining to the number of potential referrals they can make within a specific time frame. No pressure, though! Make it totally positive and comfortable for them to take on. Remember, this assignment is a high honor.

Note: I would not offer a reward of compensation for referrals. Research shows that it not only will be a disincentive for some people but also will take integrity away from the premise of leveraging your Sneezers and the positive intent they naturally bring to the table. They will recruit people for the right reasons and not need an extrinsic element to get in the way.

Culture Recon

Another way to think of the Sneezers is as a culture reconnaissance team. They can be your eyes and ears who unlock the mystery of what's really happening within the culture. Here's a stern warning. Ensure you do *not* put them in a position to be perceived as "snitches" or "narcs." If that happens, then all your good intentions will go down the drain, and you will put them in a vulnerable position where others see them as the secret police. All trust will be lost. It is vital that you keep any information they share with professionalism and in great confidence. Plus, do not solicit them for the dirt on individuals or leaders within the organization.

Change Agents

Again, the Sneezers can be your eyes and ears as to how engaged people are in the culture. For example, if you've just enacted a huge change initiative in the organization, then ask the Sneezers how people are feeling about it, and what could be done to clarify the initiative and encourage buy-in. Ask them how the message is getting through (or not). They can also directly influence the communication process if you ask them to help get the message out through their role.

Engagement Pulse

Instead of just investing in rolling out the same old engagement survey, tap into the Sneezers to evaluate the state of your culture. They will surface real-time, specific data in a street language form that is often far more useful than the complex consultant-speak analysis.

If you still want to do an engagement survey, then great! Here's an idea to gauge how accurate it is. Before you administer the survey, gather the Sneezers to answer the questions (from the perspective of their respective divisions). Then, when you get the broader results, you can compare those results to the Sneezer prediction and likely feel confident they are fully aware and accurate as pulse takers of culture engagement.

Engagement Catalysts

After the survey results are in, tap into the Sneezers for ideas on how to improve results in engagement. You can do this by gathering the team for a brainstorming session to focus on specific issues from the survey, and by asking them to take the lead within their departments to facilitate action planning. Realize that they have a deep understanding of what is happening underneath the surface of the culture, including a sense for whether people in general are a flight risk to leave the company. You can be proactive to improve retention by getting ahead of issues that cause people to start looking elsewhere.

Key Takeaways

- Uncover the powerful change-agent force that represents the very best of your culture.
- Identify the Sneezers in your organization and invite them to take part.
- Train Sneezers for their special role of influencing others within the culture.
- Leverage Sneezers as your
  o culture think tank,
  o change implementers at the ground level, and
  o recruiters.
- Retain your best talent. The Sneezer program gives them a unique, special, and honored role that adds to their learning and development—and increases their likelihood of staying with your company.

10

The Customer Amplifier

When it comes to corporate values, "customer focus," or "the customer comes first," or some other phrase about the sanctity of the customer is a stated value at 98 percent of all companies. It's such a no-brainer, I wonder why anyone would need to put it in writing. In the "Company Amplifier" chapter (chapter 9), we discussed how to take the value of "customer focus" and make the expectations clear on what this value looks like in action. This chapter is about leading to the next level by putting the customer front and center as a purpose that amplifies meaning.

Nearly everyone, from top to bottom, has a sense for the importance of the relationship with the customer. But many people in the rank and file don't clearly see how they personally influence the outcome. Your opportunity comes from making a connection for people in ways that amplify the importance of their work and sense of meaning as it relates to the customer. Explicitly designating the customer as a purpose unlocks one of the most potent ingredients for engagement within your culture: creativity. If you give people creative freedom to surprise and delight your customers, they will rise to the occasion in ways that will engage them in the high-impact pursuit of building your brand.

Remember, your company's brand is the essential promise you make to the customer. And it's a promise you must keep. Businesses live or die on the tipping point of their brand promise. I love the expression Zappos's legendary founder and CEO Tony Hsieh used to make the connection. He would say, "The brand is simply a lagging indicator of the culture."[1] It's so true. If you're healthy as a culture on the inside, then you'll delight the customer on the outside. And, if we make the connection between customer focus and brand promise, and then empower people to delight customers, they will find the experience deeply meaningful.

The following are some search-for-meaning questions people ask themselves:

- Do I understand how my role directly impacts the customer?
- Do I know why our customers choose to do business with us?
- Do I have the ability to apply new ideas to impact the customer experience?
- Do I have the opportunity to interact directly with the customer?

CUSTOMER EMPATHY UNLOCKS ENGAGEMENT

> Great companies don't offer us something to buy. Great companies offer us something to buy into.
>
> —Simon Sinek

One of the only things I was fully qualified to do after I graduated from college was to be a DJ on the radio. In my first job in the working world, I was hired to do the overnights on a rock station in Jersey Shore, Pennsylvania. The graveyard shift was a great way to earn some street cred, and as an unexpected bonus, I learned how kooky people can be in the middle of the night when they call in for a request. For a rookie like me, the hectic multitasking of running a radio station by myself was challenging enough, but the hardest thing of all was opening up your mic and talking to thousands of people you couldn't see. Our super-smart programming director Mark Bell coached our DJ team to sound authentic and speak to our listeners as if we were in the back seat of their car. He did something creative to help us visualize it. He blew up a life-sized poster picture of a man and woman in a car and placed it in the soundproof window that separated the main studio from the production studio. Here's the catch: The picture was of the back of their heads as if taken from the back seat of their car. So, standing in the studio literally felt like you were taking a ride together with the listener. It helped me relax and talk about the music as you would to a couple of good friends instead of freaking out that I had to entertain the masses. We absolutely knew who our listeners were at WSQV, and this became my first lesson in the power of empathy for the customer to amplify meaning and performance.

Branding guru Denise Lee Yohn nails the connection between empathy for the customer and meaning, saying, "The most extraordinary experiences aren't just about relevance, meeting a need or fulfilling a want; they're about meaning, conveying something important or connecting through shared values."[2]

So, it prompts the question, what might we do to intimately know our customer's values and their needs? I believe this question will reveal answers that will dial your culture into the creative sport of building your brand from the inside out. The creativity to reshape the customer experience is turbocharged by the in-depth knowledge people have of the customer and their motivations for doing business with you. That needs to happen at every level. The ownership of the effort goes far beyond your marketing or branding team. The customer amplifier is a full-on culture initiative.

THE PURPOSE OF YOUR CUSTOMERS

When customers engage with your brand, does it give them meaning? Yes, it's inherent in any transaction that satisfies a need. The stronger your brand, the more it fulfills a definitive promise for the lives of your customers. That is how great brands build loyalty by delivering a differentiated experience that connects emotionally.

In the last chapter, I described your brand as a promise. But here is the payoff you might underestimate. If you understand and fully appreciate how this mental and emotional transaction takes place in the mind of your customers, then your culture can engage to deliver a differentiated experience. Fulfilling a promise for your customers is meaningful to them *and your employees.* The pursuit of delivering your brand promise has the power to engage your employees, but only if they see how their role makes a difference. It might surprise you how much it matters to people. I've seen firsthand how far people will go in terms of applying their own discretionary effort if empowered to do so. Instead of employees just thinking it's their obligation or duty to serve the customer, they will willingly go the extra mile if the effort feels meaningful. Let's explore how to build the bridge from employee to customer that amplifies meaning.

Revealing Customer Purpose

In only 20 years, QVC had gone from a long-shot start-up to an $8 billion multichannel retailer. But we were way overdue for a brand refresh. Instead of just doing some tweaks to our logo—a new tagline, or fresh graphics, for example—we went headfirst into the deep end of the branding pool to learn about our customers. The effort was led by our new chief marketing officer (CMO), Jeff Charney. Incidentally, years later, Jeff went on to create the Flo character series of commercials for Progressive Insurance and was named 2021 Brand CMO of the year by *Advertising Age*. His inspirational style, creative drive, and passion for excellence made an enormous difference in QVC's rebrand success.

We wanted to answer a key question: What was it about QVC that caused our customers to be so loyal and engaged with us? One remarkable piece of evidence about their relationship with QVC was that customers would post reviews of their product purchases at four times the average rate of other dot-com retailers. Customers viewed shopping on QVC in the same way a sports fan is passionate for their home team. They built their own organic community for the shopping experience. We were aware of this dynamic but wanted to learn more, so we hired the famed design agency IDEO to reveal the secret of the relationship.

IDEO pioneered the methodology of "design thinking," an "observer" style of research that weaves a real-life, behind-the-scenes view of how people interact with a product or brand. For our QVC project, they went to people's homes for an entire day and observed how they lived, when they went on-line, and how they watched TV. In one experiment, they invited a group of QVC customers to a dinner party and invited a control group of non-QVC customers to a dinner party with the same food, venue, entertainment, and so on, but on a different day. The groups were not told why they were together, or what they had in common (i.e., being a QVC customer or not). They only knew it was a dinner party with a chance to meet some new people and have good food and drink. The team from IDEO observed something that blew us all away after conducting multiple dinner events. The dinner parties with the groups of our QVC customers were consistently super fun and unbelievably energized, while the control group dinner parties were a good time, but nothing unique or special. IDEO described QVC customers as uniquely full of energy, easy to laugh, warm and welcoming, and optimistic about life. It explains why the wine-and-dine events became a rockin' party. And more important, it explained why they connected so well to the vibe of our show hosts who emulated being "trusted neighbors over the backyard fence."

What do you do with valuable reconnaissance like that? Essentially, we built our entire brand experience around creating an emotional connection with customers that was positive and uplifting to reinforce their "glass-half-full" mojo for life. In other words, their purpose for life became our purpose for creating our brand. Here's one way we did it that reveals the magic of engaging employees in the effort.

The Meaningful and Emotional Connection with Customers

We had an idea. What if we shared the epiphany discovered by IDEO with our customer service reps? After all, they had conversations with customers thousands of times per day. Who could relate better than them? We wanted to find out if they could go to the next level to create a positive and uplifting emotional connection. Realize, we already had amazing customer service levels that were monitored constantly in our four call centers. Any improvement would be a high bar to jump.

We created a plan and curriculum to train customer service teams while setting up control groups of customer service teams that would not receive training. We called the workshop "Brand Champions." All teams were measured for employee engagement using our five standard "engagement driver" questions, and we chronicled their pretraining "contactor scores" (our way of measuring customer service directly from our customers via outbound calls).

Here's the content flow of the Brand Champions workshops:

1. **Branding 101:** This was a deep-dive course into the psychology of consumer behavior. Our reps ate it up because it's such a fun and fascinating subject all could relate to for their own lives. It answered the *why* question regarding the choices consumers make that inevitably separate great brands from the rest of the pack.

2. **QVC's Brand:** We unpacked all the research from IDEO on the emotional connection and shared demographic data and trends in our product sales. The reps doubled down on everything they heard with their own anecdotal stories in working with customers. It was a validating experience for all. Some told me on the side they'd never been treated with such respect in having people teach them the way the business runs from the inside. Wow.

3. **Creating an emotional connection:** Although we had some ideas, we let the reps brainstorm how they might do it first. Their ideas were creative and relevant and made the ones we came preloaded with seem average. One idea, for example, was listening for background noise on their calls, like a barking dog or a baby crying, and then making an appropriate and fun comment like, "Gee, I hope the dog doesn't eat the package when it arrives. He sounds hungry." The reps were thrilled to inject their own personality into calls and the creativity of being able to go off script to connect as human beings.

After the workshops, we turned them loose, armed with new knowledge of branding and the customer, and with the empowerment to create an emotional connection. A number of leaders were nervous that their "talk time" (the average call length of customer rep conversations with customers, which QVC monitored closely) would go through the roof and creating emotional connections would be costly to pull off. But what we measured four weeks later confirmed the power of the customer amplifier. Not only did their contactor scores improve significantly, but their employee engagement scores jumped double digits compared to the control groups. And they accomplished this with only a three-second increase in their average talk time. Clearly the reps loved the freedom to satisfy the customer, while sensing more meaning in their work. The Brand Champions workshops were a slam-dunk success.

Among many things that amazed me from this experience included the insight that front-line workers are highly enamored and interested to learn about "business" strategy. Too many leaders, myself included, used to assume it would be either boring, irrelevant, or inconsequential to people in the rank and file. To overcome the false assumption that it's a waste of time, you might need to experience it for yourself. Seeing how the deep dive to learn about QVC's customer relationship was a launching pad to engagement and their ability to perform creatively was a game changer for me as a leader. Their eagerness was illuminating. Lesson learned: Challenge your assumptions about your culture's desire to learn and innovate. What might you do to use the deep dive to amplify meaning for employees at all levels in your organization?

Here's my encouragement to you. Every organization can and should do this type of Brand Champion immersion training with employees, whether they have direct contact with customers or not. Making the brand connection, treating people with respect to share the inner workings of your business, and then empowering them to act upon ideas is a surefire recipe for employee engagement. You have the knowledge inside your organization to make it happen, but you must be intentional about it. Your efforts will pay off and be deeply meaningful to everyone involved. Here's how to determine if you're ready.

ARE YOU READY TO TURN ON THE CUSTOMER AMPLIFIER?

It's important to gauge your culture readiness to become aware of your strengths and liabilities in making progress in delivering your brand. I've created a Culture Gap Analysis tool to guide you on where to concentrate your efforts. There are three key culture attributes you must have as core values to be ready to execute as a cohesive innovative force: *accountability*, *respect*, and *collaboration*. The impact of these values is both internal and external. The three additional attributes of *brand advocacy*, *customer intelligence*, and *clarity of purpose* round out the externally focused capacities that grow both the intelligence and the mind-set necessary to drive ideas. Elite customer-driven organizations score high in all six cultural attributes.

The Culture Gap Analysis

The Culture Gap Analysis tool shown in figure 10.1 lists positive characteristics of the attributes in the right column and the opposite negative expressions in the left column. Weigh the comparison of characteristics in action within your culture and assign the corresponding number for each attribute. The tool is valuable to use in conversations with senior team members to gain alignment on priorities. I have also used it successfully with culture council teams and with leaders of business units. The data provides a gauge that forecasts your readiness to reshape your customer experience.

Culture Gap Assessment

POOR ▼	Attribute (GREAT ▼)	GREAT
• Victim attitude. • Blame game. • Pessimistic and powerless. • Mistakes are punished.	**Accountability** 1 2 3 4 5 6 7 8 9 10	• An ownership attitude. • Proactive problem solving. • Drive for results – clarity of goals. • Mistakes are leveraged for learning.
• Leaders antagonize via micromanagement. • Ridged controls are toxic to initiating results. • Input is discouraged and unsupported. • No feedback for improvement.	**Respect** 1 2 3 4 5 6 7 8 9 10	• Leaders act as trusted advocates. • Autonomy is a catalyst for results. • Input encouraged and supported. • Coaching-rich environment for improvement.
• Change is perceived as threat. • Meetings are unproductive. • Politics create bureaucracy. • Stuck with no creative process.	**Collaboration** 1 2 3 4 5 6 7 8 9 10	• Innovation is highly valued. • Meetings are highly effective. • Collective results surpass politics. • Creative competence and agility.
• No consideration given to the strategic differentiation of your brand. • Undisciplined approach to execute upon the brand promise. • No ownership of outcomes.	**Brand Advocacy** 1 2 3 4 5 6 7 8 9 10	• Deep understanding of your brand differentiation and why it matters. • High awareness of their role in executing upon your brand promise. • Accountability to satisfy and delight.
• Lack of customer empathy. • No knowledge of customer needs, motivations, and demographics. • No interaction with customers.	**Customer Intelligence** 1 2 3 4 5 6 7 8 9 10	• High customer focus and empathy. • Deep knowledge of customer needs, motivations, and demographics. • High interaction with customers.
• No communication on business strategy. • Intentions and expectations are not evident or obvious. • The future is perceived as negative or uncertain.	**Clarity of Purpose** 1 2 3 4 5 6 7 8 9 10	• Deep understanding on the strategic success factors of the business. • Intentions and expectations are extremely clear and evident. • The future is perceived as compelling.

Figure 10.1 Culture Gap assessment.

THE DIRECT CONNECTION

What is the magic that happens in the exchanges we have with customers that is so meaningful? Wharton superstar professor Adam Grant uncovered the answers in his now famous study on students doing fund-raising. Their results went "hockey stick" after the students were given a chance to meet with the people who benefited from their fund-raising efforts. Grant summarized the three primary benefits of getting employees connected directly with the customer:

1. *Impact:* People can see for themselves how their hard work benefits others.
2. *Appreciation:* People feel valued by the end user.
3. *Empathy:* People have a deeper understanding of the customers' problems and needs and, therefore, are more committed to help.[3]

If we want to share and spread the magic, then our next creative challenge is getting as many people in the organization as reasonably possible to have their own encounters with customers.

Making the Direct Connection

Sometimes the direct connection opportunity is right in front of us. But we still must feel empowered and make the choice to step up and make it happen. One of my all-time best friends, Kevin Hennigan, loved to tell me a story that shaped his beliefs about surprising and delighting customers. Kevin is a super creative inventor and entrepreneur, and his first foray was running a 7-Eleven franchise. At lunchtime, the 7-Eleven would become packed with people anxious to get their "grub" quickly so they could get back to work or life. 7-Eleven had just introduced a fast-serve pizza option that was amazingly tasty. One day, when the checkout line seemed out of control, Kevin stepped up to own the situation. He went over to the pizza display, pulled out a pie, and cut each slice into thirds, and promptly served everyone waiting in line a sample treat. The customers' anxiety was immediately transformed into delight. Kevin said people knew his name from that day forward, and he was able to build a rapport that was profoundly fulfilling every time they came into the store. The personal relationships made the hard work and pressure of running a high-volume 7-Eleven meaningful. Here's the other kicker. After sacrificing many $7 pizzas, his pizza sales grew faster than any other 7-Eleven on the east coast. Kevin exemplified the direct connection equation: direct contact plus accountability plus creativity equals breakthrough results.

What do you do, though, if your customers are virtual, or your employees never have the opportunity to interact because of proximity? Here are two high-impact tactical ideas we led at QVC you can implement:

1. **Assign a direct contact experience into your onboarding.** Whatever your opportunity is to connect, your goal is to transform the way employees perceive your customers—from just being "statistics" to understanding them as humans. No matter where your customers are located, they are connecting with your organization *live* in some manner. Even if customers only interact via website transactions, then participating in a live chat would still have an impact. Our live direct connection at QVC took place through our call centers, so new employees were given the assignment to take a listening tour by sitting in with supervisors monitoring the calls for quality.

2. **Create events where employees and customers interact.** I realize this big idea might be beyond your budget or capacity to execute, but I want to share it with you to spark your own customized and applicable version. At QVC, we created a customer "Red Carpet Weekend" event for some of our very best customers. We invited hundreds of customers to come to our Studio Park headquarters for a two-day QVC immersion experience. We bought their plane tickets, put them up in a nice hotel near QVC, bused them over to our studios, and had a meet-and-greet dinner event. We also set up one of our warehouses like a trade show with our very best merchandise vendors on display so they could shop and give feedback. The entire experience was meant to treat them like rock stars and learn from them. We broke them into focus groups to ask about ideas to make our broadcasts and website experience more enjoyable. They gave us priceless feedback on how to up our game. But here's the other way we leveraged this initiative. We invited employees to interact with them on the trade show floor and in the focus groups. The positive feedback from employees was remarkable. They were re-energized from the experience and armed with their own firsthand wisdom for why customers loved us so much. It lifted people's spirits to make the meaningful direct connection with customers. The creative ideas that germinated from this event took us to the next level.

AMPLIFYING MEANING FOR THE CUSTOMER—
THE BOOMERANG EFFECT

Engaged employees do this almost seamlessly: They choose to apply their energy, talent, and care toward delighting customers. It's baked into some people's character. I saw this in action in a place you might not expect: the Quest Lab where I would go for blood tests. As you probably know firsthand, a blood lab is a very routine, process-driven experience you hope begins and ends as quickly as possible. On this occasion, it was completely different. It started when one of the phlebotomists came out into the crowded waiting room and cracked a sarcastic joke that got the entire room to laugh. Then when it was my turn, I had the fortune to have her as my blood-drawer. She made a fun comment about my hat, asked me what I do, and struck up a rapport. She saw that I was nervous (I hate needles and can't watch) so she told me ripping the tape off my hairy arm was going to be way more painful than the needle. Then, she engaged me in a deeper discussion about the economy. She said it was proof the economy was picking up because there were so many people coming in for employment screenings. Wow, the entire visit for me was a positive experience. Think of the alternative—a loathsome experience that you hope to forget. But this was uplifting and meaningful for me. I told her how much I appreciated her personality and for being so kind. Humanity and personality can rise to the surface, but only if your employees make that choice. What might you do to show them the positive alternative?

Billy Joel is someone who takes this to a whole new level. You'd think being a music legend would cause you to become numb to your audience after performing for years on the road. It evidently has the opposite effect for Billy Joel, and he has a way to keep it energized. I learned recently that he would never sell the front-row seats of his concerts because bored rich people typically buy them up. Instead, Billy would ask his road crew to go out into the audience to people in the worst seats in the arena and take them down to the front row. Imagine their reaction, and the mind-blowing energy they would give back during the show: real fans giving back the love to Billy Joel within arm's reach, singing at the top of their lungs. It's no wonder he had the EQ (emotional intelligence) insight early in his career to write the epic chorus, "Sing us a song, you're the piano man. Sing us a song tonight. Well, we're all in the mood for a melody, and you've got us feelin' alright." In Billy's case, the "feelin'" works both ways.

When I started Culturology, I went from having a comfortable salary to having zero. That's a shockwave that knocks all start-up entrepreneurs right on their tush. I needed to make some immediate money just to help keep the family above water. I accepted a part-time job as a gardener at Longwood Gardens in Kennett Square, Pennsylvania. The job started at 6:30 a.m. and ended at 2:30 p.m., so I'd have time to schedule meetings with potential Culturology clients at the end of the day. Longwood is one of the most revered public gardens in the entire world. It was a stunning and inspiring work environment. But I admit the physically challenging work was an endurance test for me. One thing I noticed was that our team of hardworking gardeners craved the opportunity to answer questions from guests even if we were covered in dirt and exhausted. Many of the guests were wide-eyed, cheerful tourists from all over the country. We took it upon ourselves to point out things they may have missed in the garden, simply to make their experience at Longwood something extra special. I also noticed that when guests were around, I'd weed and do my tasks with more energy and conviction. There was a super high bar of excellence at Longwood, and even something as low level as weeding suddenly became extra meaningful to me.

VIRTUAL CONNECTIONS

Almost every online shopping site has created sophisticated techno-wizardry to grab attention and your credit card. Yet, the evolution has gone the other direction when it comes to personal touch and a sense of humanity. All the key factors that bring meaning into play have been replaced by algorithms and automated processes. Mostly gone are *live* people to help you shop or solve customer service problems. Even live chat seems robotic, cold, and distant. This sets up an opportunity to stand out and break through as a differentiated brand experience that connects with customers. It also creates the conditions for your employees to make progress in meaningful work.

One of the very best e-commerce leaders who is knocking it out of the park as a brand is Backcountry.com. They specialize in outdoor gear and clothing for skiing and snow sports. I've been a skier for many years and even worked in a ski shop for the perks. For the most part, I still know my stuff and love to have the latest and greatest gear for my ventures out west. This occasion, I was ordering some things to prep for a trip to Big Sky, Montana, but had a question about one of the jackets I was considering. Backcountry offers live chat of course, but a *live number* inviting me to speak with one of their "Gearheads" (a real title) caught my attention. I called and was blown away by the experience. Gearhead Ashleigh McClary answered my questions with grace and ease but then proceeded to build rapport by asking about my trip. She told me some tips about Big Sky and even checked the long-range snow forecast. Talking to Ashleigh was like connecting with a good friend who shared the same passion for skiing as me. I was so enamored for how she worked with me, I asked if I could "interview" her to learn how she developed her service skills and what Backcountry.com was doing to empower her. This is what I learned.

Ashleigh had been with Backcountry.com for four years and described it as the best job she's ever had. I asked why, of course, and her answer centered on the positivity of her coworkers and leaders, plus the constant customer feedback. Internally, the company invested in creating a culture with high accountability standards and the expectations for living up to their guiding principles. Everyone has visibility to each others' goals, which means they can motivate each other to perform and support each other. Ashleigh said, "It's the great way they treat you here and the energy they give employees. They care." That attitude translates outside to the customer experience. Gearheads are empowered to build long-term relationships for the purpose of growing people's passion for the outdoors. I asked Ashleigh how that purpose made a difference for her personally. She said, "I see direct results by being in a unique position to help people make smart choices. I get them ready to have fun on their next adventure. The positive feedback makes it meaningful. You might not expect selling gear to have that kind of an impact, but it happens every day here" (personal communication with the author, March 4, 2021). I can attest that it happened that way for me, and now I'm a raving fan.

Being a virtual business doesn't preclude you from building meaningful connections with customers; however, your people must feel empowered and supported to let their personality and creativity shine through. It might take a complete reengineering of your customer connections and a major investment in your culture to create live encounters. But consider how much brand equity you build in every conversation. What might those positive brand impressions be worth to your business?

I put my creativity gift to work a few years ago and invented and patented a unique ergonomic garden tool called the Mulch Fork. The process to go from concept to prototyping to manufacturing and launching it live on QVC was one of the most daunting challenges of my life; however, to bring an idea to fruition at that scale was deeply meaningful. Today, each package that I ship to customers includes a handwritten thank-you note signed, "Steve the Inventor." I also include in the note a comment that is specifically relevant to gardening in the customer's state. If they are from Texas, for example, I might say something like, "I hope this Mulch Fork is helpful and you get out to your garden before the Blue Bonnets are up." Interestingly enough, of the hundreds that I've shipped, I've never had a single Mulch Fork returned to me. I write the note just to be nice, but it must resonate with my customers in such a way they emotionally connect back to me as the inventor. I must be making a virtual connection the old-fashioned way. What might happen if you asked your team to write notes to their customers?

CREATIVITY AND THE CUSTOMER

What would it take to create a meaningful experience for the customer if you worked on the shop floor of a manufacturing plant and never actually encounter customers? It takes creativity applied to empathy, plus the accountability to pursue a great idea. I was amazed to see this example take place with one of my most beloved clients, Miller Ingenuity in Winona, Minnesota. One of their products is a heavy-duty assembly kit containing many parts for overhauling trucks (wheels) on locomotives. One of the managers in charge of shipping had an idea to determine how to customize customer orders. He received the green light to investigate, and he traveled to observe customers working on locomotives in the field. He detailed the exact sequence they went through to assemble the parts and noted that customers struggled with the logistics of heavy items packed in a random order. A big idea revealed itself. If Miller Ingenuity packed the kits in the opposite order, then customers would unpack the kits in the exact order they needed to do their job safely and efficiently. This absolute brilliant customization became the industry standard. Empathy unlocked a breakthrough idea.

CONNECT INNOVATION TO YOUR BRAND

Ideas like customizing the packing of the truck part kits don't happen by accident. The CEO of Miller Ingenuity, Steve Blue, made the commitment to create the conditions for innovation. Here's what he told me, "When we added *innovation* to our existing set of six *values*, we did it to make a statement, and to begin the shift in attitudes. We knew we literally had no other choice if we wanted to grow in the short term, and even survive in the long term. This gave us the latitude to provide a new promise to our customers and established something vital from an internal cultural perspective that cannot be underestimated" (personal communication with the author, February 2, 2018).

Many leaders underestimate the scope of the challenge involved in shaping their culture to become innovation centric. Once you have truly decided to make the change within your culture, you must gain a full buy-in. Innovation culture change is not something that happens with a single edict from on high, or by changing a simple process-step out on the floor. The effort consists of a full-blown campaign—both top down and bottom up—that requires winning the hearts and minds of your employees.

Start with Beliefs and Attitudes

Employees will be creative and innovative if they have the desire to support and serve their customers in any way possible. That desire begins with their beliefs and attitudes about customers. If you influence the deeply held beliefs and attitudes employees have toward customers, they will act in ways that reflect and support those beliefs.

Imagine employees who have the following *beliefs and attitudes* about their customers:

- Customers are a pain and make my life difficult.
- Customers' demands are unreasonable.
- I do not enjoy my interactions with customers.
- It's okay to fool or manipulate customers for short-term gains.

With such beliefs and attitudes, you can anticipate their *behaviors* to look like this:

- They will avoid or minimize their interactions with customers.
- They will do what's required by the book and not give customers more than they expect.
- They will protect themselves and the company from customers' demands.

Now imagine the flip side with these employee beliefs and attitudes:

- Customer interactions are opportunities to super serve and win them over.
- I enjoy the challenge of learning what customers really want and need from us.
- I play a vital role in creating a brand promise with customers that must be kept.

As you can expect, the behaviors will also be quite different:

• They will go out of their way to ensure customers' needs are met and exceeded.
• They will put the customer first in their decision-making process.
• They will explore ideas that elevate our brand experience.
• They will share ideas and best practices with others on the team that enhance our customer service.

Reversing negative attitudes and beliefs about customers won't be easy. This is where your personal creativity as a leader and the collaboration of the senior team truly come into play. If you can confidently answer these two questions, and relentlessly pursue the quest to bring them into reality, then you will succeed in shaping an innovative, customer-centered culture.

1. What is the promise we are making to our customers?
2. How might we become even more effective in delivering upon the promise?

If you're really at a loss for creating this foundation, then you may need to pull in an outside perspective, a trusted business coach, or a consultant.

Keep in mind that it's very tempting to just train for behaviors. It seems easier. Behaviors are obvious and on the surface. They are easier to wrap your arms around because they are observable. The problem is that you can modify behavior in the short term, only to have it revert back to the "way things have always been done around here." Establishing the new and preferred belief and attitude set is more challenging, but doing so creates a foundation that makes behavior change sustainable for the long haul.

Training for Innovation: Increasing Creative Intelligence

Once employees have positive beliefs and attitudes about customers, they are primed to accept creativity and innovation as part of the company culture. I asked Miller Ingenuity CEO Steve Blue how innovation became a value within his firm's culture. He said,

> We wanted to impact the way we looked at everything on the shop floor and in our offices. If we were to succeed, creativity had to become a sweet spot discipline for us in the same way we excelled with the hard-nosed determination to execute. If the team could generate more ideas on a consistent basis, then we would fill our innovation pipeline. Execution was always one of our strengths that we knew we could leverage. So, the front end of generating ideas became a high priority. (Personal communication with the author, February 2, 2018)

One question you may be asking yourself is, "Can you actually teach, or train people to be more creative?" The answer is a resounding *yes*.

One of the first goals for the training is to define what we mean by creativity. It's not just about painting and poetry. We make certain we are talking about the very essence of problem-solving. Reframing creativity as problem-solving makes it highly relevant to people. It's about giving them confidence and a conviction that the creative aspect of their work is something you highly value. It's also something people engage in every day, even if they don't realize it. We define creativity as the disciplined thought process to explore possibilities and generate ideas; innovation is defined as the next step in making it happen—to implement the idea. It makes the important "relevance" connection.

Thus, the first step in the challenge for any organization is to instill employee creative confidence within your culture. Again, it is making the connection for *why* it's important and valued as the genesis for innovation, as well as the direct relevance to impact customers. The second step is to teach people how to generate ideas. This includes generating ideas on their own, and by collaborating with each other as a team. You must get very tactical with these skills and began by learning the basics of brainstorming.

Brainstorming 101

Many people have formed a negative feeling toward brainstorming because they've attended ineffective meetings in the past. Sometimes brainstorming can go awry by coming across as goofy and frivolous with no true business focus. Or maybe the session ends up generating a decent number of ideas only to have them disappear into a black hole never to be seen again. No one followed through. Or maybe they experience a power struggle in the room with only the politically strong surviving with their ideas at the top of the priority list. There are many things that can go wrong, and have gone wrong in the past, to justify the negative feeling toward brainstorming.

Miller Ingenuity is an example of an organization committed to doing it right. I'm convinced now that, by doing so, they not only consistently generated more ideas with higher impact but also experienced something that transformed their culture (and it can transform your culture). Everyone from top to bottom felt included in the business, and you could sense a new level of respect among the team. By including people in the process of creative problem-solving, you will be activating one of the most powerful things you can do as a leader to amplify the meaning of their work. This is the proverbial secret sauce that so many leaders seem to miss. Brainstorming is like a 3-for-1 special: (1) You utilize an effective process to solve problems. (2) You engage the team far beyond the session itself by making progress in meaningful work. (3). You find new ways to delight customers to deliver your brand promise. People should use the discipline of brainstorming in everyday conversations in the hallway. It doesn't have to be relegated to a formal brainstorming session. The discipline translates to any type of conversation. When every conversation resembles a brainstorm, then you have arrived as an innovation-ready culture wired to elevate your brand.

THE CUSTOMER AMPLIFIER PLAYBOOK: THE REAL RULES OF BRAINSTORMING

I made the mistake once of leading a brainstorming session without reminding the group of the rules. I assumed they knew, and it would feel parochial to go through the list with them. After all, this particular group was made up of highly motivated senior leaders, who dealt with problem-solving every day as a regular part of their job. They would surely know how to brainstorm effectively, right? *Wrong!* It was a train wreck.

We didn't get five minutes into the brainstorm before an argument broke out as to why an idea wouldn't work. Then, people proceeded to piggyback on the negativity regarding all the things that were going wrong in the business. There was no way to get the brainstorm back on track. I made a promise to myself that I'd never lead a brainstorm again without reviewing and enforcing the rules.

It takes practice to get good at brainstorming. It's the same as any sport or musical instrument we've taken on in life. In a sport like football, you have the proven fundamental techniques for blocking and tackling. The team that executes these consistently well wins nearly every game. If you are learning to play an instrument, the instructor always starts you out with the basic fundamentals called "rudiments." Once you learn these, it unlocks the possibilities for playing music.

Brainstorming has its fundamental rules as well. Ironically, the rules are actually liberating to the creative process as opposed to constraining. Once you learn and practice them consistently, you will experience more creativity that results in highly effective ideas.

Here are the five essential rules of brainstorming:

1. **Suspend judgment:** Treat every idea as a good idea.
2. **Be curious, not critical:** Say, "Yes, and . . . " *not* "Yes, but . . . "

3. **Think it . . . say it . . . write it:** Let it fly and capture them all. No idea is too outrageous.
4. **Quantity creates quality:** Look for the second right answer and beyond.
5. **Piggyback on ideas:** Combine and build on ideas to create new possibilities.

These rules are the blocking and tackling basics of brainstorming. Be certain that your team knows and practices the rules so that it becomes second nature anytime you're problem-solving together. It's the key to winning with ideas that delight customers and enhance your brand. Here's why and how they work.

Brainstorming Rule #1: Suspend Judgment

Treat every idea as a good idea.

There are five essential rules for brainstorming. But, if I was forced to pick only one to guarantee success, I'd choose *suspend judgment*. Ironically, it's probably the toughest one for people to do. Our human nature is to voice opinions and criticisms almost immediately. In fact, we almost always go to the dark side and negatively evaluate things we don't fully understand, especially if it looks or sounds different. Most people dislike change, and ideas change things. That makes suspending judgment very challenging.

The best way to suspend judgment comes by eliminating the language that is toxic to ideas. The language of judgment often comes out in the form of "toxic phrases." They're like a poison that snuffs out ideas. Some classics include "It's not in the budget," "We tried that before," "That will never work," "Not the right timing," "Legal will never approve it," and even "Let's form a committee to look into it." I use a proven technique to eliminate these phrases. Nerf-ball bopping! Pass a Nerf ball out to everyone in the brainstorm and give them permission to Nerf-ball bop any violators who judge with toxic phrases. It's fun and effective as an instant reminder.

Here are two reasons why judgment is toxic to effective brainstorming:

1. *Judgment slows the process down.* Rather than thinking of new ideas, all the energy of the group gets applied to whether the idea is viable. It becomes a black hole from which few return.
2. *Judgment intimidates.* People will hold back on sharing ideas that haven't been thought through. Or if they feel they might be shot down right away, they won't take any chances. The truth is that hardly any great

ideas are ever completely formed at the beginning of the creative process. It's important to create an environment that encourages ideas even if they aren't fully baked initially.

Generate better ideas by resisting the temptation to judge them prematurely. It takes discipline to stay in the divergent-thinking stage instead of jumping ahead to the converging stage where the ideas are judged and prioritized. Judgment is built into the process, but it must come later with its own purposeful focus.

If you suspend judgment and treat every idea as a good idea in the diverge stage, you will be more efficient and energized to generate lots of ideas, plus you will encourage participation from everyone. When people take more risks, great ideas are more likely to surface and become potential difference makers. Be certain to remember the first rule of brainstorming and suspend judgment, plus remind others on your team to do so as well.

Brainstorming Rule #2: Be Curious, Not Critical

Say, "Yes, and . . . " not "Yes, but . . . "

One of my three dogs is a smart little rescue mutt named Tally. She doesn't look like any one specific breed but is this cool combination of unique and endearing characteristics. When I talk to Tally or make a strange sound, she pops her antenna-like ears up in the air and then tilts her head from side to side. She seems desperate to pick up every detail with her built-in satellite dishes tilting back and forth to get the perfect reception. I've come to the conclusion that the tilted head is the universal symbol for curiosity.

Curiosity is all about being open, inquisitive, and interested. It's an eagerness to want to know more; it's a desire to understand and learn the true meaning. That's exactly what Tally demonstrates with her head-tilting technique.

Why is curiosity so important that it would be one of the five rules of brainstorming? The ability to be curious unlocks the potential in our mind to respond positively to ideas and to build cognitive connections that improve upon them. Creative advertising legend Leo Burnett said, "Curiosity about life in all of its aspects, I think, is still the secret of great creative people."[4]

Curiosity expands our own ability to be creative, and in the dynamics of brainstorming, it causes everyone to be more effective as a group.

So how do we apply the secret and respond with curiosity more often?

1. *Say, "Yes, and . . . " not "Yes, but . . . "* Improv theater comedy players have a hard and fast rule that makes the difference between a skit that

is creative, hilarious, and interesting, and one that is a complete bomb. You must think "yes, and . . . " to the line the person is throwing you and simply go with it. "Yes, and . . . " thinking allows you to build and expand upon the line using the momentum of the creative flow. If you say "No" or "But . . . " then the skit will consistently fall on its face. They have learned this rule by studying tapes of their performances. The proof is overwhelming. This same phenomenon applies to brainstorming. It's no wonder that a highly effective brainstorming session resembles improv theater well done.

2. *Be aware of the questions you ask.* Do they help unlock and open possibilities, or do they shut things down with a tone of critical judgment? What questions might you ask if you wanted to fully understand others and learn more about their thinking? These good questions are proof-positive signs that you're being more curious: "Can you tell me more?" "What does that look like?" "How might it work?"

3. *Pause before responding.* Since our natural knee-jerk reaction to an idea is typically negative, take a momentary "chill pill" before saying anything at all. Then, apply the discipline of first thinking what is positive about the idea. If that's a stretch, then consider what is interesting about the idea. This new thinking pattern puts you in curiosity mode first. Creativity guru Chic Thompson (author of *What a Great Idea*) calls this the PIN technique (Positive, Interesting, and Negative).[5] By reversing the natural order, you become curious first and establish a creative pattern that is highly effective for ideation.

Curiosity takes discipline and practice like any worthwhile skill. And, like all the rules of brainstorming, it really can be applied to everyday conversations to make them even more effective, too.

Listen to the words you use in response to others and be more aware of your underlying thinking. A heightened awareness will give you better choices to be curious first. Oh, and tilting your head works, too!

Brainstorming Rule #3: Think It . . . Say It . . . Write It

No idea is too outrageous . . . let it fly and capture them all.

The lightbulb is rightfully the symbol for ideas because it is one of the most iconic inventions of all time. It's right up there with the wheel, fire, and the iPhone. There is another reason. It has to do with the quintessential moment in which an idea "flashes" in our head. The experience is akin to suddenly flicking on a bright light in the dark space of our mind. You'd call it an enlightening experience (pun intended). Ideas illuminate something new, different, and exciting that wasn't perceived before in the darkness. It's often described as a *wow* or "brilliant" moment. The lightbulb metaphor is appropriate for so many good reasons.

People who are prolifically creative recognize and embrace their lightbulb moments. They not only seek purposeful ways to turn on the switch but also are confident to tell people what they see once the light is on. They think it and say it, plus they take another important step to write it all down.

Here's how to enlighten a brainstorm:

- When an idea hits you, resist the temptation to pull back and self-judge it. Often introverts will want to think it through first before *saying it* out loud. Without the processing time introverts desire, they might not say it at all. If that sounds like you, then flex your creative muscles and take more risks to say it even if it isn't perfected or if it seems outrageous.
- Extroverts have such an easy time *thinking it . . . and saying it* that they sometimes dominate the airtime in the brainstorm. Maintain your enthusiasm and be aware to give others the grace to participate. You might need to invoke some techniques of "going around the room" for idea sharing, or use a ball, tossing it to random people for shout-outs. These will ensure a fair balance of airtime.
- When it comes to *saying it*, be short and sweet like billboards and tweets. People often get lost in their explanations of ideas and end up being a buzzkill to the group's energy. What's the headline? Also, avoid overselling and trying to convince people your idea is the greatest thing ever. You'll have a chance to do that during the converge stage of brainstorming.
- The act of *writing it* down sends a huge message to everyone that their idea matters enough to be captured. It also provides the important practical application of allowing everyone to see what has been generated. It's vital to visually represent the ideas so you can later build, sort, and evaluate them. Always write down every idea and assign a scribe if you need some help. Post-it notes and flipchart paper are your best friends.

Think it . . . say it . . . write it is one of the five essential rules of brainstorming because it encourages people to step up and participate whether their idea is big, small, crazy, or conservative. Writing it down creates idea democracy and inclusion. Everyone has a say, and all ideas will be considered.

Realize that some ideas are like blinding halogen beams, and others are as subtle as the soft flicker of a candle. Sharing your vision is the only way they will see the light of your creativity.

Brainstorming Rule #4: Quantity Creates Quality

Go for the second right answer and beyond.

I've grown a lot of plants from seeds over the years. It's very satisfying. For example, you buy a packet of tomato seeds for around $2 and end up with a bodacious harvest of red juicy orbs of organic goodness to give away to delighted friends and neighbors. Seed packets contain about 30 seeds. But here's the thing. Even in a fairly large vegetable garden like mine you'd never plant more than eight plants. So why do they give you 30 seeds? That's practically enough to put Del Monte out of business. The reason is simple. You germinate 30 seedlings but then are able to selectively choose the healthiest and robust plants that are guaranteed to thrive and produce. Quantity gives you a better choice to plant, grow, and harvest quality tomatoes . . . and the same exact principle applies to idea generation.

When it comes to ideas, it's tempting to take the first one that "germinates" and simply run with it. Task accomplished, check the box, *next*! But step back and look at the bigger picture. If your ultimate goal is to achieve something remarkable, then the way to truly have a breakthrough is by evoking the discipline to seek the second right answer and beyond. The process of going for *quantity creates quality*.

Here are some techniques to generate quantity and quality:

- Challenge each other to "fill the flipchart page" with ideas. Don't stop until it's full.
- Ask better questions. Great brainstorming questions are focused yet flexible. The flexibility allows for a ton of potential answers. For example, "How might we increase sales in the fourth quarter using social media?" or "What might we do to increase repeat purchases from our first-time customers?"
- Use creative constraints to drive more ideas. For example, "What might we do if the budget was no object?" or "What might we do if we had to deliver the idea in only 24 hours?" or "What might we do for free?"
- Borrow unique perspectives as stimuli. For example, "What would scare the competition the most?" or "What would we *never* do?" Then convert the answers to a positive action step. Or say, "How might Pixar approach this challenge?" or "What is this problem like?" Create a metaphor and generate ideas from the new perspective.

School trained us to think there is just one right answer to a question, and it can only be found in the back of the teacher's edition. Our complex business challenges have more than one right answer, and some will be more "righter" than others if you're patient enough to go for them. Albert Einstein once said, "It's not that I'm so smart, it's just that I stay with problems longer." His second right answers changed the world.

Remember, the best way to get good ideas is to get lots of them and then throw away the bad ones. And like the healthy tomato plants, you will harvest some seriously juicy results.

Brainstorming Rule #5: Piggyback on Ideas

Combine and build on ideas to create new possibilities.

Many people say there really aren't any new ideas but, instead, only improvements to existing ones. Whether or not that's true is probably worth debating over happy hour. What's definitely true is the power of piggybacking on ideas in a brainstorming session to generate something remarkable. One of the most effective ways to produce great ideas is to combine and build on others to create new possibilities.

Did you know that Apple did not invent the mouse? Xerox invented the mouse. When young Steve Jobs witnessed it in action at the legendary Xerox PARC innovation lab, he got frantic with excitement. He saw the future. The only problem was the Xerox mouse broke down every two weeks. It had three complicated buttons and cost $300. Jobs asked his designers at Apple to build a durable mouse—with one button and a price tag under $15. In one of the most savvy piggybacks of all time, the Macintosh was launched shortly thereafter with the revolutionary new mouse that we all know and love.

The people I'd consider to be "masters" in the art of brainstorming share a particular trait. They continually use the expression "What if . . . ?" as part of their dialogue. These two powerful words reflect the thinking and attitude that unlocks possibilities.

The elite and all-powerful "Yoda Jedi Masters" of brainstorming take it one step further. They combine the *curiosity attitude* of "Yes, and . . ." with the *possibility catalyst* of "What if . . . ?" to piggyback on the ideas of others. Achieving this level requires listening with curiosity and a sense of optimism that sparks creative intuition. Steve Jobs said, "Yes, and what if . . . ?" when he saw the mouse for the first time.

If you're thinking it sounds like a silly exercise in semantics, be curious enough to try it in your next brainstorming conversation. If you say, "Yes, and what if . . . ?" out loud, you'll be amazed at the creative direction it will take you. The good news is that all of us have the capacity to do so even if we don't consider ourselves at Steve Jobs's level of genius.

In the brainstorming sessions I've led, I've witnessed many times how an idea that was average or half baked turned into a something remarkable through the power of piggybacking on ideas. Yes, and what if you and your team all became Jedi Masters of brainstorming? What are the remarkable things you might accomplish together to turn the customer amplifier up to full power?

11

The Community Amplifier

A better vision for the workplace is a community—a place where people bond around shared values, feel valued as human beings, and have a voice in decisions that affect them.

—Wharton professor Adam Grant, author of *Give and Take*

The tug of altruism compels us to do extraordinary things in the service of others. We are wired for the purpose of helping others. Giving ourselves away is an act of compassion and love. I believe love is a universal purpose, and when scaled, that bond forms a community.

One day I was killing some time on LinkedIn and saw a picture that had evidently gone viral. It was of a simple, hand-drawn sign taped on the door of a dry-cleaning shop. The sign read, "If you are unemployed and need an outfit clean for an interview, we will clean it for free." With its profound simplicity, it touched me and the hearts of thousands of people by emoting something meaningful. It was the gift of grace offered to someone in need. And then I thought about the owner and the workers of that shop. Their gift wasn't given just to individuals; it was for the entire community. Even through the gritty hard work of being a dry cleaner, they had the power to extend themselves in that way to give the gift. Anyone who read that sign and patronized that dry cleaner was automatically enrolled into the meaningfulness of the community through association. Imagine what the interactions typically feel like between customers and these dry cleaner workers. One simple sign is a priceless payback in community altruism.

I later learned the same wonderful offer of helping people who were unemployed was being carried out on a larger scale by dressforsuccess.com. This
women's charity provides out-of-work women with an interview suit or outfit
to help them nail their interviews with confidence. It's a great example of how
we can stretch our community comfort zones to be creative in the service of
others. Think of the positive impact your unique organization can make by
discovering what niche need might be served. What are your employees passionate about? What are your customers passionate about? Your brand should
act as a creative catalyst to reveal possibilities that are worthy of becoming your
community purpose.

An interesting thing happens when your company's culture includes a focus
on reaching out to the community: It becomes a community of its own. In this
chapter, we will talk both about the external and internal community—the
community in which your company operates and your customers work and
live, plus the community that *is* your company's culture.

The following are some search-for-meaning questions people ask themselves:

- Is our company an asset to the community?
- Does our company give back in ways that I can participate in?
- Am I proud of what our company represents to the community?
- Do I feel included within the community of our company culture?

The Unsung Hero of Your Community Impact

It seems completely unfair, but the idea of a business making a profit has been
given a bad rap more recently in some political circles. A lot of people have
formed the belief that profit signifies corporate greed, and there are enough
dreadful high-profile stories that have gone viral to justify this feeling. But,
in reality, these stories represent the exception, not the norm. The detrac-
tors never pause to consider the broader positive socioeconomic impact of a
successful business and assume only greedy owners benefit. In my opinion,
leaders need to stop feeling gun shy or self-conscious about touting the success of their business. Here's why. The financial health of your business is an
unsung hero that fosters a community worthy of being your purpose. I get
the feeling that few leaders step back long enough to analyze the positive impact and proudly communicate their community impact as a purpose being
fulfilled.

It's not profit versus purpose; it's success so you can live out your purpose.
No one needs to feel compelled to make a mutually exclusive or binary choice.

Activating this amplifier of meaning requires expanding your definition of stakeholders beyond the obvious and traditional considerations. The economy you create is the lifeblood and enhancer of the literal community in which you operate. I'm not referring to the charitable causes that are most often associated with community. The socioeconomic health of community itself is the purpose that too often goes unrecognized and unappreciated. Sometimes it sadly remains hidden until a business goes away.

Back in the 1980s, Billy Joel wrote the popular song called "Allentown," which bemoaned the loss of the steel industry and the devastation to the steel industry communities, such as the titular Allentown, Pennsylvania. For many of us who grew up in that era, the feeling hit very close to home. My hometown of Williamsport, Pennsylvania, was actually hit harder than Allentown with the loss of Bethlehem Steel and Piper Aircraft. I remember my dad and grandpa, who were both dentists, having worried discussions at the Sunday dinner table about the thousands of employees losing their benefits and not being able to get dental work done. It directly impacted our family financially. My dad and grandpa often would do work for unemployed patients and not bill them. These patients would sometimes stop by the house months later offering venison or jars of honey from their beehives as a reciprocal gesture of goodwill.

Williamsport was a tight-knit community made up of honorable people who were somewhat gritty and definitely hardworking. When a business closed down, everyone knew about it and could feel the loss financially and emotionally. Williamsport was featured on the cover of *U.S. News and World Report* for being the real Allentown of economic malaise. If it wasn't for our fame of being the home of Little League baseball, we might have lost our identity, although never our pride.

Your business matters to the community more than you might consider. As a first step, it would be a good analytical exercise to determine the actual financial impact your business makes on your community. Then, as a second step, think holistically and systemically on the socioeconomic impact. Here is an example:

Step 1: Conduct a socioeconomic calculus. How many people do you employ, and how much do you pay them? When you start breaking it down, it may be an impressive number. For example, if you have 100 employees and pay them an average of $50,000, then you are pumping $5 million into the local economy just from the salaries alone. That doesn't even take into account the many local businesses that generate their own direct income servicing and supplying your company. That would include the landscaping crew, the office supply company, the janitorial service, the real estate firm, the tax accountants, the consultants, and the copier repair service, just to name a few. Each of these companies produces income affecting *their* employees' lives as well.

Step 2: What does the salary income translate into holistically? Other people benefit as a result of your employees. How many grocery clerk jobs, music teachers, car repair mechanics, babysitters, dry cleaners, schoolteachers, pastors, restaurant servers, mortgage brokers, and electricians earn a living as a result of your employees living within the community? What about the number of parents being able to pay for their kids' college? Consider the doctor's offices, coffee shops, hospital workers, and dentists it takes to serve your employees. For example, QVC essentially paid our family's mortgage, my son Ryan's college, and my addiction to cool plants for my garden from the local nursery. How could I not be QVC's biggest fan for being highly successful? I'm immensely grateful.

If you can quantify this data and make the impact connection, then you have an amazing story to tell that puts your community amplifier front and center as a purpose. It may feel like an enormous challenge, but you are responsible for the security and well-being of your employees who feed the health of the community. Hardly anyone seems to make this their explicitly stated purpose. It is a vast opportunity missed. Share your story through social media, at town halls, or at your church, rotary, or business mentor groups. Be proud of the impact. Once your employees understand their hard work matters in achieving success for the purpose of having an altruistic impact, they will engage. Do you remember Jimmy Stewart's character George Bailey from the movie *It's a Wonderful Life* (1946)? Clarence, his guardian angel, shows him what the community would be like without him in the world. It shocks George Bailey into the emotional epiphany that his life and work mattered far beyond him. You don't need to wait for something bad to happen to have that revelation. Work on it now with intention to prove to yourself and others that your business success—success that your employees are making possible—has high impact and is vital to the community. If someone asks you what your purpose is as an organization, just tell them to look around at people living their lives within the community as they drive to your office. You don't live in the Allentown of the 1970s.

Imagine if the purpose an individual employee now sees for their contribution in making the company succeed is tied to the beehive mentality of the socioeconomic lifeblood of their community. I want that for my fellow humans and for the community in which I live.

A Community of United Fans

During week 14 of the 1989 NFL season, there was an unusual call for unity as a community. In a game against the Seattle Seahawks, Cincinnati Bengals fans started throwing beer bottles and trash on the field after a controversial call by officials. The Seahawks refused to continue the game until the Cincinnati Bengals could get things under control. After failed attempts by the referees to calm the mayhem, Bengal head coach Sam Wyche grabbed the stadium microphone from a befuddled ref and did what any good Cincinnatian would do: He made fun of Cleveland. The coach belts out into the PA system, "Knock it off! You don't live in Cleveland; you live in Cincinnati!" Fans got it right away. The sarcasm worked and raised the bar of dignity where the crude behavior of throwing stuff on the field is not tolerated—except in Cleveland. Whether it's fair to use Cleveland to make the point, it was made nonetheless, and the game proceeded. One *CBS Sports* announcer declared that Coach Wyche summed up the Bengals-Browns rivalry with those nine words.

Football fans are one of the most fun and extreme examples of community. It's a sport unto itself to proudly display your loyalty, passion, and identity as a fan. They create a community for which it's worth sacrificing their dignity with tailgating debauchery, face painting, or, of course, wearing fake cheese on their head. If you're not convinced that community amplifies meaning, you've never attended a packed stadium on a Sunday afternoon.

Boomer Community

If you've wondered how fulfilled you and your family will be after retiring, you are not alone. So, what is one of the most important keys to a happy and healthy retirement? According to the American Society of Aging, it's community. Surrounding ourselves with positive social connections and neighbors has a significant impact on our lifespan. More adults 55 and older are considering communities to keep an active social life, and it's easy to see why. Community touches or fulfills nearly every level of Maslow's hierarchy of needs.

Optimism for the Human Spirit

Repeatedly, we've all seen examples of communities coming together following disasters. Whether it was 9/11, Hurricane Harvey flooding in Houston, or the Hurricane Katrina aftermath in Louisiana, the human spirit proves itself as inherently good. People want to come together to get involved, to contribute to something of value to others. Community falls within the zone of altruism.

A sense of community is the opposite of being alone. Loneliness is one of the unexpected consequences stemming from the COVID-19 pandemic. I would describe it in the business context as virtual loneliness—people separated from each other physically. Working to build community shouldn't require a disaster, however. Leaders can be proactive and creative without having to rely on the emotional drama factor to pull people together with a sense of community.

The Pull of Community: A Family Story

The following story comes from my son Ryan. As with many others, COVID-19 led to a reassessment by Ryan and his wife, Nina. Driven by a longing for community, they changed their lives in one of the most dramatic ways you'll ever hear about. Here, in Ryan's own words, is Ryan and Nina's story:

> The first night that I met my future wife, Nina, we shared with each other that we both wanted a farm some day. The words seemed to fall out of my mouth as we were talking, though they seemed somewhat far-fetched. At that point I hadn't given farming much thought. While I loved nature, I grew up in suburban Philadelphia. The closest I had come to farming was working on landscaping projects and helping my dad out around our yard.
>
> After graduating from college, Nina and I left our Pennsylvania roots for sunny San Diego. Years of exploration, growth, joy, and challenge followed. Though we were almost 3,000 miles from everything we knew, we came home to ourselves, individually and together.
>
> We got married and started to wonder what was next for us. As the events of 2020 unfolded, we found ourselves isolated as many did. We didn't see our family for over a year, and missed most of the things that we loved about San Diego during that time. While we were incredibly fortunate, we felt a shift and a slow-growing longing for something more. It became clear that we were missing community, and ultimately lacking purpose.
>
> We were reminded of our first conversation and asked ourselves, "What if we moved home and started a farm?" I was now working remotely as a result of the COVID-19 pandemic, and for the first time it became possible for us to live anywhere while still allowing me to pursue my career in technology.
>
> We put the wheels in motion and started to build our dream farm. We worked harder than we knew was possible, driven by a sense of meaning in the work and a vision of the future. Many long days, late nights, and lots of dirt, sweat, and humbling lessons reaffirmed our purpose to be stewards for our land and for the people around us.

Now that our dream has become our reality, it is sweeter than we ever could have imagined. We grow healthy food for our community, and host events that bring people together in fun, learning, and spiritual development. Every day we have the joy of supporting our neighbors in nourishing their families with food that we grew on the farm. We are able to provide people with the opportunity to get their hands dirty in our fields, and to reconnect with parts of themselves that they forgot existed.

Just like plants, communities take time to grow. They need to establish their roots and receive regular nourishment to thrive. While Nina and I may not get to eat the fruit from every tree that we plant in our lifetimes, we will continue to plant the seeds.

The Importance of Community for Safety and Security

Natural disasters, including hurricanes, wildfires, and floods, are obviously life changers for all involved. Hurricane Sandy caused the deaths of more than 230 people and caused nearly $70 billion in damage when it hit the northeastern United States in 2012.

What moved the people impacted by Hurricane Sandy toward recovery? According to a four-year study by Purdue University, it was strong community involvement, including support from neighborhood groups, faith-based organizations, and local agencies. These groups—providing food, shelter, clothing, and more—proved to be the glue that bound the community together in the face of crisis.[1]

Our nation will continue to be challenged by crises, but possibly none has been more impactful than the COVID-19 pandemic. Life as we knew it came to a screeching halt, forcing many small businesses to close their doors permanently. And that's when celebrity blogger Dave Portnoy, creator of Barstool Sports, got involved. Portnoy said in a December 2020 Twitter video:

New York City just closed indoor dining. What do they think is gonna happen? They're done. The bar and restaurant industry and small businesses have been squeezed and squeezed and squeezed. They've been as creative as they can be to save their livelihoods. And now a few politicians in New York are like "eh, you're done, we're shutting it down." How do you expect these people to survive?

The right to earn a livelihood is being stolen by a few politicians. Politicians are taking away the right to earn a living. It's that simple, and it's insanity. I don't know what the answer is, but it is insanity.[2]

In a classic schoolyard dare, Marcus Lemonis, the star of CNBC's *The Profit*, responded with a tweet to Portnoy: "Put your money where your mouth is . . . I'll put up 500k if you match it to create a relief fund for NYC-area restaurants."[3] Portnoy contributed $500,000 of his own money, and in December 2020, the Barstool Fund was launched.

The Barstool Fund—allowing any small business across the country maintaining payroll throughout the pandemic to apply for relief money—was announced on social media in a December 2020 tweet. The deal: To apply, small business owners needed to disclose information including number of employees and how much money the business has lost. Selected businesses received recurring payments until the economy stabilized and the pandemic was under control.

Portnoy and Lemonis weren't the only contributors. New England Patriots wide receiver Julian Edelman, Darren Rovell of the Action Network, poker star Daniel Negreanu, Tom Brady, Guy Fieri, Kid Rock, Penn National Gaming, and 231,044 people across the country donated. At the time of this writing, the Barstool Fund has raised nearly $42 million and saved more than 500 businesses from the brink of collapse due to COVID-19.[4]

The Charitable Community

I'm so enamored with the depth of involvement I'm seeing with charitable causes. Many organizations are doing incredible work inviting volunteerism at all levels with a full commitment to change people's lives in the community. The impact is twofold, with the other beneficiary being the volunteers themselves: volunteerism provides employees with the opportunity to get involved and make a difference.

Volunteerism is now among the top considerations for candidates when determining their next employer. Making a difference beyond normal work has become an expectation of college graduates. They come prewired to make an impact. Not having community purpose to tout as an attraction can be a major obstacle for a company striving to achieve their recruiting goals. How you serve the community makes a big statement to people about who you are, and the anticipated experience of working for you. Here's a gut check: Is your highest profile charitable community purpose worthy of being on your homepage, included within job descriptions, and shared in a first interview? If not, then maybe a reboot or upgrade to the effort is required.

Researchers and survey companies have been accumulating statistics for a number of years that prove the importance of volunteerism and a company's positive community impact on employee engagement, well-being, and desire to work for the company. Here is a sample:

According to Gallup, one in three job seekers say it is extremely important that their organization has a positive impact on communities. Also, employees who strongly agree that their organization makes a positive impact on people and the planet, compared with other workers, are

- 3.6 times more likely to recommend their organization as a place to work;
- 57 percent more likely to intend to not be looking for another job;
- 3.1 times more likely to be extremely satisfied with their organization as a place to work; and
- half as likely to be burned out often or always.[5]

According to Deloitte's 2017 Volunteerism Survey of working Americans,

- 77 percent of respondents said that company-sponsored volunteer activities are essential to employee well-being;
- 89 percent believe that companies who sponsor volunteer activities offer a better overall working environment than those who do not; and
- 75 percent said that volunteering was essential to their sense of well-being.[6]

Experiencing What Matters

The biggest purpose payoff comes when employees can see with their own eyes the difference they are making. I'm not against having mechanisms for charitable donations such as the United Way, Special Olympics, or American Red Cross, but the old idea of just giving money and hoping it will do good somewhere is not satisfying enough for people with high expectations for being directly involved. When Vynamic committed to refurbishing the after-school technology room for kids at the R. W. Brown Community Center in North Philadelphia, our entire team went there to put the paint on the walls and celebrate with the kids when the new space was reopened. We didn't just give money; we owned it. The community purpose that was amplified is still loud and clear in my mind when I think about the incredible experience of being part of Vynamic's culture and team. So whatever your charitable purpose, the creative question is this: "How might we provide a clear line of sight for people so they can experience the positive outcome directly?" You may already have a community purpose, but the answer to this question is the surefire way to amplifying meaning.

Charity and Brand

Selecting a charitable cause that reflects your brand is one of the most impactful decisions you can make. Doing so aligns your effort with the same things your customers care about. Chris and John Trogner, cofounders of Troëgs Independent Brewing of Hershey, Pennsylvania, have a history of keeping their corner of the world a better place. In addition to supporting more than 100 charities, the brewery purchases its ingredients, including barley and honey, from local suppliers.

During summer 2021, the brewery announced its latest commitment to its community. Proceeds from their Scratch #439, a crispy Kolsch-style brew, would be donated to the Susquehanna Area Mountain Bike Association to help create 30 miles of new mountain bike trails in Lykens, Pennsylvania. This is just the latest philanthropic endeavor to add to the company's long history of helping nonprofit organizations, small farms and businesses, and local charities.

Fallout from the COVID-19 pandemic resulted in the closing of schools and restaurants throughout the country, creating a serious threat to Pennsylvania's dairy farmers. In an attempt to help save these local dairy farms, Troëgs partnered with the Giant Company and Caputo Brothers Creamery and created a line of beer cheese. To date, the partnership has helped keep two dairy farms running and has the potential to save even more.[7]

Software company Salesforce's philanthropic efforts are ingrained in the company's culture. Each employee is given seven days off per year to volunteer, leading skill-based volunteer efforts that spearhead pro bono campaigns and engage in employee-inspired acts of giving. Additionally, Salesforce is part of the Pledge 1% campaign, which challenges organizations to pledge 1 percent of their time and resources to charitable causes.[8]

Our final example comes from a very special community-minded restaurant in Denver called the Same Café. They allow people to pay whatever they are able for their meal, or they can work for their food. Some patrons pay three times the perceived value.

THE COMMUNITY OF YOUR CULTURE

It's inspiring to have a culture that is so purpose driven that you're willing and able to invite customers into your community. Zappos has done this right from the beginning by listing one of their values on every delivery box. The boxes also proudly proclaim to the customer they are delivering "Happiness." The Zappos concept invites you to think about how well your community of culture is defined. If you can articulate your community concept on a box or a postcard, then you've defined it with powerful clarity. For example, I bought a pair of ski goggles directly from the superb brand Oakley. In the packing materials was a message printed on an oversized postcard on thick, high-quality stock. Here's what it said: "Welcome to the community. We are individuals compelled by the pursuit of self progression—IN SPORT AND IN LIFE. Lead life on your own terms and stay motivated to reach your potential." As a customer of Oakley, I have no doubt in my mind as to what they stand for as a community and what the culture is centered upon there. I was tempted to send them my resume.

Company cultures have the potential to become so deeply relationship centered that they become a community unto itself. One of the most devastating cultural consequences of the pandemic was the separation of people and their ability to bond as a community. Leaders who recognized the loss were desperate to reboot the connectivity that was so valuable in galvanizing their culture and the positive relationships that are nurtured through the organic community of working together. It's all the things that happen on their own behind the scenes, like having drinks, getting together on the weekend, exercising together, shopping together at lunch, and supporting each other in general with words of encouragement. It's about people having the prospect to make friends. If you're lacking that community within your culture as a result of being virtual or physically separated, then be proactive and create events and experiences that bring people together.

It is possible to intentionally flip the culture script on work-life balance to become a life-work blend. Dan Calista, the founder and CEO of the health care consulting firm Vynamic, was 100 percent committed to grow his company in a healthy way that leveraged the best of the culture he had carefully orchestrated as a start-up. Culture was the centerpiece of Vynamic's employee value proposition right from the beginning, but as the company rapidly grew, the challenge of crossing the tribal threshold—going beyond 50 team members—required even further focus. Dan hired me as team member number 53 to help with the articulation and integration of the Vynamic culture as a proactive strategy for future growth and success. The company's employees had already become an amazingly nimble and cohesive team committed to succeeding together. Bonding and friendships ran deep because people felt they were all a part of an exciting breakthrough experience with unlimited potential as a consulting powerhouse.

Many of the Vynamic team members had come from the typical "churn-and-burn" cultures of the consulting world. In contrast, they were exceedingly grateful to be within a healthy culture at Vynamic. But we had reached the tipping point of needing to hire many more people to join the team and realized it might be difficult to maintain the healthy close-knit tribal bond of community that was so fulfilling to people. We addressed the challenge by creating a series of monthly excursions after hours that tied to our values. We called them "Thrive LIVE" events and got super creative, using Center City Philadelphia as our playground. Thrive LIVE was funded enthusiastically by our CEO Dan Calista, and he fully participated with great joy. The team engaged in everything from wine and chocolate tastings, sports stadium tours, and flying airplanes. We were growing fast, but Dan still knew everyone's first name and, through rapport and shared experiences, made people feel special. The one rule we applied was no "forced fun." In other words, if someone didn't want to participate or felt uncomfortable physically, they could sit it out with zero pushback or peer pressure. Vynamic built community from the inside, and it paid off in a sustainable, healthy high-performance culture.

Building Community from the Inside

I've been impressed with the work of many other organizations to create community from the inside of their culture. The concept is fairly simple but requires some creativity to empower employees to connect on their special interests. Creating special interest groups (SIGs) can be a dynamic force that will shape an inclusive culture from the inside. The idea is not new. For example, softball and bowling teams have been around forever. Now, the possibilities are almost endless when you consider how diverse people's interests are. The good news is you don't have to come up with the group designations on your own. Give people the invitation to form together organically. Provide initial ideas on the variety of SIGs you're willing to support, and then let people self-select or create their own. New groups will form that you could never imagine. One of my clients had a murder mystery book group. It's a good example of how niche the groups can be. I've also seen a new mother's group, a rock-climbing group, and a gluten-free cooking group. Here are some categories and examples to show you how creative and diverse community can be for your employees.

- Sports/exercise: Beyond softball, bowling, and golf leagues, there is hiking, pickleball, Pilates, skiing, and mountain-biking groups.
- Food/cooking: Beyond having chef experts give classes, there are progressive dinners, in-office food competitions, restaurant review groups, and bar crawls.

- Hobbies/interests: Beyond gardening, fishing, and music groups, there is beer making, Netflix groups, drone flyer groups, entrepreneur groups, and antiquing.
- Healthy living: Beyond yoga and weight loss accountability groups, there is organic gardening, breathing classes, meditation, and spiritual growth groups.
- Travel/culture: Beyond group trips, there are second-language groups, motorcycle travel groups, camping, and music festivals.
- Volunteering: Beyond Habitat for Humanity, there is green restoration, mentoring for kids, community watch groups, elder assistance, prison mentoring, and disaster relief trips.

These are just a few of the many internal communities to consider.

Depending on the size of your organization, you may need a dedicated resource to communicate the opportunities and organize the logistics. Give people a chance to promote their good work and fun experiences on whatever communication platforms you use. Employees will recognize your commitment not only when you provide a budget but also, more important, when you participate. If you build it, they will come. Better yet, if they build it, they will own the experience. Remind yourself of the enormous payoff. When people get together to share their passion, talent, or knowledge, meaningful relationships germinate and engagement blooms.

A Word about Hobbies

The word *hobby* seems a bit dated, but once your employees start exploring their common interests and looking for internal groups to join, it becomes quickly clear that hobbies are thriving! Most important, as innovative thinker Seth Godin argues in a blog, hobbies today offer a chance for people to contribute to others and to the community. Hobbies are changing from self-focused activities such as woodworking or candlemaking, Godin says. "This might be the golden age for a new kind of hobby, one that's about community, leadership and producing public goods, not private ones."[9]

THE COMMUNITY AMPLIFIER PLAYBOOK

This playbook is intended to unlock an essential leadership competency: communicating to earn trust. Although this mind-set and skill would apply to nearly any challenge at work or in life, I'm sharing it here in the context of amplifying purpose through community. All the community amplifier ideas we reviewed require you to gain acceptance from your stakeholders for positive change to take place. Simply having the authority may not be enough to influence your ideas and get the buy-in and commitment from others on your team to execute the initiatives.

Amplifying purpose through community is a significant undertaking that can go south quickly if people at all levels aren't bought into the effort. Whether it's shaping your culture as a community, launching a community charity, or forming employee special interest groups (SIGs), your success depends on people trusting in the value of the effort, and you as the sponsor. As leaders, we earn trust at the highest level when people cognify our messaging through the lenses of its rational impact and its emotional impact.

I developed a communication template (figure 11.1) as a checklist to ensure your messaging gets through and is trusted by leveraging the rational and emotional connection. For any project launch, vital town hall meeting, conference with stakeholders, or interview with the press, the checklist should be used with discipline to ensure you communicate to maximize buy-in and commitment. There are three expanding building blocks of trust that shape beliefs about you as the leader and the issue at hand. Here are the beliefs you want to influence from the stakeholder's perspective in this sequence:

1. "I believe the leader and the team are competent. I am confident we can do what is being asked of us." *Note:* The "competence" building block of trust earns a rational belief that forms trust by answering the *what* items on the checklist.
2. "I believe the leader and this team are accountable. We will walk the talk and own the challenge." *Note:* "Accountability" is the building block that bolsters trust through rational and emotional beliefs answered by the *how* items on the checklist.
3. "I believe you're my advocate. This organization and the leader care for me. I believe this challenge is in my best interest." *Note:* Earning trust at the level of "advocacy" happens when your communication is received at both the rational and emotional level by others. Answer the *why* checklist items.

Communicate for TRUST Playbook

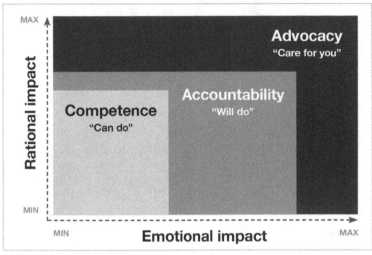

WHAT we plan to do (Prove Competence)

☐ What success looks-like (clear goal)

☐ Strategic reason for the direction

☐ What we have the capacity to do

☐ What strengths we are leveraging

☐ What I (the leader) will do specifically in the process

HOW we will execute (Exhibit Accountability)

☐ Clear expectations for communicating with each other

☐ The teams and people who own the specific outcomes

☐ How we will measure progress

☐ How I (the leader) will coach and communicate to get results

WHY it matters (Establish Advocacy)

☐ The ultimate purpose of the effort

☐ Acknowledge the sacrifice and hard work people will experience

☐ How I (the leader) will support teams and people to be successful

☐ Why it matters to me (the leader)

Figure 11.1 Communicate for trust playbook.

12

The World Society Amplifier

I think people get satisfaction from living for a cause that's greater than themselves. They want to leave an imprint.

—Dan Pink, author of *Drive*

Never before has there been a greater desire for employees to benefit world society through their work. This movement has been turbocharged by the green crusade and by millennials and Generation Z themselves, who have grown up with a renewed sense of idealism when it comes to serving a greater purpose. Both millennials and Gen Z are generations that have witnessed their baby boomer grandparents and Generation X parents toil for the materialistic brass ring all their lives. They've often seen those same parents and grandparents disheartened with the lack of return on true happiness upon arriving in the so-called upper echelon. These new generations seem very determined to avoid falling into the same trap and are more keenly focused on doing something that really matters for others. They are actively seeking meaning through their work. The world society amplifier has become significant enough for them, and every generation, to stand tall and make a bold and obvious statement about its importance.

The following are key questions people ask themselves:

- Does the work I do inevitably benefit people to live better lives?
- Does this company leave the world in a better condition than if it were not here?

- Am I leaving a positive mark, doing my share, and creating a better world for others?
- Does the work we do add to the joy, peace, or benefit of humankind?
- Does this company make the world a better place?

Categorically, only a few businesses actually have a direct and overt connection to benefiting world society through the natural outcome of their work. Some examples would be companies that create vaccines, climate change solutions, life-saving drugs, or technological breakthroughs that allow millions to participate within the world community. For everyone else, the effort must be intentional—a deliberate decision.

Companies like Patagonia with their environmental focus, Newman's Own with their charitable and sustainable donations, and TOMS shoes with their amazing "One for One" concept have made meaning an integral part of their brand. Each of them recruits and retains a highly engaged workforce with a compelling and noble cause that plays a central role in their brand promise and is the very heart of their purpose.

I can understand if you're thinking this amplifier maybe out of reach for you because of the inherent nature of your work or your company's specific industry, which may seem too remote to benefit world society. I get that, yet there are some great opportunities revealed by thinking more broadly about what your employees are capable of doing. You might need to go beyond the limited nature of your business. This chapter will share examples with you as creative fuel to spark ideas you can implement.

One of the most stunning examples to stretch our imagination is TOMS shoes. TOMS lives by the motto, "We're in business to help improve lives," and for every new pair of TOMS shoes purchased, its One for One initiative donates a new pair of shoes to a child in need. Under the same initiative, the newly launched TOMS eyewear division donates a pair of eyeglasses for every new pair purchased, helping to restore sight to people in need around the world. Not only is One for One a powerful business model, but it's also a purpose that carries intrinsic meaning for all involved. It amplifies so much meaning that customers stay loyal to the brand, employees rally around the ideal, and new hires line up to be a part of this kindhearted movement. TOMS understands what is important to employees. And they connect the dots for employees because they know that employees are the key to their success. TOMS allows them to see the full picture by taking their employees to Argentina and South Africa to give new shoes to children in need. For TOMS employees, it's not just a job; it's a purpose with meaning.[1] Again, if your organization does not have a direct connection, you can still turn on this amplifier of meaning by considering creative possibilities. In this case, what might you "give back" each time someone purchases your products or services?

THE POWER OF ONE PERSON

> The greatest legacy of Live Aid for me personally, is the example of how Bob Geldof's leadership demonstrated the power of the individual. How the voice and action of just one person could start a movement that could make a difference.
>
> —Live Aid production manager Andy Zweck[2]

After seeing a BBC News report on the famine in Ethiopia in the 1980s, Bob Geldof, at the time the lead singer of the Boomtown Rats, decided that something had to be done. With images of the starving children surely burned into his brain, Geldof quickly organized the supergroup Band Aid to record a song to raise money to fight the famine. Band Aid consisted mainly of some of the biggest British and Irish stars at the time, including such names as Bono, Phil Collins, and George Michael. Geldof's only criteria for selecting members for his supergroup were how famous they were, and if they were willing to give their time for free.

Geldof and Band Aid were given only one day to record their song. On December 3, 1984, "Do They Know It's Christmas?" was released to the public. The single was able to raise £8 million within 12 months of release, with all the money going toward famine relief.

That wasn't enough for Geldof. On July 13, 1985, Live Aid was held. Hosted simultaneously at Wembley Stadium in London and John F. Kennedy Stadium in Philadelphia, it broadcast 16 hours of rock music to more than 1.6 billion people around the globe. Through the combined powers of the 75 groups playing, and Geldof allegedly yelling, "Give us your f-ing money!" to the crowd, Live Aid was successful in raising £150 million for famine relief.

What can be learned from Bob Geldof is that it only takes the power of one person determined to make a change to start a movement.

DECLARE A PURPOSE

Aaron Hurst, the founder of Imperative, recommended in his epic book *The Purpose Economy* that college students should declare a "Purpose" instead of a

"Major."[3] I know for myself, declaring a major put a box around what I was capable of doing initially after graduation. Imagine the expanded choices and possibilities that would have unfolded if we had contemplated our purpose first and foremost at that critical tipping point in our lives. It's never too late to lock into another purpose path heading in the direction for what we truly care for now.

PLEDGE TO A PURPOSE

Michael and Amy Port, world-renowned performance coaches and co-founders of Heroic Public Speaking, hold a very unique event in Philadelphia each year called Heroic Public Speaking LIVE. It's a highly energized deep dive into taking your speaking or teaching ability to a whole new level. They've created a purpose-driven experience that taps into a speaker's deepest reservoir of intrinsic motivation. Here's one of the steps they take to gain commitment and amplify meaning: They created a pledge that identifies the key behaviors to act upon at the event (and as a professional speaker); plus, it also acknowledges the impact speakers make through their profession. As a ritual beginning and ending each day of the three-day training, hundreds of passionate speakers in training stand up together to recite the Heroic Public Speaking LIVE pledge:

> I will take chances
> Try new things
> Make big choices
> And crush my fears.
> YES! And . . .
> I will listen to faculty
> Won't poke holes
> Do more together
> Than we can alone.
> YES! And . . .
> I'll be a performer
> Not a critic
> And I'll save the world one speech at a time.
> YES! And . . .

Most professional speakers believe with great confidence their personal platform can "save the world" in some way. If you ask a speaker about their platform, you can almost guarantee that you'll see this sentiment in their eyes as they answer your question. They consistently exude a personal pride or ownership for their subject. The pledge tapped into this underlying emotion because we believe that about ourselves and our platform. That's a brilliant amplifier of meaning!

It's universal that speakers are passionate for their platform—but not just in a vacuum. I'm convinced they are passionate for their platform because they have experienced the positive change they can enact upon others. The change they've witnessed is so compelling that it becomes an overarching purpose in most speakers' lives. For the record, I've never met a successful speaker who lacked an authentic passion for enlightening others. I can speak to this first-hand. It's why I personally love what I do so much. The day I lose that feeling is the day I'll do my final mic drop.

Can you elicit the same feeling of purpose and passion in your employees? Have you made the connection on how their work has the potential to change the world? Finding the right pledge for your company's employees may tap into their inner emotions and desires to do something important, just as the Heroic Public Speaking Pledge does for the speakers who recite it.

Bringing the Experience of Volunteering to Work

In the "Community Amplifier" chapter (chapter 11), we talked about volunteering and the impact it has on employees and the local community, but volunteering can be further magnified when it impacts world society. Dr. Travis Bradberry, author of *Emotional Intelligence*, says, "Volunteering is a powerful experience that feels good and expands your network at the same time."[4] I have found this to be true in all my volunteering experiences. I am in total agreement with Travis's question, "Have you ever met anyone who made volunteering a priority and wasn't changed for the better by the experience? Neither have I."[5]

We know that volunteering and giving back has many benefits to multiple stakeholders. Volunteering not only helps the larger society, it helps people feel they are part of something bigger than themselves. We know that we often can't fulfill our altruistic needs or make the time to volunteer outside of our busy work schedules and family. So what if we bring the experience of volunteering through work itself with the goal of giving employees the chance to impact the greater good of world society?

HOW TO DO WELL BY DOING GOOD

> Profit for a company is like oxygen for a person. If you don't have enough
> of it, you're out of the game. But if you think your life is about breathing,
> you're really missing something.
>
> —Peter Drucker

Today's curious, creative, compassionate, confident business leaders are imagining how they might create *shared value*—creating monetary value for the business while creating societal value by addressing the *real* needs of people and communities. In doing so, they amplify the meaning of work by creating a return on *energy*.

Lara Heacock and Kelly Stewart cohost the *Doing (Good) Business* podcast. They talk with people in business who have amplified meaning while finding that doing good business is possible, profitable, and packed with opportunities.

Let's consider just two examples from the many people they've talked with—one from the real estate investment world and one from an industry that dates to the 15th century.[6]

Everyday people helping everyday people stay in their homes. This is Automation Finance's mission. They have a proven track record of saving homeowners from foreclosures. They buy distressed debt at a discount, work with the borrower to get them back on track, and pay their investors up to 8 percent return. In a world where people shouldn't have to choose between paying their medical bills and keeping their homes, Automation Finance has "developed workflows to maximize the predictability of outcomes" (that sounds very business-y, doesn't it?) and uses that knowledge to work with families to help them avoid foreclosure (that's addressing a very real need, isn't it?).

Sheets & Giggles loves sleep and is making bed sheets while not sacrificing quality for sustainability—or vice versa. Now, take a deep breath and marvel at what they've created:

1. Their sheets are made from eucalyptus lyocell (a renewable natural resource).
2. They plant trees for every customer.
3. They give back to their local community in Colorado.
4. They donate to help save koalas harmed by wildfires in Australia.
5. They've provided tens of thousands of dollars in cash and bedding to COVID-19 relief efforts in Colorado.

They also encourage others to "do good" by giving a 10 percent discount for customers for who provide picture proof of donating their old sheets.

And their very funny style is sure to put a smile on your face.

What are the specific, actionable ideas from their stories you can use to create shared value and, in doing so, amplify meaning at work?

Let's take a few ideas Kelly Stewart uses in shifting the tone and direction of strategic conversations to help her clients achieve more of what they want while working toward a triple bottom line of people, planet, and profit.

1. Start thinking like a start-up. Explore *what might be* with all the people essential to your success and keep asking, "How good could it get?"
2. Make the invisible visible by asking generative questions that inspire divergent thinking. (Hint: They're questions for which you do not already have the answer.)
3. Recall high-point experiences and how they reflect the organization's strengths and duplicate those proven track records of success.
4. Identify leading metrics that indicate you're on the right path. The error in measuring lagging indicators is metaphorically like managing through a rear-view mirror. You miss the opportunities in front of you that allow for course correction.

WHY SHOULD BUSINESSES CARE ABOUT WORLD SOCIETY?

One word: reputation.

Joan Jett may not give a damn about a bad reputation; in fact, that's the title of one of her albums. We don't "live in the past; it's a new generation," she sings in her song "Do You Wanna Touch Me (Oh Yeah)."[7] That said, corporations compete in the public eye as they face scrutiny under the BuzzFeed limelight of corporate social responsibility (CSR). There is no safe place to hide from the far reaches of viral news, crowdsourcing opinions, or global report indexes that measure, compare, and disclose corporate environmental, social, and governance insights.

Walmart is a prime example of how companies and leadership can use CSR to not just uplift a poor reputation and brand but also increase engagement and bring people together over a common cause. Back in 2012, Dr. Ante Glavas, who holds a PhD in organizational behavior, said: "At Walmart, a company widely criticized for its work conditions, CSR became the main source of employee engagement." Since the early to mid-2000s, the height of Walmart's aggressive anti-union tactics, they have made drastic changes to their public image by implementing CSR. To some degree, Walmart has changed the media narrative by going green and addressing abuses and major risks to the dignity of workers in their supply chain.[8] According to Kate Patrick, a lead editor at *Industry Dive,* "the company has invested $100 million in programs to help workers advance their careers in retail, and is funding training for one million farmers at the supplier level." Patrick also says that Walmart is actively seeking to address problems including human trafficking and unfair labor practices within the supply chain.[9]

WHAT DOES CSR MEAN TO EMPLOYEES?

We talked about how corporate social responsibility can improve a company's brand and reputation. And I also mentioned that it increases employee engagement—but how exactly? What's in it for employees? In a nutshell, it happens when corporations and management (starting from the top down) embrace CSR, according to Dr. Glavas and CSR researcher Dr. David Jones. Jones says "employees find greater meaningfulness and values congruence at work. Specifically, CSR allows for companies to go beyond formal values statements that tend to be words on paper to actually living out these values. This in turn sends signals to employees about the values of the company. . . . Moreover, CSR can also be a pathway for finding greater meaningfulness at work."[10]

What about being a conservative, buttoned-up vertical industry like the financial sector? Vanguard is also doing some amazing things for world society. They're attracting millennial employees and customers alike by offering two low-cost, socially responsible, exchange-traded funds or ESG (environmental, social, and governance) funds. Kiplinger, a publisher of business forecasts and personal finance advice, honed in on Vanguard funds "that blend a desire to do good with exceptional investment results." Using sustainability ratings from Morningstar, Kiplinger reports, "These funds invest only in companies that earn high marks on green, social and workplace issues, including how mindful the firm is of its environmental impact, whether it treats employees, customers and suppliers well, and whether it follows policies that align the interests of management and shareholders."[11] Vanguard's crewmembers—that is, their employees—seem to feel pretty good about their alleged stodgy and traditional company doing something hip and progressive in this realm.

Vanguard is not only committed to socially responsible funds but also an industry leader in the surrounding communities and in the world society. They also offer retirement plans, work-life programs, and employee charitable giving to their favorite causes that has a meaningful impact on their crewmembers and families throughout the world, including North America, Europe, Australia, and Asia.

Vanguard is what I consider a positive business in terms of a quadruple bottom line (QBL) of

Purpose: leadership, culture, governance
People: employees, community, society
Planet: Earth-friendly responsible decisions
Prosperity: profitably reinvesting in purpose

Vanguard is doing something that is wildly and wonderfully different. It creates *real* value for *others* by creating *meaning* for *all* of the people essential to the company's success, not only the people who profit from it.

What Does It Mean to Be a Positive Business?

Creating meaning for employees, clients, suppliers, partners, and other stakeholders is a multifaceted endeavor. At the highest level, it involves connecting people with the purpose at the heart of your business. Leaders who answer the *why* question amplify meaning in ways that engage people. They are building a culture that attracts and retains top talent positioned to deliver on a brand promise that is highly compelling. High-performance organizations are in a war for talent and looking for a competitive advantage. Making the commitment to be purpose driven via the world society amplifier is a differentiator for your employment brand and all your stakeholders.

Let's take Heinz, for example. Heinz ketchup is an all-time favorite staple in almost every American home, and it is one of the most prolific brands of all time. So how does a food-processing company connect meaning to its thousands of manufacturing employees grinding away in its factories? For starters, they introduced the "plant bottle." You might have heard of the slogan "Red Goes Green," which accompanied the rollout of what was actually the first recyclable bottle to hit store shelves.

This initiative tells employees that their company cares about world society, but on its own, a recyclable bottle does little to connect employees on an emotional level.

One of the real drivers of purpose and meaning at Heinz is in the way they honor their employees. Even the farmers and tomato pickers realize the importance and ascribe meaning to their jobs. "Our team carefully selects Heinz tomatoes for color and quality, so only the best tomatoes make it into our ketchup."[12] Wow! Now that's some strong attribution for a job that might be perceived as monotonous without the direct knowledge that every tomato counts! Even more attractive than Heinz's high standards and quality product is their environmental initiatives. They rally their employees around environmental protection, the sharing of innovative ideas and best practices, building communities, and other initiatives designed to improve nutrition and education. For instance, they are dedicated to fighting the hunger epidemic and saving lives, and they distribute their micronutrient powder to regions where people suffer from undernourishment.

The point is, employees are proud of their jobs at Heinz, they experience a sense of giving back that is much like that of volunteering, and it reflects in the work they do. Heinz's "Grown Not Made" is not just a slogan to the company and its employees; for them it's a way of life.

I wanted to quickly mention the emotional connection that Heinz makes with its employees and its philanthropic mission. Gallup talks about turning customers into true believers. They define customer engagement as the emotional connection between your customers and your company. But you and I know emotional connections and customer satisfaction begins with engaged employees who enjoy serving customers and consequently gain customer excellence. So, in reality, if your employees aren't "true believers" of your company, the company risks its survival.

WORLD SOCIETY AMPLIFIER PLAYBOOK: CREATING A PURPOSEFUL EMPLOYEE VALUE PROPOSITION

Developing a strong employee value proposition (EVP) is a key element of any successful recruiting and retention effort. Your EVP should have direct alignment with your consumer brand promise and borrow the same tone and language used to articulate your leading principles. An EVP represents a focused expression describing the total work experience you provide to your employees.

If done well, an EVP quickly tells the story as to *why* people want to come work here. It helps to both qualify and disqualify potential recruits as they search for companies that match up to their desired culture. The EVP can spark the immediate motivation to apply if it's inspiring and connected to the recruit's personal values. It is especially essential to communicate your commitment to benefit world society if you are engaged in doing so. More and more people are looking for cultures that are proud enough of their efforts to state it up front in the recruiting process.

Here are some examples of how organizations express portions of their EVP:

Shopify: "We're Shopify. Our mission is to make commerce better for everyone—but we're not the workplace for everyone. We thrive on change, operate on trust, and leverage the diverse perspectives of people on our team in everything we do. We solve problems at a rapid pace. In short, we get shit done."[13]

Starbucks: "Connect to Something Bigger. Connecting with each other, with our customers and the communities we are a part of, fosters a deep sense of purpose at Starbucks. We believe we can all become a part of something bigger and inspire positive change in the world around us. That's why we go out to do community service as a team throughout the year, partnering up with organizations to revitalize and enhance the neighborhoods we serve."[14]

Yelp: "We work hard, throw Nerf darts even harder, and have a whole lot of fun."[15]

EVP Creation Template

Use these fill-in-the-blank statements that follow to craft your responses. Review what's most aligned to your consumer brand and your leading principles. Leverage the aligned responses as the foundation of your EVP story. Create your EVP story narrative and leverage it throughout every touchpoint in the recruiting process. Train your interviewers on how to tell the story using examples that bring it to life and make it authentic.

You can achieve _____ by working here.

We give back to make the world a better place by _____

_____.

We uplift and support our community by _____

_____.

Customers are inspirational to us because _____

_____.

Our company has a bright future because we believe _____
_____.

When you work on a team here, the experience is like _____
_____.

We support each other as unique, diverse individuals by _____
_____.

We want our team members to experience the satisfaction of _____
_____ by working here.

You can only experience _____ by working here.

Our culture is like _____
_____.

As a culture, we thrive on _____
_____.

We hope you join our organization because _____
_____.

13

The Spirituality Amplifier

> Management deals with people, their values, their growth and development—and this makes it a humanity. So does its concern with, and impact on, social structure and the community. Indeed . . . management is deeply involved in spiritual concerns—the nature of man, good and evil.
>
> —Peter Drucker, *The New Realities*

Although it may seem out of bounds these days to consider the role of spirituality at work, those who dismiss it are simply not facing an important truth. Spirituality does matter greatly for many people to the extent it is their ultimate amplifier of meaning. Spirituality can be not only an amplifier for work but also for people's whole lives. People who are inspired spiritually do not want to check their soul at the door at work and pick it up later as they exit to go home. It's just not something that can easily be separated within their conscience. For them—and I'm one of them—the experience of work must harmonize with what they believe to be of the ultimate importance. Even if work is not a person's primary amplifier of spirituality, it should at least provide a sense of acceptability that doesn't rub against the morals of their faith.

Back in the golden age of TV advertising, there was a cute and ingenious TV commercial for Hebrew National kosher-certified hot dogs. The commercial called out the list of quality regulations that Uncle Sam (via the U.S. Department of Agriculture) applied to the production of hot dogs. But Hebrew National found a clever way to tell the consumer they go well beyond the baseline of government rules. Here's what they said: "We answer to a higher authority." It was a *wow* that perfectly communicated their own extra measures of quality and integrity. What a great way to get across their brand message as differentiator.

In a similar way, people who have spirituality as a powerful amplifier of meaning in many ways answer to a higher authority that goes far beyond you as their boss. You may be their boss, but you're not their only boss.

I've heard little kids say to each other, "You're not the boss of me!" It's such an in-your-face way of saying, "Buzz off, and quit trying to tell me what to do." We need to be more aware that if our actions or approach as the boss are in violation of someone's deeply held moral beliefs, then they will likely default to "You're not the boss of me." This will become their attitude toward us. We don't need to be "walking on eggshells" with this factor, however. Here's the saving grace: If our actions are tethered to respect, then the good will of our intent should trump any misunderstandings in the long term. I always want to give people the benefit of the doubt and assume positive intent. I would expect them to reciprocate.

The following are key questions people ask themselves:

- Is my work aligned to my highest sense of ideals?
- Does my work help me live out my life's destiny or higher calling?
- Is the work I'm doing in harmony with my conscience on what is right and wrong?
- Is my work at this organization in harmony with what I believe about my higher purpose in life?

THE COMMON GROUND OF LOVE

> Love is the answer. What is the question?
> —Ken Blanchard, author of *The One Minute Manager*

I acknowledge there are significant differences and contentions in spiritual beliefs that have caused wars and atrocities throughout the woeful history of humankind. That's obviously one of the reasons most thought leaders don't approach the subject at all. I intend, however, to explore the spiritual amplifier in a positive way, and I want to be inclusive to all. I believe it's far more useful to find the high ground together—the common ground that all major beliefs, religions, and denominations are anchored upon: love.

I will openly share with you some of the things I believe about love and our spirit. If I held back, then my words would be a nonauthentic perspective that violates one of my own personal values. Instead of being dogmatic, my intent is to do the best job possible denoting the common ground we all value. I'll follow the advice of the Beatles for this amplifier of purpose: "All you need is love. Love is all you need."

I share the view that our universal purpose is *to love and be loved.* Take a moment to reflect on whether that is true for you. Are you making progress on this purpose? How might that change the meaning you feel for life if love was even more evident and vivid in your relationships? How might that impact the people you love and potentially change their lives?

The English term *love* is better expressed by the romantic Greek language. The Greeks articulated *love* using four terms to describe its nature and origin. Let's review them for the purpose of awareness and relevance to spirituality.

1. *Eros:* A physical or sexual love. It's the root word for *eroticism.*
2. *Storge:* A love for family. It's a natural or instinctual affection, such as a mother for her child.
3. *Philos:* A warm affection or friendship love. Philos is the root word for Philadelphia, "the city of brotherly love."
4. *Agapē:* The sacrificial and unconditional love of God. Agape is a transcendent love. When humans express agape, it is the highest form of applied empathy and selflessness. In a sense, it is the willingness to give oneself away to another with no preconditions.

Here's an additional description of the attributes of love by the Apostle Paul from the Bible. Love is often referred to as the fruit of the spirit.

> Love is patient, love is kind. It does not envy, it does not boast, it is not proud. It does not dishonor others, it is not self-seeking, it is not easily angered, it keeps no record of wrongs.
>
> Love does not delight in evil but rejoices with the truth. It always protects, always trusts, always hopes, always perseveres. Love never fails. (1 Corinthians 13:3–8)

Just for a moment imagine these attributes as competencies for leadership. It describes the type of person who would be a dream to work for or work with. I want to be that person. If these attributes of love are the fruit of the spirit, then it means spirituality in the context of business is completely relevant and highly desired. Mary Baker Eddy, author of *Science and Health*, says, "To love and to be loved, one must do good to others. The inevitable condition whereby to become blessed, is to bless others."

Lifting Others Up

The only way to be loved is to be and to appear lovely, to possess and display kindness, benevolence, tenderness, to be free from selfishness and to be alive to the welfare of others.

—John Jay, Founding Father and president of the Continental Congress

There is more hunger for love and appreciation in this world than bread.

—Mother Teresa, Roman Catholic Religious Sister and missionary

How is it possible for others to feel unconditional love from us? It starts by simply raising their spirit. Whether you view their "spirit" simply as a "mood," or something far greater on a cosmic scale, it doesn't matter. Just do it. We can't go wrong here. Raising someone's spirit with a positive, uplifting, and affirming expression is an act of love. Even for just a moment, we have the capacity to help others feel unconditional acceptance and belonging with the simplest of choices. It's the choice to step across the invisible line that separates our "all about me" thinking from the empathetic "all about you" thinking.

It comes down to a willingness to give ourselves away for the sake of the other person. Conduct an inventory of the people in your life who do that for you. Now, do an inventory of the people for whom you're willing to do the same. The power and strength of our own spirituality amplifier is in direct proportion to the love you're willing to give and the priceless people from whom you receive it. For example, I've been remarkably blessed with a dear friend, Doug Thompson, who has an unshakable faith. Every major step of the way in my life, he willingly checks in with me to ask how he can support me. His prayers for me and my family encourage my spirit to preserve through challenges large and small. He helps me recognize my ultimate anchoring point for decision-making. It's my faith that gives me clarity of perspective. Although it's not his motivation at all, I'm certain Doug would say he's the one who's uplifted as a result of giving himself away.

Let's consider how we can begin to make a more conscious decision that raises the spirit of others. It may come from the habit of making a very simple inquiry, such as, "Please let me know how I might encourage and support you to live out your purpose." Imagine the response we'd get from others. The ensuing conversation may become the breakthrough in your relationship that forever bonds you together.

If that feels too forward or overt, then simply go to your empathetic kindness mode. The situational opportunities to raise someone's spirit will organically reveal themselves. You may have no idea of the far-reaching impact just one kind comment will have upon someone. For example, I started the journey to become a master level gardener because of one compliment. My wife and I were getting ready to sell our first home, a small house on a very small property. Our real estate agent, Janet Colantonio, was visiting to strategize the selling process. Janet seemed delighted by the colorful flowerbed I had planted along the side of our driveway. She told me how nice it looked and that a buyer would value the love I had put into the effort. Then, she said something I'll never forget. "I can't wait to see what you do at your new house." Mic drop! She just laid down a challenge that changed everything for me. Just one comment elevated my spirit and gave me a new purpose and accompanying vision. I saw how much the simple flowerbed thrilled her.

It motivated me to advance my fledgling passion for gardening into something meaningful. I wanted to go from a weekend novice to a highly skilled horticulturalist. I studied at Longwood Gardens where I earned two certificates in ornamental horticulture. Now I'm fully living out the satisfaction that comes from gardening and have developed a deeper appreciation for creation. I use it as my own form of "give back" by sharing my knowledge and passion with kids and adults to get them into gardening. Delighting people with a walk through my gardens is one of my greatest joys in life. Gardening went from a transactional purpose to a transcendent one for me. Looking back, it was one lovingly kind compliment that planted the seed.

FREEING THE SPIRIT

Here are two reflective questions to amplify the universal purpose:

- What is the one thing you might do that, having done it, would free your spirit?
- What is the one thing you might do that, having done it, would free someone else's spirit?

Platinum Rule at Work

How do you allow people to feel their work is in harmony with their highest ideals? This can be a deal breaker that turns off the spiritual amplifier. It's such a challenge because everyone comes prewired with a conscience that delineates what is right or wrong. Integrity is nonnegotiable for people seeking harmony. We can find common ground for integrity by following a rule that applies to all. Just as love is core to every major religion, a version of "the golden rule" is also universally embraced. The more appropriate version applied to business is called "the platinum rule." *Treat others the way they want to be treated.*

Whatever your business makes, services, or sells matters little compared to whether your company is living up to the platinum rule. It provides a valuable gut check to assess the way you treat customers and employees. If people sense there is a disconnect, it will turn off their spiritual amplifier. On the other hand, if people feel they can say with conviction that the organization does the right thing by people, for the right reason, then this amplifier projects a positive beam that aligns a person's spirituality to the integrity of the organization.

Spirituality serves as the "North Star" for many people. It provides a confident direction that weathers every storm. We need that more than ever in our lives to survive the relentless pace of change that is dragging us into the unfamiliar. At the same time, we've also experienced the demise of institutions as dependable sources of truth. For example, the once reliable media is all but gone as an unbiased filter. As a result, we've lost an important sense of security and confidence that used to come from trusted moral authorities.

Everyone needs a solid foundation to anchor their beliefs. It seems many people are now insecure with no "North Star" of purpose in their life. The great resignation triggered by the COVID-19 pandemic is emblematic of people seeking to fill the void. Let's look at it as an opportunity. If we create and uphold high integrity businesses with healthy, respectful cultures, then we provide the desperately needed anchoring point for people. The search for meaning and satisfaction at work will be found within environments that embrace the platinum rule. Those leaders and those organizations will be the heroes that amplify purpose at a time when it is needed the most.

THE SPIRIT OF RESPECT

> Love goes very far beyond the physical person of the beloved. It finds its deepest meaning in its spiritual being, his inner self. Whether or not he is actually present, whether or not he is still alive at all, ceases somehow to be of importance.
>
> —Viktor Frankl

What is the most universal value in business? In other words, what is the most immutable, indispensable, must-have value that applies across the board to every organization? I can answer that question without a doubt. It is *respect*.

Respect is won or lost in the trenches. It happens one conversation at a time.

At the very core of the spirituality amplifier is respect. At the very least, a person must feel respected for having a belief that is personal, even if it differs from yours philosophically. Respect is different than "buy-in." Where people sometimes seem to get hung up on this one is not understanding that you must respect the person, even if you don't buy in to their belief, or lack of belief. None of this suggests that people need to label themselves, or in any way become "approved." Generally speaking, people aren't overtly asking others to believe the same thing as they do; however, people do demand the respect to be themselves without oppression or censure. If the work environment is rich with respect, then the amplifier of spirituality can play in rich, clear harmony.

Why is respect so sought after yet a struggle to attain? People don't intend to come to work to be disrespectful or to be disrespected. What ends up happening is that too many people stop seeing their own accountability for the impact they have on others. The people who are the respect catalysts in a culture have developed a higher level of emotional intelligence (EQ). Their awareness allows them to make smart choices in crucial relationships to grow respect. Here are the three quickest ways to instantly demonstrate respect:

1. **Ask, "How might we . . . ?"** Asking for an opinion is a creative and respectful act. Questions are the great engager of mind and spirit in ways that amplify the meaning of work and your relationship.
2. **Say, "I'm sorry . . ."** What do you need to repair in your relationship? Be the person who's willing to make the first move to show how much you care.
3. **Tell, "Here's what I'm working on, and why it matters . . ."** If you're the boss, make this a daily habit. You'll give people a powerful sense of inclusion—a key to feeling respected.

Did you ever consider the irony of the term *paying last respects*? Isn't it revealing that the last thing you do for a person after they have passed away is to "pay them respects"? It's obviously baked into our DNA as human beings and reflected in our world culture as a value. Respect is so important; we give respect even in death. Memorializing people is a vital attribute of our culture that honors the purpose of the life that has been lost. Doing so challenges us to pick up the torch and do well by them in the way we live our lives going forward. We receive meaning through the honored person and the purpose they represented.

Here's a challenge to us all. Why not do a better job of giving respect to people while they are alive, so they can receive their "payment" now? I'm willing to start, one conversation at a time. Let's give the roses *now*.

THE PURPOSE OF YOUR GIFT

I watched a stunning interview on TV during the pandemic that left me teary eyed with admiration. A reporter was speaking with a Chicago schoolteacher named Joe Ocol. He was petitioning the school to teach on site instead of forced remote learning. Even though he was facing life-threatening cancer, Ocol said, "I believe my role should be in the classroom with my students. I feel, despite my battling cancer, I still have a role to play. Right now, I just want to make my life relevant somehow—the thought that I can still be of service to my students and can touch their lives and make a difference in their lives."[1]

Joe Ocol had a gift, and he wanted to use that gift in a profound way that mattered. All of us feel that same tug to some degree. The concept of having a gift is another piece of common ground most every faith embraces. Our spiritual purpose is driven by acting upon the gifts we've been given. When we use our gifts, it gives us the fulfillment and meaning that we are repaying the giver. If we don't know our gift, or put it to use, then we get frustrated and feel trapped by our circumstances.

During the pandemic, a lot of us felt desperate to use our gifts. It explains why the shutdown fueled the search for meaning and triggered the great resignation. People scrambled to seek out the new job, entrepreneurism, side hustles, family time, and deep hobby pursuits. People mindful of their spirit perhaps heard an even louder prompting that "we have these gifts; we *must* use them." People became creative in finding ways to use their gifts. For many, it may have felt like an obligation of self-efficacy, but also coming from a place of gratitude. The pandemic also caused people to stop and look around at how blessed they were, while empathizing with others. I was reminded of this perspective: We don't have to look very far to find someone who is better off than us. We only have to look half as far to find someone less fortunate.

What could be more fulfilling than honoring the gifts from God, or whatever higher power you believe in, by acting upon your spiritually driven superpowers? I believe it's fair to say that reaching for your potential by using the strengths of your gifts at work is an approachable way for people to connect work to their faith. It then becomes another amplifier of purpose that simply gives people a sense that what they do matters to their higher authority.

THE EMOTIONAL INTELLIGENCE OF SPIRITUALITY

Even though we may think of emotional intelligence as mostly a business competency, it is completely applicable to our spirituality. At the core, EQ is about self-awareness and our ability to make good choices. Here's the direct connection I see. Our reading, listening, learning, and praying to whom we follow spiritually shine a light of awareness on our current state. It tells us how we're living our lives in accordance with the teaching of our faith. The light of awareness almost always reveals a better choice or decision to be made about the way we are living our lives. It's not a surprise that the path to salvation, enlightenment, or a higher order requires you to make a choice. This is a universal truth embraced by every major denomination or recognized religion. So, it can be said with confidence that high emotional intelligence is principally relevant to our spiritual fulfillment because awareness gives us choices.

I witnessed firsthand how prison causes inmates to consider their choices. Several years ago, I began volunteering through my church to teach a weekly Bible study at the Chester County Prison in West Chester, Pennsylvania. I confess, this is literally the last thing I wanted to do, and I was enormously afraid for what I'd experience there on top of the pressure of presenting the good news to them. Added to this apprehension was an extra challenge: I'd be presenting in English and would have a Spanish interpreter since a large percentage of the inmates only knew Spanish. Talk about a stretch of my zone of comfort.

After my first few experiences at the prison, I began to notice something remarkable about the men. All of them voluntarily came to the study. Some came just to kill time, but others were exceedingly grateful and hungry to learn and to have fellowship with me, Yone (my interpreter), and other like-minded inmates. Even in the midst of confinement they possessed dignity as a purpose and humility as their character virtue. Many would come up to us before being taken back to their cell blocks and express their belief that God had put them into prison for a reason. They viewed it as their wake-up call that turned their life around and potentially saved it. The men technically had their freedom taken away but found something that was even more freeing and profound.

I watched how they responded to Yone and me. Being there and treating them as equals, under the same God, we showed them respect and gave them the dignity they needed to feel they still mattered as men. I was humbled and forever changed by the experience of seeing men with a commitment to spiritual purpose within the dreaded circumstance of being in prison. Viktor Frankl, who suffered and survived Auschwitz to grace us with *Man's Search for*

Meaning, depicted this phenomenon so poignantly: "The one thing you can't take away from me is the way I choose to respond to what you do to me. The last of one's freedoms is to choose one's attitude in any given circumstance."[2] The men I encountered at the Chester County Prison made the choice to turn bad into good for their lives and the families they would be reunited with.

YOU GO FIRST

How do we begin to have conversations on spiritual purpose with people at work? It may feel as intimidating as teaching in the prison was for me. If you have built a solid foundation of trust and rapport, then be willing to share your personal connection to how you ultimately desire to live out your spiritual calling or purpose. It's totally fair to share what is working in your life. Also, consider including what is incongruent or a struggle between your spiritual purpose and the work you're doing. I didn't "preach" to the men in prison. They simply connected to Yone and me because we shared of ourselves openly—the good, the bad, and ugly. It's always a strong testament of vulnerability to acknowledge your battles. But be certain to include what you intend to do about it as a result. Doing so turns the weakness of vulnerability into a strength of character that gains trust.

This is a bonus. Maybe they can help amplify meaning back to you by acknowledging the impact you're having on people, the positive example you're setting, or some other hidden nugget of gold that opens up your eyes as how you're living out your spiritual purpose in ways you were unaware.

I recently had a trusted colleague call out that I must have a strong moral compass. I hadn't thought of it that way and didn't realize my decision-making process was that apparent. It was a positive confirmation to me that I was attempting to do the right thing, and that she noticed. When others feel they are helping you in this regard, then by default, they will increase their own sense of meaning.

It's important that conversations on spirituality are simply centered on the expectation of building rapport and understanding. If the person you're speaking with trusts you in this regard, then it is possible they would be more likely to reciprocate by sharing their own spiritual purpose. You have the best opportunity to amplify meaning for them by understanding where they are coming from.

Be willing to go first with your perspective if you ever hope to learn theirs. Also, never assume they have ever even thought this through for themselves. This might be the first time, or at least it might have been a long time since they've broached the subject with someone other than a very close family member. If they appear to associate no value in having a spiritual purpose, then be willing to just let it go for now. There are plenty of other amplifiers to consider.

THE SPIRIT WITHIN CULTURE

If we define culture as the common and accepted expectations of working together, then that should include the spirit within the team. It's not just the observable behavioral work ethic expectations that make a difference. The attitudinal expressions that either quench or uplift our spirit are in play as well. When CEO Steve Blue first took the helm at Miller Ingenuity, he was taken aback by the language used on the shop floor. The team members were using "F-bombs" as linking verbs to communicate with each other. He said it had reached the point of being over-the-top extreme and cringe worthy. It was dragging down the professionalism, self-respect, and spirit of their entire culture. In a bold move, Steve implemented a one-strike-and-you're-out rule. He drew more than a red line in the sand. Open swearing would be a fireable offense. Instead of just making it a parochial rule without context, he explained the *why* behind it. If Miller Ingenuity were to grow and succeed, the culture had to be the driving force. The foul language was getting in the way. The team responded remarkably with just one exception. Steve Blue's commitment to set a new high-bar expectation jump-started the culture transformation at Miller Ingenuity. If you can elevate the spirit of your culture, then everything else will follow in the positive wake you create.

I'm not surprised the no-swear rule had such a positive impact. First, it came from a remarkable leader like Steve Blue, and it was championed by a stellar team of committed senior leaders. Second, it tapped into something deeper within all of us that can be sanctified by cleaner, respectful language. The heart is the universal symbol for love. Think Valentine's Day. The choices we make with our language come from the heart and reflect our spirit. My pastor uses an analogy that has always stuck with me. He often says, "The tongue is the dipstick of the heart." In other words, what you say simply reveals the nature of the spirit within you. When I think about the many times I've been gut-checked by this concept, I'm completed busted. I wish I could say it causes me to come clean every time. I'm grateful, though, for the times when it does move my conscience enough to make a change. What's the reading on the dipstick to your heart?

THE PURPOSE OF A GRATEFUL SPIRIT

A generous man will prosper; he who refreshes others will himself be refreshed.

—Proverbs 11:25

Every organization has people who are lost in the weeds at work. Let's explore what it means to be lost in the weeds and what we can do about it. Here are some questions to reflect upon:

- Can you picture the people who desperately need to have their spirits lifted?
- Are you "blessed" by the opportunity to work with them?
- Do you feel it's an honor to have them within your life at work?
- Are they helping to bring out the best in you and make the work experience joyful and fulfilling?

If you can answer "yes" to any of these questions, then you owe it to them to let them know—*now*.

How ironic that internal, heartfelt sentiments of appreciation are rarely shared, except on someone's last day at work, or as a retrospective when someone is ill, and you may be saying your goodbyes. I love the expression, "Give me my roses now." Why do we hold back and wait? Is it too hard for us to be so personally vulnerable when we find ourselves in the professional setting at work? Do we assume an emotional expression of gratitude is either out of bounds at work or not desired by the other party? What a huge mistake and missed opportunity to deeply connect with people.

It doesn't matter what religion or belief system you subscribe to. Hearing these things from others confirms we are making a difference and, in some way, living out our life's calling. All of us seek to reaffirm we are on the right path, yet often we find work to be a hollow echo chamber deep in the weed patch.

Do you see yourself and your role as a sounding board to let people hear it, absorb it, and be uplifted? There are so many things in this life that pull us down. We all desperately need others to lift us up out of the weeds, not for our ego's sake but because we so easily forget that we add meaning to people's lives. When each of us recognizes how we are blessing others, I believe it brings us in closer fellowship to our creator. It helps us feel worthy (not perfect), to approach God in ways that sanctify our spiritual relationship. Personally, I hunger for that feeling.

As managers and coworkers, or even complete strangers, we can be the nourisher who starts the process for others. It's totally within our control. The most wonderful thing about this entire subject is the paradox of meaning—it's a "give to gain" phenomenon. The times when I've felt rich, deep meaning in my life is when I've opened my heart of gratitude toward others and witnessed their astonished response. I'm always surprised to the extent it softens the guarded exterior and releases something genuine in others that is refreshingly human, vulnerable, and precious.

What's standing in the way? I realize many of us are not gifted with an awareness of the power of gratitude. We're also not comfortable in the actual expression. We often feel intimidated in knowing how to communicate it. It seems far easier to say nothing. I can tell you from my own experience as an introvert, saying something always came hard for me. The only way I've gained the ability to share appreciation with others is simply by stretching my zone of comfort through practice, practice, practice. It's allowed me to be more forthcoming, bold, and even spontaneous.

I've never once received a negative response from others, so in my own mind, the fear is mostly gone. I still start by asking permission. Let's face it, who's going to say, "No, I don't want to hear your kind and reaffirming thoughts about me"? Simply saying, "I'm grateful and blessed to work with a person like you," is the launching point to paint the picture as to *why* they have purpose in our world. That's how you pull people out of the weeds.

THE QUESTIONS ARE THE ANSWER

The two most important days in your life are the day you are born, and the day you find out *why*.

—Anonymous

What a wonderful thought it is that some of the best days of our lives haven't even happened yet.

—Anne Frank, *Anne Frank: The Diary of a Young Girl*

There is a very popular concept that illuminates the three big questions of life. The questions are highly effective to stimulate deep reflection. Although there are several variations of the three questions from different sources, I'll share with you the ones I've heard from Pastor Chris Swansen based in Chester Springs, Pennsylvania.

These are the three big questions:

1. Where did I come from?
2. Why am I here?
3. Where am I going?

I created a reflective process that considers a sequence of lifelong milestones to outline—what I call a personal life narrative. This is a creative piggyback on the story-writing technique Pixar uses to pitch their movie scripts. My version is related to the script of our personal lifelong journey. This is an exercise to gain clarity on the three big questions. Crafting your life narrative from the beginning can be an eye-opening and somewhat cathartic experience. It was for me at least.

Following this template, I've listed my personal answers in italics simply as an example and creative spark for your own reflection. Take the time to write yours down for each milestone and descriptor and watch how your story comes to life.

Life Narrative Storyline

I was born in _____ (city and state, etc.) and raised by
_____ (adjectives for parents or caregivers).

I grew up in _____ (community/
hometown) during the _____era.

I got my kicks _____
(your kid-focused activity, sport, hobby).

After high school, I transitioned in adulthood by _____
_____ (college, military, or vocation, etc.) and indulged by
_____ (social group, sport, activity).

I launched into life doing _____
(first focus or career field beyond college or high school).

I made my mark by _____ (career maker).

I grew my family by _____
_____ (spouse, kids, pets).

I stretched my wings by _____
_____ (major achievement, new role, challenge, endeavor).

I still have fun doing _____ (current
hobby, sport, interest, focus area).

I want to top it all off by _____
_____ (life-long dream, goal, bucket list, accomplishment).

Looking back, I hope I can say _____
_____ (concluding purpose for family, work, society, spirituality).

After I pass, I'm going _____
(final destination, if personably applicable).

As an example, here's what my life narrative story line sounds like using the
template provided:

I was born *on an army base in Ft. Belvoir, Virginia* (city and state, etc.) and
raised by *an amazing dentist and super-talented wonder-mom* (adjectives for
parents or caregivers).

I grew up in *central Pennsylvania* (community/hometown) during the *Vietnam,
moon landing, Woodstock, and Watergate* era.

I got my kicks *riding motorcycles and playing every sport in a nonstop neighborhood Olympics* (your kid-focused activity, sport, hobby).

After high school, I transitioned into adulthood by *going to Susquehanna
University as a communications major* (college, military, or vocation, etc.) and
indulged by *playing in a rock band, captaining the tennis team, and being on the
radio* (social group, sport, activity).

I launched into life *working for a radio station and then moving into sales and marketing* (first focus or career field beyond college or high school).

I made my mark by *leading the culture at QVC* (career maker).

I grew my family by *marrying Kara, having Ryan and Julianna, and adoring many special dogs and cats* (spouse, kids, pets).

I stretched my wings by *inventing and patenting a garden tool, obtaining horticulture degrees from Longwood, and writing a book* (major achievement, new role, challenge, endeavor).

I still have fun *skiing, gardening, golfing, and studying history* (current hobby, sport, interest, focus area).

I want to top it all off by *moving to an A-frame house in the mountains of Colorado* (lifelong dream, goal, bucket list, accomplishment).

Looking back, I hope I can say *that I touched a lot of people with my work, made my friends and family happy to be around me, and led folks to discover their creator* (concluding purpose for family, work, society, or spirituality).

After I pass, I'm going *to stand before God and account for my life He has blessed me with* (final destination, if personably applicable).

SPIRITUALITY AMPLIFIER PLAYBOOK: TRUTH TO POWER

We've all witnessed the devastating trend of people taking immediate offense to expressed opinions or coaching that assumes the worst possible motives of people. In a way, it's almost as if it has become acceptable and popular in our social culture to hot-wire our reptilian amygdala brain that signals fight or flight. How can anyone look at what has happened and think this represents a positive advancement of our culture? The toxic thinking has spilled over from social media and politics, and now into corporate culture. How ironic that at a time when psychological safety is needed to fully collaborate and engage effectively, some have created an environment where everyone is walking on eggshells fearing that any form of candor will be misconstrued. I'm advocating that people must continue to be open to challenge each other if we want to break out of the limiting box of self-victimization triggered by the slightest provocation. For example, when people are willing to point out what's wrong that is out of alignment with the values of your culture, it forms a foundation of expectations. Clarity is always the ultimate catalyst for the healthy behavior that leads to results. I've yet to come across a healthy high-performance culture that wasn't genuine, transparent, and authentic about their expectations for communicating with each other. They all have a positive *potent* point of view one way or the other that is grounded in respect. We can hate an opinion without hating the person.

Assuming Positive Intent

I'll speak to this personally. When I jump to conclusions about a scenario, or an emotionally fraught situation, I'm usually dead right. So what? There have been too many times when I've been dead wrong, and I've paid a price for being stuck in my own self-righteousness. This is the lesson that may take a lifetime for me to get right. I know it, and I'm working on it. I realize I'll never be completely free of poor assumptions, but it's worth the effort to free myself of those limiting beliefs that get in way.

I sense that a great number of people don't even have an awareness—let alone any sort of desire—to change their thinking mode. Many people have created an exterior that makes it appear dangerous for anyone to offer their own healthy perspective of coaching. Some have inadvertently locked out the potential to be helped by others. When this happens in large numbers at work, it tips the balance for a culture that lacks honesty and the ability to self-correct.

For the record, I personally believe that a person should have no cause to be offended unless the perpetrating alleged "offender" actually meant to do so. Instead, the emotionally intelligent response should be anchored in empathy. Yes, of course, there are rotten apples who go on offense with the worst intent. But what is the value in assuming everyone is operating in that mode? On the receiving end, a healthier response from empathy might express disappointment, compassion, curiosity, or humor—not indignation. The goal should be to have future-focused dialogue. It's amazing that some people seem to obsess in being the "gotcha" gurus of offense. Worse yet is when someone is offended on behalf of others when, in reality, they have no clue how that makes others feel. Being offended automatically puts you in the mode of "I'm right, and you're not only wrong, but reprehensibly wrong, and worthy of being ignored and dismissed." It's not going to end well.

Figure 13.1 shows a model that depicts the attitude of our assumptions. Awareness gives us choices. I have seen firsthand how people can make better choices that lead to respect by becoming aware of the dynamics and ramifications of their attitude. Obviously, no one is perfect and able to take the high road every single time—myself included. It takes training, discipline, and repetition for any of us to change.

I hope the model is a powerful reminder to assume positive intent. Healthy, honest, and respectful dialogue is only one conversation away for each of us.

When I'm at the top of my game, I'm tapping into my deepest positive spiritual grounding as my first filter. Doing so puts me into the mind-set of empathy and altruism that has never failed me. That mind-set is a purpose I desperately want for my life. It's no accident that the spirit-driven amplifier of purpose reminds me of an important paradox. For a person to save their own life, they must be willing to give it up first.

Attitudes of Assumption

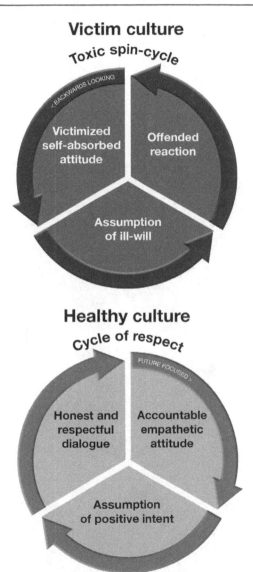

Figure 13.1 Attitudes of assumption model.

Epilogue

The Transcendent Purpose Challenge for Leaders

A purpose is the eternal condition for success.

—Revealed in a fortune cookie

It's hard to imagine that a fortune cookie could capture the essence of what it means to take the transcendent purpose challenge. My wife and I had just finished dinner at our favorite Chinese restaurant. She cracked open a cookie and revealed the saying to me with a wry smile: "A purpose is the eternal condition for success." As a first reaction, it humbled me. After all, at this point I had been working on *The Search for Meaning at Work* manuscript for several years with obviously a lot of thought poured into this subject. I felt jealous that eight words could be so spot-on perfect in telling the transcendent purpose story. But then, after thinking about it, the saying spoke comfort to my soul. I realized if the fortune cookie is true, then it confirms that the journey is indeed the destination. In other words, if we make the quest for a transcendent purpose, then everything we do in the long journey to reach that purpose is truly meaningful. If we recognize the purpose of our eternal journey, then success can be defined by whether any of this life was meaningful. That's deeply comforting because we have the power as individuals to make that choice. I have the tiny, yet mighty, fortune cookie paper strip hanging on my office wall to keep me humbled.

YOUR JOURNEY TO THE TOP

Sow a thought and you reap an action; sow an act and you reap a habit; sow a habit and you reap a character; sow a character and you reap a destiny.

—Ralph Waldo Emerson

With "enlightenment" at the tip-top of the pyramid, Maslow's hierarchy of needs inadvertently sets an objective that appears too high for many people to consider. Reaching enlightenment seems unobtainable. The daunting cliché comes to mind of having to scale the dangerous heights of a mountain peak to learn the secret from the mysterious sage at the top. How ironic that, all along, it is each step upward in the quest that enlightens and illuminates purpose. We don't have to wait to reach the pinnacle. I'm convinced the sage at the top would simply say, "Congratulations, you took the intentional steps to get here. That has been your purpose all along!"

I believe enlightenment is the realization that you don't truly need to reach the top to have purpose and meaning for your life. Each step becomes meaningful by knowing what you're seeking at the top. You must feel confident the quest is worthy of your life's work. The meaning of our life is the sum of the gratitude we feel for being able to take the journey, which begs an essential question: What might be the appropriate response to express your gratitude? The only natural response is to complete your calling by paying it forward to the next generation.

So that's the transcendent purpose challenge. It's ours to accept or ignore. The journey starts by identifying the purpose that sits atop the mountain that is unique to you. Then you must choose to climb the steps to get there. Whatever the purpose you choose, keep in mind it should complement and align with all the other amplifiers we've reviewed through this book. If we can get all the amplifiers playing together in harmony, then everything we do will feel abundantly meaningful.

GIVING YOURSELF AWAY

> Man's main concern is not to gain pleasure or to avoid pain but rather to see a meaning in his life.
>
> —Viktor Frankl, Holocaust survivor and author
> of *Man's Search for Meaning*

> When we work hard for something we don't believe in, it's called stress. When we work hard for something we love, it's called passion.
>
> —Simon Sinek, author of *Start with Why*

Chapter 1 defines transcendent purpose as a purpose for life and your being. It's important to note that every purpose I've examined points in the direction of benefiting others. Again, it's the give-to-gain paradox. It's never about benefiting ourselves directly. For me, this is further confirmation that we are driven by a higher power. If humankind only followed the linear path of evolution, then "survival of the fittest" would cancel our capacity to desire a transcendent purpose. Instead, transcendent purpose drives people to do selfless acts of service and sacrifice that defy the dead-end logic of evolution. Love's triumph over primal instinct is emblematic of our divine humanity. Living our purpose is a celebration of that blessing.

I recently was introduced to a remarkable individual whose work in the field of pediatric cancer treatment deeply moved me. I asked Dr. Ayyappan Rajasekaran if I could interview him for insights on how he came to dedicate his life's work to benefit children suffering with cancer and the harsh side effects of treatments. Dr. Raj, as he is called, began his transcendent journey at the young age of 13. His father was a nurse in a cancer ward in India and often brought him into the ward to interact with the young children. They could relate to Raj and share their feelings. He witnessed the tragic death of many of these dear kids. The experience imprinted on him a commitment to find out why cancer spreads and how to stop it. He acted upon his passion and curiosity to later seek out an education at some of the best medical schools in the world, including New York University, Cornell, and the University of California at Los Angeles. He discovered answers that could impact others' lives. He reflected to me that he knew early on that he was blessed with a capability and high work ethic. His ambition drove his desire to help people and to save lives. He turned down opportunities that would have earned a far greater salary in order to stay focused on the kids. Dr. Raj has gone on to become the founder and chief researcher of the Cancer Vision Foundation, an organization dedicated to advancing the proper treatment of kids with leukemia and the education of cancer prevention. He also speaks to kids in school on early detection and cancer prevention. I asked Dr. Raj if he could summarize the driving force and passion for his work. He said, "Saving life and giving hope to the children is what I want to achieve for my life" (personal communication with the author, February 3, 2022). He's a great example of a person who finds meaning by being willing to give himself away in the service of others.

SUPERHERO OF PURPOSE

On August 28, 2020, actor Chadwick Boseman succumbed to colon cancer. It wasn't until his passing that I realized just how special this man really was.

He's left a legacy that all of us can learn from if we pay close attention to what it means to live a purpose-driven life.

In May 2018, Chadwick Boseman returned to Howard University, his alma mater, to deliver the main address of the university's 150th commencement. Just 18 years prior, he was the one graduating with a BA in directing.

During his commencement speech, Boseman told the graduates, "Purpose is an essential element of you. It is the reason that you're on this planet at this particular time in history. Your very existence is wrapped up in the things you are here to fulfill. Whatever you choose for a career path, remember the struggles along the way are only meant to shape you for your purpose."[1]

Chadwick was diagnosed with stage 3 colon cancer in 2016 and endured a four-year fight as the cancer progressed to stage 4. We know now that Boseman delivered his moving commencement address in the middle of his battle, which makes his message even more poignant today.

"I don't know what your future is," Boseman said in his commencement speech. "But if you're willing to take the harder way, the more complicated one, the one with more failures at first than successes . . . then you will not regret it."[2]

Chadwick Boseman passed away at the age of 43. Despite a life cut tragically short, Boseman left behind an illustrative legacy in film. In addition to T'Challa, leader of utopian nation Wakanda in the Marvel movies, he was known for his powerful portrayals of black Americans including baseball great Jackie Robinson in *42* (2013), future Supreme Court justice Thurgood Marshall in *Marshall* (2017), and soul singer James Brown in the musical biography *Get On Up* (2014). Chadwick Boseman's life was much more than dazzling on the big screen. He lived his life with passion, purpose, and conviction. His legacy of encouraging others to find powerful meaning in their lives to use as a guiding force for good resonates and will influence many to change their lives for the better.

OPENING YOUR UNIQUE GIFT

The high-bar lives of people like Dr. Raj and Chadwick Boseman should not discourage us from acting on our own transcendent purpose. Instead, they should inspire us to discover and act upon our unique gifts that can be used large or small to manifest our purpose. Compared to Dr. Raj, I can only hope to have a fraction of the life-changing impact as a result of my life on this planet. But I'm convinced it's not just the scope of our impact but also the fact that we do have impact that matters. Taking the steps to make progress toward that purpose gives us meaning. How that manifests itself for you is as unique as your fingerprint. Each of us leaves a lasting mark that continues beyond our mortality.

YOUR PATH AS A LEADER

We've traveled a long purpose path together. The challenge I offer you is simply this: Will you lead people to find meaning at work? Is the challenge worthy to become your transcendent purpose as a leader of people?

If you say "yes," then I hold my glass high and offer this toast to you:

For all the ideas we've explored together. For revealing the joy of creating better lives for your team members and families. For each step of progress to create small wins. For the honor of helping others belong. For the deep fulfillment in seeing them grow and thrive within the culture you create. For believing in them, listening, caring, and advocating for their success. For laughing and crying together. For winning as a team and a trusted colleague. For engaging them to do what no one thought was possible. For finding our purpose by inspiring their best. This transcendent challenge is for you. Amplify purpose! Cheers!

WITH GRATITUDE

If I have helped you in your search for meaning at work, then my purpose has been amplified through you. I'm grateful that we've taken part in this journey together. If my words have made a difference for you, then it means I have indeed lived my life's purpose. Thank you for that gift. I wish you all the best in your journey through life and as treasured leader of the people within your care.

Positively,
Stephen Van Valin

Appendix

The Internalized Questions That Express a Search for Meaning at Work

THE SELF-SATISFACTION AMPLIFIER

- Do I feel respected here?
- Does the work stir my interest and challenge me in a positive way?
- Can I capitalize on my true talent and use my strengths doing this work?
- Am I proud of the way my work reflects on me as an individual?
- Does the work provide an intrinsic value that goes beyond the exchange of my time for extrinsic compensation?
- Do I have the ability to influence and change the way the work is done?

THE FAMILY AMPLIFIER

- Is my family proud of me because of the work I do and who I work for?
- Does my job live up to the standard of respect that reflects my family values?
- Does my work allow me to pursue and fulfill my family priorities?
- Do I feel I'm a good provider for my family?
- Does my family think favorably about the people and organization where I work?
- Does my family believe I am treated fairly and with respect at work?

THE WORK PARTNER AMPLIFIER

- Does my work partner "have my back" and support me even when I'm not with him or her?

- Do I have a bonded relationship at work that brings out the best in both of us?
- Do I have a work partner relationship in which we help each other learn and grow?
- Am I inspired to work with my work partner for the sake of interacting and achieving something together?
- Do I have a work partner who accepts me and respects me for who I am?
- Do I have a work partner I can confide in and trust to be my advocate?
- Do I have a work partner who will give me honest feedback and advice?
- Is my bond with my work partner strong enough to make me want to stay here?

THE TEAM AMPLIFIER

- Do I feel I belong as an accepted member of this team?
- Does my effort make a difference to the performance of the team?
- Do the people on my team support me and value my ideas?
- Do I believe in what this team stands for?
- Does our team have a bond that motivates us to accomplish things together?

THE MANAGER AMPLIFIER

- Is my manager *for* me or *against* me? Is my manager my advocate or my antagonist? (Am I a plus or a minus in his or her mind?)
- Does my manager respect me and the work I do by giving me meaningful recognition?
- Is my manager willing to do what it takes to support me and the work I am doing?
- Does my manager show me respect by coaching me to be accountable for my work, allowing me to gain a sense of ownership in what I do?
- Does my manager make a deliberate effort to develop an open, personal relationship with me that includes clear, timely, and (whenever possible) face-to-face communication?
- Can I count on my manager to help move the work forward and make progress? (Is my manager a catalyst or inhibitor of progress?)

THE DEPARTMENT AMPLIFIER

- Do I clearly understand how my work impacts the goals of the department?
- Is the purpose and vision of this department motivating me to perform at my very best? (Am I connected to the meaningful purpose of our department's work?)
- Do I trust the leadership of the department and feel confident in the direction they have set?
- Do I feel I can grow my reputation and career aspirations by working within this department?
- Are we making progress as a business unit toward a meaningful purpose?
- Am I inspired and motivated by a clear rally cry for the mission of our department's work?

THE COMPANY AMPLIFIER

- Do I know what this company stands for and our purpose for being in business?
- Does my work make a difference to the success of the company?
- Does the company culture allow me to be at my best and thrive?
- Do I value the same things that the company values?
- Am I proud to say I work for my company?

THE CUSTOMER AMPLIFIER

- Do I understand how my role directly impacts the customer?
- Do I know why our customers choose to do business with us?
- Do I have the ability to apply new ideas to impact the customer experience?
- Do I have the opportunity to interact directly with the customer?

THE COMMUNITY AMPLIFIER

- Is our company an asset to the community?
- Does our company give back in ways that I can participate in?
- Am I proud of what our company represents to the community?
- Do I feel included within the community of our company culture?

THE WORLD SOCIETY AMPLIFIER

- Does the work I do inevitably benefit people to live better lives?
- Does this company leave the world in a better condition than if it were not here?
- Am I leaving a positive mark, doing my share, and creating a better world for others?
- Does the work we do add to the joy, peace, or benefit of humankind?
- Does this company make the world a better place?

THE SPIRITUALITY AMPLIFIER

- Is my work aligned to my highest sense of ideals?
- Does my work help me live out my life's destiny or higher calling?
- Is the work I'm doing in harmony with my conscience on what is right and wrong?
- Is my work at this organization in harmony with what I believe about my higher purpose in life?

Notes

CHAPTER 1

1. Mark Royal and Y. J. Yoon, "Engagement and Enablement: The Key to Higher Levels of Individual and Organisational Performance," *Journal of Compensation and Benefits* 25 (September/October 2009): 13–19; Richard S. Wellins, Paul Bernthal, and Mark Phelps, "Employee Engagement: The Key to Realizing Competitive Advantage," Development Dimensions International, 2005, 5, http://theengagementeffect.com/wp-content/uploads/DDI-EmployeeEngagementMonograph.pdf; Kenexa Research Institute, "The Impact of Employee Engagement," 2009, quoted in Bruce Rayton, Tanith Dodge, and Gillian D'Analeze, "The Evidence: Employee Engagement Task Force: 'Nailing the Evidence' Workgroup," Engage for Success, November 2012, https://researchportal.bath.ac.uk/en/publications/the-evidence-employee-engagement-task-force-nailing-the-evidence-.

2. James K. Harter, Frank L. Schmidt, Emily A. Killham, and Sangeeta Agrawal, "The Relationship between Engagement at Work and Organizational Outcomes: 2012 Q12® Meta-Analysis," Gallup, February 2013, https://employeeengagement.com/wp-content/uploads/2013/04/2012-Q12-Meta-Analysis-Research-Paper.pdf, quoted in Rayton, Dodge, and D'Analeze, "The Evidence: Employee Engagement Task Force."

3. Jerry Krueger and Emily A. Killham, "The Innovation Equation," *Gallup Business Journal*, April 12, 2007, https://news.gallup.com/businessjournal/27145/innovation-equation.aspx; David MacLeod and Nita Clarke, "Engaging for Success: Enhancing Performance through Employee Engagement," Department for Business, Innovation and Skills, July 2009, https://dera.ioe.ac.uk/1810/1/file52215.pdf, quoted in Rayton, Dodge, and D'Analeze, "The Evidence: Employee Engagement Task Force."

4. Corporate Leadership Council, *Driving Performance and Retention through Employee Engagement: A Quantitative Analysis of Effective Engagement Strategies* (Washington, DC: Corporate Executive Board, 2004), quoted in Rayton, Dodge, and D'Analeze, "The Evidence: Employee Engagement Task Force."

5. Gallup, *State of the US Workplace Report*, January 7, 2022.

6. "Survey: Individual Purpose Trumps Popcorn for the Post-Pandemic American Worker," Blu Ivy Group, April 25, 2022, https://www.prnewswire.com/news-releases/survey-individual-purpose-trumps-popcorn-for-the-post-pandemic-american-worker-301531863.html. Respondents were among a nationally representative sample of full-time and part-time employed Americans.

7. Teresa Amabile and Steven Kramer, *The Progress Principle: Using Small Wins to Ignite Joy, Engagement, and Creativity at Work* (Brighton: Harvard Business Review Press, 2011).

8. Aaron Hurst, *The Purpose Economy: How Your Desire for Impact, Personal Growth and Community Is Changing the World* (Seattle: Imperative, 2018), 66.

9. Amabile and Kramer, *The Progress Principle*, 95.

10. Francesco Gino, "To Motivate Employees, Show How They're Helping Customers," *Harvard Business Review*, March 6, 2017.

11. Thomas Heath, "Why She Left a $185,000 Job to Launch a D.C. Fitness Chain," *Washington Post*, April 12, 2015, https://www.washingtonpost.com/business/economy/why-anne-mahlum-left-a-185000-job-to-launch-a-dc-area-fitness-chain/2015/04/10/dd2f4b0a-de3d-11e4-a500-1c5bb1d8ff6a_story.html.

CHAPTER 2

1. Esther Perel, "Esther Perel's Post," LinkedIn, accessed April 20, 2022, https://www.linkedin.com/posts/estherperel_the-quality-of-our-relationships-determines-activity-6863562124287975424-9LJe/.

2. Seth Godin, *Tribes: We Need You to Lead Us* (New York: Penguin Portfolio, 2008).

CHAPTER 3

1. Brendon Burchard, *The Motivation Manifesto* (Carlsbad, CA: Hay House, 2014), x.

2. James W. Adie, Joan L. Duda, and Nikos Ntoumanis, "Autonomy Support, Basic Need Satisfaction and the Optimal Functioning of Adult Male and Female Sport Participants: A Test of Basic Needs Theory," *Motivation and Emotion* 32, no. 3 (2008): 189–99.

3. Teresa M. Amabile, "How to Kill Creativity," *Harvard Business Review*, September–October 1998, https://hbr.org/1998/09/how-to-kill-creativity.

4. A. Wrzesniewski, J. E. Dutton, and G. Debebe, "Interpersonal Sensemaking and the Meaning of Work," *Research in Organizational Behavior* 25 (2003): 93–135.

5. Lisa Bodell, *Kill the Company* (New York: Routledge, 2012).

6. Stephen M. R. Covey with Rebecca R. Merrill, *The Speed of Trust: The One Thing That Changes Everything* (New York: Simon & Schuster, 2006).

7. Covey with Merrill, *The Speed of Trust*.

8. Rob Asghar and Fred Tuffile, "Study: Millennials Are the True Entrepreneur Generation," *Forbes*, November 11, 2014, https://forbes/com/sites/robasghar/2014/11/11/study-millennials-are-the-true-entrepreneur-generation/#2fe4dc9873dc.

9. Shankar Vedantam, host, "You 2.0: Dream Jobs," NPR, July 30, 2018, accessed September 26, 2018, https://www.npr.org/templates/transcript/transcript .php?storyId=634047154.

10. Jay Yarow, "This Is the Inspirational Quote Apple Employees Receive on Day One," *Business Insider*, May 7, 2012, https://www.businessinsider.com/this-is-the -inspirational-quote-apple-employees-receive-on-day-one-2012-5.

11. "Logos, Website, Graphic Design, Product Design, Naming & More," Crowd-spring.com, accessed September 26, 2018, https://www.crowdspring.com/.

12. Aaron Hurst, *The Purpose Economy: How Your Desire for Impact, Personal Growth and Community Is Changing the World* (Seattle, WA: Imperative, 2018).

CHAPTER 4

1. M. P. Muchinsky, *Psychology Applied to Work: An Introduction to Industrial and Organizational Psychology*, 10th ed. (Summerfield, NC: Hypergraphic, 2012).

2. J. Pfeffer, "Organizational Demography," *Research in Organizational Behavior* 5 (1983): 299–357.

3. Peter Crush, "Engagement Surveys: Gallup and Best Companies Face Criticism," *HR Magazine*, March 24, 2009, http://www.hrmagazine.co.uk/article-details /engagement-surveys-gallup-and-best-companies-face-criticism.

4. William B. Swann Jr., Chris De La Ronde, and John G. Hixon, "Authenticity and Positivity Strivings in Marriage and Courtship," *Journal of Personality and Social Psychology* 66 (1994): 857–69.

5. Brie Weiler Reynolds, "FlexJobs 2019 Annual Survey: Flexible Work Plays Big Role in Job Choices," FlexJobs, 2019, https://www.flexjobs.com/blog/post/survey -flexible-work-job-choices/.

6. "Talent Accelerator: The Forces That Are Shaping the New Working World," Citrix, December 2020, https://www.citrix.com/content/dam/citrix/en_us/documents /analyst-report/talent-accelerator.pdf.

7. Melody Beattie, "Today's Daily Meditation," MelodyBeattie.com, accessed April 22, 2022, https://melodybeattie.com/gratitude-2/.

8. Stephen M. R. Covey, with Rebecca R. Merrill, *The Speed of Trust: The One Thing That Changes Everything* (New York: Free Press, 2006).

CHAPTER 5

1. Dick Winters, interviewed in *Band of Brothers*, directed by Phil Alden Robinson et al., written by Erik Jendresen et al., aired September–December 2001, on HBO.

2. Roy F. Baumeister and Mark R. Leary, "The Need to Belong: Desire for Interpersonal Attachments as a Fundamental Human Motivation," *Psychological Bulletin* 117, no. 3 (1995): 497.

3. Warren Bennis, *On Becoming a Leader* (New York: Basic Books, 2010).

4. Carolyn Manno, CNN Headline News, November 6, 2021; see also "Somali-Dutch Wins Bronze Medal and Helps Other Runner to Keep Pace," YouTube, August 9, 2021, https://www.youtube.com/watch?v=00L-BOrYBpc.

5. Annamarie Mann, "Why We Need Best Friends at Work," Gallup Workplace, January 15, 2018, https://www.gallup.com/workplace/236213/why-need-best-friends-work.aspx.

6. Gallup, "Item 10: I Have a Best Friend at Work," Gallup Workplace, May 26, 1999, https:/www.gallup.com/workplace/237530/item-best-friend-work.aspx.

7. Gallup, "Item 10: I Have a Best Friend at Work."

8. Mann, "Why We Need Best Friends at Work."

9. Gallup, "Item 10: I Have a Best Friend at Work"; see also Mann, "Why We Need Best Friends at Work."

10. Richard Sheridan, *Joy, Inc.: How We Built a Workplace People Love* (New York: Penguin, 2013).

11. Laurie Williams and Robert Kessler, *Pair Programming Illuminated* (Boston, MA: Addison-Wesley, 2003).

12. Williams and Kessler, *Pair Programming Illuminated*, 15.

13. Williams and Kessler, *Pair Programming Illuminated*, 17.

14. Williams and Kessler, *Pair Programming Illuminated*, 18.

15. Williams and Kessler, *Pair Programming Illuminated*, 18–19.

16. Mann, "Why We Need Best Friends at Work."

CHAPTER 6

1. B. W. Tuckman, "Developmental Sequence in Small Groups," *Psychological Bulletin 63, no. 6* (1965): 384–99, https://doi.org/10.1037/h0022100.

2. Anthony Mazzocchi, "Why Students Really Quit Their Musical Instrument (and How Parents Can Prevent It)," Music Parents' Guide, February 17, 2015, http://www.musicparentsguide.com/2015/02/17/students-really-quit-musical-instrument-parents-can-prevent/.

3. Teresa Amabile and Steven Kramer, *The Progress Principle: Using Small Wins to Ignite Joy, Engagement, and Creativity at Work* (Brighton: Harvard Business Review Press, 2011).

4. Amabile and Kramer, *The Progress Principle*.

5. Laura Delizonna, "High-Performing Teams Need Psychological Safety: Here's How to Create It," *Harvard Business Review* 8 (2017): 1–5.

6. Delizonna, "High-Performing Teams Need Psychological Safety."

CHAPTER 7

1. Jack Altman, "Don't Be Surprised When Your Employees Quit," *Forbes*, April 27, 2018, https://www.forbes.com/sites/valleyvoices/2017/02/22/dont-be-surprised -when-your-employees-quit/#66bb7893325e.

2. Jim Harter and Amy Adkins, "Employees Want a Lot More from Their Managers," Gallup Workplace, April 8, 2015, https://www.gallup.com/workplace/236570 /employees-lot-managers.aspx.

3. Annamarie Mann and Nate Dvorak, "Employee Recognition: Low Cost, High Impact," Gallup Workplace, June 28, 2016, https://www.gallup.com/workplace /236441/employee-recognition-low-cost-high-impact.aspx.

4. Dale Carnegie, *How to Win Friends and Influence People* (New York: Simon & Schuster, 2009), 249.

5. Gallup, *State of the Global Workplace* (New York: Simon & Schuster, 2017), 107.

6. Mark C. Crowley, "Employee Engagement Isn't Getting Better and Gallup Shares the Surprising Reasons Why," LinkedIn, December 8, 2015, https://www .linkedin.com/pulse/employee-engagement-isnt-getting-better-gallup-shares-mark-c -crowley.

7. Denise M. Breaux, Pamela L. Perrewé, Angela T. Hall, Dwight D. Frink, and Wayne H. Hochwarter, "Time to Try a Little Tenderness? The Detrimental Effects of Accountability When Coupled with Abusive Supervision," *Journal of Leadership & Organizational Studies* 15, no. 2 (2008): 111–22, https://doi.org /10.1177/1548051808321787.

8. The terms and concepts used in the Progress Playbook are based on the breakthrough research published in Teresa Amabile and Steven Kramer, *The Progress Principle: Using Small Wins to Ignite Joy, Engagement, and Creativity at Work* (Brighton: Harvard Business Review Press, 2011).

CHAPTER 8

1. Cleve R. Wootson Jr. and Tyler Pager, "A Kamala Harris Staff Exodus Reignites Questions about Her Leadership Style—and Her Future Ambitions," *Washington Post*, December 4, 2021, https://www.washingtonpost.com/politics/2021/12/04/kamala -harris-staff-departures/.

2. Brené Brown, *Rising Strong: How the Ability to Reset Transforms the Way We Live, Love, Parent, and Lead* (New York: Spiegel & Grau, 2015), 182.

3. Teresa Amabile and Steven Kramer, *The Progress Principle: Using Small Wins to Ignite Joy, Engagement, and Creativity at Work* (Brighton: Harvard Business Review Press, 2011).

4. Wikipedia, s.v. "Learning Pyramid," last modified January 18, 2022, 06:49, https://en.wikipedia.org/wiki/Learning_pyramid.

5. Neal Chalofsky and Vijay Krishna, "Meaningfulness, Commitment, and Engagement: The Intersection of a Deeper Level of Intrinsic Motivation," *Advances in Developing Human Resources* 11, no. 2 (April 2009): 189–203, https://doi.org/10.1177/1523422309333147.

6. Patrick M. Lencioni, *The Advantage: Why Organizational Health Trumps Everything Else in Business* (New York: Wiley, 2012).

CHAPTER 9

1. Martina Olbertova, "Meaning Is the Soul of Your Company," *Brand Strategy Insider*, November 9, 2018, https://www.brandingstrategyinsider.com/meaning-is-the-soul-of-your-company/.

2. Denise Lee Yohn, "Build a Culture to Match Your Brand," *Harvard Business Review*, December 17, 2019, https://hbr.org/2019/12/build-a-culture-to-match-your-brand.

3. Olbertova, "Meaning Is the Soul of Your Company."

4. Jim Collins and Jerry I. Porras, *Built to Last: Successful Habits of Visionary Companies* (New York: Random House, 2005).

5. Hubert Joly, "Creating a Meaningful Corporate Purpose," *Harvard Business Review*, October 28, 2021, https://hbr.org/2021/10/creating-a-meaningful-corporate-purpose.

6. Joly, "Creating a Meaningful Corporate Purpose."

7. Arne Gast, Pablo Illanes, Nina Probst, Bill Schaninger, and Bruce Simpson, "Purpose: Shifting from Why to How," *McKinsey Quarterly*, April 22, 2020.

8. Aaron Hurst, *The Purpose Economy: How Your Desire for Impact, Personal Growth and Community Is Changing the World* (Seattle, WA: Imperative, 2018).

9. Teresa Amabile and Steven Kramer, *The Progress Principle: Using Small Wins to Ignite Joy, Engagement, and Creativity at Work* (Brighton: Harvard Business Review Press, 2011).

CHAPTER 10

1. Tony Hsieh, "What Is *The Zappos Culture Book*?" Zappos Insights, accessed May 10, 2022, https://www.zapposinsights.com/culture-book.

2. Denise Lee Yohn, "It's the Experience, Stupid!" *Porchlight* (blog), November 11, 2015, https://www.porchlightbooks.com/blog/changethis/2015/it-s-the-experience-stupid-.

3. Adam M. Grant, Elizabeth M. Campbell, Grace Chen, Keenan Cottone, David Lapedis, and Karen Lee, "Impact and the Art of Motivation Maintenance: The Effects of Contact with Beneficiaries on Persistence Behavior," *Organizational Behavior and Human Decision Processes* 103, no. 1 (2007): 53–67.

4. Leo Burnett, *Communications of an Advertising Man* (privately published, 1961), 26.

5. Charles (Chic) Thompson, *What a Great Idea* (New York: Random House, 1994).

CHAPTER 11

1. Cynthia Sequin, Satish Ukkusuri, Shreyas Sundaram, and Seungyoon Lee, "A Little Help from Your Friends Is Key to Natural Disaster Recovery, Purdue Research Study Suggests," *Purdue University Research Foundation News*, October 12, 2018, https://www.purdue.edu/newsroom/releases/2018/Q4/a-little-help-from-your-friends-is-key-to-natural-disaster-recovery,-purdue-research-study-suggests.html.

2. Dave Portnoy (@stoolpresidente), "Politicians Are Stealing the Basic Right to Earn a Living," Twitter (video), December 11, 2020, 12:46 p.m., https://twitter.com/stoolpresidente/status/1337453710822285316.

3. Marcus Lemonis (@marcuslemonis), "Put Your Money Where Your Mouth Is," Twitter, December 11, 2020, 10:46 p.m., https://twitter.com/marcuslemonis/status/1337604798200258566.

4. Sequin et al., "A Little Help from Your Friends."

5. Gallup, "The Gallup Sustainability 5 (GS5) Index: The Will of the Workplace for Environmental, Social and Governance," Gallup Workplace, 2021,https://www.gallup.com/workplace/352118/environment-social-governance-reporting-perspective.aspx#ite-352124.

6. "2017 Deloitte Volunteerism Survey," Deloitte, June 2017, https://www2.deloitte.com/content/dam/Deloitte/us/Documents/about-deloitte/us-2017-deloitte-volunteerism-survey.pdf.

7. Terrell M. Martin, "4 PA Businesses That Are Prioritizing Philanthropy," Pennsylvania Department of Community and Economic Development, August 31, 2021, https://dced.pa.gov/paproudblog/4-pa-businesses-that-are-prioritizing-philanthropy/.

8. "Companies That Give Back," Robbins Research International, 2022, https://www.tonyrobbins.com/giving-back/companies-give-back/.

9. Seth Godin, "Generative Hobbies," *Seth's Blog*, January 3, 2022, https://seths.blog/2022/01/generative-hobbies/.

CHAPTER 12

1. "One for One," TOMS, 2016–2018, https://www.toms.com/one-for-one-en/.

2. Wikipedia, s.v. "Bob Geldof," last modified April 27, 2022, 20:05, https://en.wikipedia.org/wiki/Bob_Geldof#:~:text=%22The%20greatest%20legacy%20of%20Live,Aid%20production%20manager%20Andy%20Zweck.

3. Aaron Hurst, *The Purpose Economy: How Your Desire for Impact, Personal Growth and Community Is Changing the World* (Seattle, WA: Imperative, 2018).

4. Travis Bradberry, "10 Uncomfortable Deeds That Will Pay Off Forever," *Huffington Post*, October 30, 2016, https://www.huffingtonpost.com/dr-travis -bradberry/10-uncomfortable-deeds-th_b_12593668.html.

5. Bradberry, "10 Uncomfortable Deeds."

6. Lara Heacock and Kelly Stewart, "Return on Energy," February 28, 2022, episode 80 of *Doing (Good) Business*, podcast, https://www.doinggoodbusiness.com /shows/2022/2/28/return-on-energy.

7. Joan Jett, "Do You Wanna Touch Me (Oh Yeah)," *Bad Reputation* (Beverly Hills, CA: Boardwalk Records, 1981).

8. Ante Glavas, "Employee Engagement and Sustainability: A Model for Implementing Meaningfulness at and in Work," *Journal of Corporate Citizenship* 46 (2012): 13.

9. Kate Patrick, "Walmart's Improved Social Responsibility Efforts Begin with Supply Chain," Supply Chain Dive, April 25, 2018, https://www.supplychaindive .com/news/walmart-corporate-social-responsibility-efforts/521961/.

10. David A. Jones, Chelsea R. Willness, and Sarah Madey, "Why Are Job Seekers Attracted by Corporate Social Performance? Experimental and Field Tests of Three Signal-Based Mechanisms," *Academy of Management Journal* 57, no. 2 (2014): 383–404. See also Ante Glavas, "Corporate Social Responsibility and Employee Engagement: Enabling Employees to Employ More of Their Whole Selves at Work," *Frontiers in Psychology* 7 (2016): 796, https://doi.org/10.3389/fpsyg.2016.00796.

11. N. S. Huang, "Vanguard Funds That Are Socially Responsible," Kiplinger, April 18, 2017, https://www.kiplinger.com/slideshow/investing/T041-S003-6 -vanguard-funds-that-are-socially-responsible/index.html. See also Kimberly McGuane, "Vanguard Looks to Woo Millennials with Socially Responsible, Exchange-Traded Funds," Vista Today, June 29, 2018, https://vista.today/2018/06/vanguard -looks-to-woo-millennials-with-socially-responsible-exchange-traded-funds/?utm _source=VISTA+Today&utm_campaign=e163a8da5c-Morning_Drive_Campaign5 _28_2015&utm_medium=email&utm_term=0_75b1fa784c-e163a8da5c-27 4836213.

12. "Grown Not Made," Heinz, accessed May 10, 2022, https://www.heinz.com /grown-not-made.

13. Quoted in Jessica Miller-Merrell, "Ten Employer Examples of EVPs," Workology, February 21, 2022, https://workology.com/employee-value-propositions-evp/.

14. "Expect More Than Coffee," Starbucks, accessed May 10, 2022, https://www .starbucks.com/careers/working-at-starbucks/culture-and-values/.

15. Quoted in Andrea Goodkin and Lauren Slipkowsky, "How an Employee Value Proposition Can Help You Win the Talent Game," Hub, last modified March 24, 2022, https://www.hubinternational.com/en-CA/blog/2018/02/employee-value -proposition/.

CHAPTER 13

1. Yael Halon, "Chicago Teacher Battling Cancer Refuses to Stop In-Person Classes," Fox News, January 5, 2022, https://www.foxnews.com/media/chicago-teacher -battling-cancer-in-person-classes-teachers-union.

2. Viktor Frankl, *Man's Search for Meaning* (Boston, MA: Beacon, 1992).

EPILOGUE

1. Chadwick Boseman, "Howard University 150th Commencement Convocation," commencement speech, Howard University, May 12, 2018, video, 34:40, You-Tube, https://www.youtube.com/watch?v=RIHZypMyQ2s.

2. Boseman, "Howard University 150th Commencement Convocation."

Bibliography

Adie, James W., Joan L. Duda, and Nikos Ntoumanis. "Autonomy Support, Basic Need Satisfaction and the Optimal Functioning of Adult Male and Female Sport Participants: A Test of Basic Needs Theory." *Motivation and Emotion* 32, no. 3 (2008): 189–99.

Altman, Jack. "Don't Be Surprised When Your Employees Quit." *Forbes*, April 27, 2018. https://www.forbes.com/sites/valleyvoices/2017/02/22/dont-be-surprised -when-your-employees-quit/#66bb7893325e.

Amabile, Teresa. "How to Kill Creativity." *Harvard Business Review*, September–October 1998. https://hbr.org/1998/09/how-to-kill-creativity.

Amabile, Teresa, and Steven Kramer. *The Progress Principle: Using Small Wins to Ignite Joy, Engagement, and Creativity at Work*. Brighton: Harvard Business Review Press, 2011.

Asghar, Rob, and Fred Tuffile. "Study: Millennials Are the True Entrepreneur Generation." *Forbes*, November 11, 2014. https://forbes/com/sites/robasghar/2014/11/11 /study-millennials-are-the-true-entrepreneur-generation/#2fe4dc9873dc.

Bartos, Jeff. "The Barstool Fund." Barstool Sports, December 2020. https://www .barstoolsports.com/the-barstool-fund.

Baumeister, Roy F., and Mark R. Leary. "The Need to Belong: Desire for Interpersonal Attachments as a Fundamental Human Motivation." *Psychological Bulletin* 117, no. 3 (1995): 497–529.

Beattie, Melody. "Today's Daily Meditation." MelodyBeattie.com, accessed April 22, 2022. https://melodybeattie.com/gratitude-2/.

Bennis, Warren. *On Becoming a Leader*. New York: Basic Books, 2010.

Blu Ivy Group. "Survey: Individual Purpose Trumps Popcorn for the Post-Pandemic American Worker." April 25, 2022. https://www.prnewswire.com/news-releases /survey-individual-purpose-trumps-popcorn-for-the-post-pandemic-american -worker-301531863.html.

Bodell, Lisa. *Kill the Company*. New York: Routledge, 2012.

Boseman, Chadwick. "Howard University 150th Commencement Convocation." Commencement speech. Howard University, May 12, 2018. Video, 34:40. You-Tube. https://www.youtube.com/watch?v=RIHZypMyQ2s.

Bradberry, Travis. "10 Uncomfortable Deeds That Will Pay Off Forever." *Huffington Post*, October 30, 2016. https://www.huffingtonpost.com/dr-travis-bradberry/10 -uncomfortable-deeds-th_b_12593668.html.

Breaux, Denise M., Pamela L. Perrewé, Angela T. Hall, Dwight D. Frink, and Wayne H. Hochwarter. "Time to Try a Little Tenderness? The Detrimental Effects of Accountability When Coupled with Abusive Supervision." *Journal of Leadership & Organizational Studies* 15, no. 2 (2008): 111–22. https://doi.org /10.1177/1548051808321787.

Burchard, Brendon. *The Motivation Manifesto*. Carlsbad, CA: Hay House, 2014.

Burnett, Leo. *Communications of an Advertising Man*. Privately published, 1961.

Cain, Aine, and Rachel Gillett. "21 Billionaires Who Grew Up Poor." *Business Insider*, August 28, 2018. http://www.businessinsider.com/billionaires-who-came-from -nothing-2013-12.

Carnegie, Dale. *How to Win Friends and Influence People*. New York: Simon & Schuster, 2009.

Chalofsky, Neal, and Vijay Krishna. "Meaningfulness, Commitment, and Engagement: The Intersection of a Deeper Level of Intrinsic Motivation." *Advances in Developing Human Resources* 11, no. 2 (April 2009): 189–203. https://doi.org /10.1177/1523422309333147.

Citrix. "Talent Accelerator: The Forces That Are Shaping the New Working World." December 2020. https://www.citrix.com/content/dam/citrix/en_us/documents /analyst-report/talent-accelerator.pdf.

Collins, Jim, and Jerry I. Porras. *Built to Last: Successful Habits of Visionary Companies*. New York: Random House, 2005.

Corporate Leadership Council. *Driving Performance and Retention through Employee Engagement: A Quantitative Analysis of Effective Engagement Strategies*. Washington, DC: Corporate Executive Board, 2004.

Covey, Stephen M. R., with Rebecca R. Merrill. *The Speed of Trust: The One Thing That Changes Everything*. New York: Simon & Schuster, 2006.

Crowdspring.com. "Logos, Website, Graphic Design, Product Design, Naming & More." Accessed September 26, 2018. https://www.crowdspring.com/.

Crowley, Mark C. "Employee Engagement Isn't Getting Better and Gallup Shares the Surprising Reasons Why." LinkedIn, December 8, 2015. https://www.linkedin.com /pulse/employee-engagement-isnt-getting-better-gallup-shares-mark-c-crowley.

Crush, Peter. "Engagement Surveys: Gallup and Best Companies Face Criticism." *HR Magazine*, March 24, 2009. http://www.hrmagazine.co.uk/article-details/engage ment-surveys-gallup-and-best-companies-face-criticism.

Delizonna, Laura. "High-Performing Teams Need Psychological Safety: Here's How to Create It." *Harvard Business Review* 8 (2017): 1–5.

Deloitte. "2017 Deloitte Volunteerism Survey." June 2017. https://www2.deloitte .com/content/dam/Deloitte/us/Documents/about-deloitte/us-2017-deloitte-volun teerism-survey.pdf.

Drucker, Peter F. *The New Realities*. New York: Routledge, 2017.

Frankl, Viktor. *Man's Search for Meaning*. Boston, MA: Beacon, 1992.

Gallup. "The Gallup Sustainability 5 (GS5) Index: The Will of the Workplace for Environmental, Social and Governance." Gallup Workplace, 2021. https://www .gallup.com/workplace/352118/environment-social-governance-reporting-perspec tive.aspx#ite-352124.

———. "Item 10: I Have a Best Friend at Work." Gallup Workplace, May 26, 1999. https:/www.gallup.com/workplace/237530/item-best-friend-work.aspx.

———. *State of the Global Workplace.* New York: Simon & Schuster, 2017.

Gast, Arne, Pablo Illanes, Nina Probst, Bill Schaninger, and Bruce Simpson. "Purpose: Shifting from Why to How." *McKinsey Quarterly,* April 22, 2020.

Gino, Francesco. "To Motivate Employees, Show How They're Helping Customers." *Harvard Business Review,* March 6, 2017.

Glavas, Ante. "Corporate Social Responsibility and Employee Engagement: Enabling Employees to Employ More of Their Whole Selves at Work." *Frontiers in Psychology* 7 (2016): 796. https://doi.org/10.3389/fpsyg.2016.00796.

———. "Employee Engagement and Sustainability: A Model for Implementing Meaningfulness at and in Work." *Journal of Corporate Citizenship* 46 (2012): 13.

Godin, Seth. "Generative Hobbies." *Seth's Blog,* January 3, 2022. https://seths.blog /2022/01/generative-hobbies/.

———. *Tribes: We Need You to Lead Us.* New York: Penguin Portfolio, 2008.

Goodkin, Andrea, and Lauren Slipkowsky. "How an Employee Value Proposition Can Help You Win the Talent Game." Hub, last modified March 24, 2022. https://www .hubinternational.com/en-CA/blog/2018/02/employee-value-proposition/.

Grant, Adam M., Elizabeth M. Campbell, Grace Chen, Keenan Cottone, David La-pedis, and Karen Lee. "Impact and the Art of Motivation Maintenance: The Effects of Contact with Beneficiaries on Persistence Behavior." *Organizational Behavior and Human Decision Processes* 103, no. 1 (2007): 53–67.

Halon, Yael. "Chicago Teacher Battling Cancer Refuses to Stop In-Person Classes." Fox News, January 5, 2022. https://www.foxnews.com/media/chicago-teacher-battling -cancer-in-person-classes-teachers-union.

Harter, James K., Frank L. Schmidt, Emily A. Killham, and Sangeeta Agrawal. "The Relationship between Engagement at Work and Organizational Outcomes: 2012 Q12® Meta-analysis." Gallup, February 2013. https://employeeengagement.com /wp-content/uploads/2013/04/2012-Q12-Meta-Analysis-Research-Paper.pdf.

Harter, Jim, and Amy Adkins. "Employees Want a Lot More from Their Managers." Gallup Workplace, April 8, 2015. https://www.gallup.com/workplace/236570 /employees-lot-managers.aspx.

Heacock, Lara, and Kelly Stewart. "Return on Energy." February 28, 2022. Epi-sode 80 of *Doing (Good) Business.* Podcast. https://www.doinggoodbusiness.com /shows/2022/2/28/return-on-energy.

Heath, Thomas. "Why She Left a $185,000 Job to Launch a D.C. Fitness Chain." *Washington Post,* April 12, 2015. https://www.washingtonpost.com/business /economy/why-anne-mahlum-left-a-185000-job-to-launch-a-dc-area-fitness-chain /2015/04/10/dd2f4b0a-de3d-11e4-a500-1c5bb1d8ff6a_story.html.

Heinz. "Grown Not Made." Accessed May 10, 2022. https://www.heinz.com/grown-not-made.

Hsieh, Tony. "What Is *The Zappos Culture Book*?" Zappos Insights, accessed May 10, 2022. https://www.zapposinsights.com/culture-book.

Huang, N. S. "Vanguard Funds That Are Socially Responsible." Kiplinger, April 18, 2017. https://www.kiplinger.com/slideshow/investing/T041-S003-6-vanguard-funds-that-are-socially-responsible/index.html.

Hurst, Aaron. *The Purpose Economy: How Your Desire for Impact, Personal Growth and Community Is Changing the World*. Seattle, WA: Imperative, 2018.

Jett, Joan. "Do You Wanna Touch Me (Oh Yeah)." *Bad Reputation*. Beverly Hills, CA: Boardwalk Records, 1981.

Joly, Hubert. "Creating a Meaningful Corporate Purpose." *Harvard Business Review*, October 28, 2021. https://hbr.org/2021/10/creating-a-meaningful-corporate-purpose.

Jones, David A., Chelsea R. Willness, and Sarah Madey. "Why Are Job Seekers Attracted by Corporate Social Performance? Experimental and Field Tests of Three Signal-Based Mechanisms." *Academy of Management Journal* 57, no. 2 (2014): 383–404.

Krueger, Jerry, and Emily A. Killham. "The Innovation Equation." *Gallup Business Journal*, April 12, 2007. https://news.gallup.com/businessjournal/27145/innovation-equation.aspx.

Lencioni, Patrick M. *The Advantage: Why Organizational Health Trumps Everything Else in Business*. New York: Wiley, 2012.

MacLeod, David, and Nita Clarke. "Engaging for Success: Enhancing Performance through Employee Engagement." Department for Business, Innovation and Skills, July 2009. https://dera.ioe.ac.uk/1810/1/file52215.pdf.

Mann, Annamarie. "Why We Need Best Friends at Work." Gallup Workplace, January 15, 2018. https://www.gallup.com/workplace/236213/why-need-best-friends-work.aspx.

Mann, Annamarie, and Nate Dvorak. "Employee Recognition: Low Cost, High Impact." Gallup Workplace, June 28, 2016. https://www.gallup.com/workplace/236441/employee-recognition-low-cost-high-impact.aspx.

Manno, Carolyn. CNN Headline News, November 6, 2021.

Martin, Terrell M. "4 PA Businesses That Are Prioritizing Philanthropy." Pennsylvania Department of Community and Economic Development, August 31, 2021. https://dced.pa.gov/paproudblog/4-pa-businesses-that-are-prioritizing-philanthropy/.

Mayer, J. D., P. Salovey, and D. R. Caruso. "Emotional Intelligence: New Ability or Eclectic Traits?" *American Psychologist* 63, no. 6 (2008): 503–17.

Mazzocchi, Anthony. "Why Students Really Quit Their Musical Instrument (and How Parents Can Prevent It)." Music Parents' Guide, February 17, 2015. http://www.musicparentsguide.com/2015/02/17/students-really-quit-musical-instrument-parents-can-prevent/.

McGuane, Kimberly. "Vanguard Looks to Woo Millennials with Socially Responsible, Exchange-Traded Funds." Vista Today, June 29, 2018. https://vista.today/2018/06 /vanguard-looks-to-woo-millennials-with-socially-responsible-exchange-traded -funds/?utm_source=VISTA+Today&utm_campaign=e163a8da5c-Morning _Drive_Campaign5_28_2015&utm_medium=email&utm_term=0_75b1fa784c -e163a8da5c-274836213.

Miller-Merrell, Jessica. "Ten Employer Examples of EVPs." Workology, February 21, 2022. https://workology.com/employee-value-propositions-evp/.

Muchinsky, M. P. *Psychology Applied to Work: An Introduction to Industrial and Organizational Psychology*. 10th ed. Summerfield, NC: Hypergraphic, 2012.

Olbertova, Martina. "Meaning Is the Soul of Your Company." *Brand Strategy Insider*, November 9, 2018. https://www.brandingstrategyinsider.com/meaning-is-the-soul -of-your-company/.

Patrick, Kate. "Walmart's Improved Social Responsibility Efforts Begin with Supply Chain." Supply Chain Dive, April 25, 2018. https://www.supplychaindive.com /news/walmart-corporate-social-responsibility-efforts/521961/.

Perel, Esther. "Esther Perel's Post." LinkedIn, accessed April 20, 2022. https://www .linkedin.com/posts/estherperel_the-quality-of-our-relationships-determines-activ ity-6863562124287975424-9LJe/.

Pfeffer, J. "Organizational Demography." *Research in Organizational Behavior* 5 (1983): 299–357.

Rayton, Bruce, Tanith Dodge, and Gillian D'Analeze. "The Evidence: Employee Engagement Task Force: 'Nailing the Evidence' Workgroup." Engage for Success, November 2012. https://researchportal.bath.ac.uk/en/publications/the-evidence -employee-engagement-task-force-nailing-the-evidence-.

Reynolds, Brie Weiler. "FlexJobs 2019 Annual Survey: Flexible Work Plays Big Role in Job Choices." FlexJobs, 2019. https://www.flexjobs.com/blog/post/survey-flexible -work-job-choices/.

Robbins Research International. "Companies That Give Back." 2022. https://www .tonyrobbins.com/giving-back/companies-give-back/.

Royal, Mark, and Y. J. Yoon. "Engagement and Enablement: The Key to Higher Levels of Individual and Organisational Performance." *Journal of Compensation and Benefits* 25 (September/October 2009): 13–19.

Sequin, Cynthia, Satish Ukkusuri, Shreyas Sundaram, and Seungyoon Lee. "A Little Help from Your Friends Is Key to Natural Disaster Recovery, Purdue Research Study Suggests." *Purdue University Research Foundation News*, October 12, 2018. https:// www.purdue.edu/newsroom/releases/2018/Q4/a-little-help-from-your-friends-is -key-to-natural-disaster-recovery,-purdue-research-study-suggests.html.

Sheridan, Richard. *Joy, Inc.: How We Built a Workplace People Love*. New York: Penguin, 2013.

"Somali-Dutch Wins Bronze Medal and Helps Other Runner to Keep Pace." YouTube, August 9, 2021. https://www.youtube.com/watch?v=00L-BOrYBpc.

Starbucks. "Expect More Than Coffee." Accessed May 10, 2022. https://www.starbucks
    .com/careers/working-at-starbucks/culture-and-values/.
Swann, William B., Jr., Chris De La Ronde, and John G. Hixon. "Authenticity and
    Positivity Strivings in Marriage and Courtship." *Journal of Personality and Social
    Psychology* 66 (1994): 857–69.
Thompson, Charles (Chic). *What a Great Idea.* New York: Random House, 1994.
TOMS. "One for One." 2016–2018. https://www.toms.com/one-for-one-en/.
Tuckman, B. W. "Developmental Sequence in Small Groups." *Psychological Bulletin 63,*
    no. 6 (1965): 384–99. https://doi.org/10.1037/h0022100.
Vedantam, Shankar, host. "You 2.0: Dream Jobs." NPR, July 30, 2018. Ac-
    cessed September 26, 2018. https://www.npr.org/templates/transcript/transcript
    .php?storyId=634047154.
Weick, K. E., K. M. Sutcliffe, and D. Obstfeld. "Organizing and the Process of Sen-
    semaking." *Organization Science* 16, no. 4 (2005): 409–21. https://doi.org/10.1287
    /orsc.1050.0133.
Wellins, Richard S., Paul Bernthal, and Mark Phelps. "Employee Engagement: The
    Key to Realizing Competitive Advantage." Development Dimensions International,
    2005. http://theengagementeffect.com/wp-content/uploads/DDI-EmployeeEngage
    mentMonograph.pdf.
Wikipedia. "Bob Geldof." Last modified April 27, 2022, 20:05. https://en.wikipedia
    .org/wiki/Bob_Geldof#:~:text=%22The%20greatest%20legacy%20of%20
    Live,Aid%20production%20manager%20Andy%20Zweck.
———. "Learning Pyramid." Last modified January 18, 2022, 06:49. https://
    en.wikipedia.org/wiki/Learning_pyramid.
Williams, Laurie, and Robert Kessler. *Pair Programming Illuminated.* Boston, MA:
    Addison-Wesley, 2003.
Wootson, Cleve R., Jr., and Tyler Pager. "A Kamala Harris Staff Exodus Reignites
    Questions about Her Leadership Style—and Her Future Ambitions." *Washington
    Post,* December 4, 2021. https://www.washingtonpost.com/politics/2021/12/04
    /kamala-harris-staff-departures/.
Wrzesniewski, A., J. E. Dutton, and G. Debebe. "Interpersonal Sensemaking and the
    Meaning of Work." *Research in Organizational Behavior* 25 (2003): 93–135.
Yarow, Jay. "This Is the Inspirational Quote Apple Employees Receive on Day One."
    Business Insider, May 7, 2012, https://www.businessinsider.com/this-is-the-inspira
    tional-quote-apple-employees-receive-on-day-one-2012-5.
Yohn, Denise Lee. "Build a Culture to Match Your Brand." *Harvard Business Review,*
    December 17, 2019. https://hbr.org/2019/12/build-a-culture-to-match-your-brand.
———. "It's the Experience, Stupid!" *Porchlight* (blog), November 11, 2015. https://
    www.porchlightbooks.com/blog/changethis/2015/it-s-the-experience-stupid-.

Index